D1715130

The Rise of the Unelected

Unelected bodies, such as independent central banks, economic regulators, risk managers and auditors, have become a worldwide phenomenon. Democracies are increasingly turning to them to demarcate boundaries between the market and the state, to resolve conflicts of interest and to allocate resources, even in sensitive ethical areas such as those involving privacy or biotechnology. This book examines the challenge that unelected bodies present to democracy and argues that, taken together, such bodies should be viewed as a new branch of government with their own sources of legitimacy and held to account through a new separation of powers. Vibert suggests that such bodies help promote a more informed citizenry because they provide a more trustworthy and reliable source of information for decisions. This book will be of interest to specialists and general readers with an interest in modern democracy as well as policy-makers, think tanks and journalists.

FRANK VIBERT is the co-founder and Director of the European Policy Forum in Pall Mall. He has previously worked as a Senior Adviser at the World Bank and a Senior Fellow at the UNU-WIDER Institute. He writes extensively on regulatory, institutional and constitutional topics and his previous publications include *Europe Simple, Europe Strong: The Future of European Governance* (2001) and *Europe: A Constitution for the Millennium* (1995).

The Rise of the Unelected
Democracy and the New Separation of Powers

Frank Vibert

CAMBRIDGE
UNIVERSITY PRESS

JF
229
.V43
2007

CAMBRIDGE UNIVERSITY PRESS
Cambridge, New York, Melbourne, Madrid, Cape Town, Singapore,
São Paulo

Cambridge University Press
The Edinburgh Building, Cambridge CB2 8RU, UK

Published in the United States of America by Cambridge University Press,
New York

www.cambridge.org
Information on this title: www.cambridge.org/9780521694148

First published 2007

Printed in the United Kingdom at the University Press, Cambridge

A catalogue record for this book is available from the British Library

ISBN 978-0-521-87239-3 hardback
ISBN 978-0-521-69414-8 paperback

789890 92

To My Parents

Contents

Boxes, tables and figures

Acknowledgements

I would particularly like to thank Professor Richard Rose, University of Aberdeen, for his encouragement and guidance; Professor Edward Page (Beatrice and Sydney Webb Professor), London School of Economics, for a very helpful set of comments; Professor Claudio Radaelli, University of Exeter, who kindly organised a seminar at the university's Centre for Regulatory Governance to discuss the themes of the book; and Dr Mark Thatcher, Reader in Public Administration and Public Policy at the London School of Economics, for his comments. Professor Dirk J. Wolfson, Professor Emeritus of Economics, Erasmus University, Rotterdam, also provided a helpful and challenging set of comments.

I would also like to thank the Progress Foundation and its Board Member Dr Gerhard Schwarz who organised a colloquium on Judicial Independence in Schwarzenberg 8–11 July 2004. The colloquium under the guidance of Professor Dr Stefan Voigt was most helpful to me in writing what is said in this book about the rule of law and the basis for an independent judiciary.

I have deliberately sought comments from knowledgeable observers outside the academic community. Those who kindly commented included Martin Summers and Paul Arlman. Cambridge University Press has been most helpful in steering the book through the publication process, and thanks in particular to Jacqueline French for her copy-editing skills. Finally, I would like to thank both Sarah Summers and Diana Munoz for their help and research assistance.

Introduction

A danger to democracy?

In modern democracies unelected bodies now take many of the detailed policy decisions that affect people's lives, untangle key conflicts of interest for society, resolve disputes over the allocation of resources and even make ethical judgements in some of the most sensitive areas. By contrast, our elected politicians often seem ill-equipped to deal with the complexities of public policy, lightweight in the knowledge they bring to bear, masters not of substance but of spin and presentation and skilled above all in avoiding being blamed for public mishaps.

The rise of the unelected is spread across the democratic world. Unelected bodies take different legal forms and different names are used to label them in different democratic settings. The variety of forms and terminology obscures the underlying growth in their importance. The key question is whether the increasing dependence of modern democratic societies on unelected bodies presents a new danger to democracy.

The alarm signals triggered by the rise of the unelected are not warnings about any sudden reversion away from democracy but about the risks of attrition. There appear, at particular points of time, to be good reasons why a problem area in public policy should be entrusted to an unelected body; but when this is repeated again and again over many of the practical issues that people face in their lives, the combined effect is a cumulative transfer of public power from elected politicians to unelected officials. Politicians compete for sound-bites but the real work of running democracies is now carried out by the unelected. We need therefore to be much more conscious about the implications for democratic theory and practice of the growing dependency of modern societies on the unelected.

The contrast between the ineffectiveness of the elected and the superior capabilities of the unelected has ancient roots. It goes back to the beginnings of democratic theory when it was formulated as a question of

1

whether societies are likely to be better off entrusting their government to elites, composed of the wise, or to democratically elected institutions with all their manifest imperfections. At first sight, the rise of the unelected seems to pose this old question in a new form. Today's rise of the unelected seems to lead to a straightforward loss to democracy – as the importance of the unelected rises, so the importance of the elected declines.

Reinvigorating democracies

The unexpected message of this book is that the rise of the unelected is not a danger to democracy. On the contrary, their rise has the potential to make democratic systems of government more robust. In reaching this conclusion this book suggests that we should take the new bodies as a whole and view them as composing a new branch of government and forming the basis of a new separation of powers. Just as the old separation of powers, between legislatures, executives and the judiciary, added to the overall strength of democratic systems of government, so too can the new separation of powers.

The danger to modern democracies is not caused by the rise of the unelected, it comes from failing to recognise the significance of the new separation of powers and from failing to adapt systems of government to it. In systems of government that fail to make good use of what the unelected do best and what only the elected can do, democratic governments will neither be able to solve contemporary problems effectively nor be able to articulate the voice of democracy. Both unelected bodies and elected bodies will be weakened. Citizens will become suspicious of both with the result that democracies will become vulnerable to populism and to arbitrary and indiscriminate exercises of power.

The new branch

What underlies the new separation of powers is a distinction between the empirical component of public policy and the value judgements. The making of public policy involves both elements – the factual evidence and the social or political judgements to be made in the light of that evidence. Unelected bodies have an advantage in dealing with the empirical components of public policy and elected bodies in choosing the values to be reflected in public policy. We are seeing a basic institutional distinction emerge between the processes of gathering information and mobilising the latest knowledge in democratic societies and the processes for passing political judgement on that information and knowledge.

Unelected bodies may sometimes be entrusted with making social or ethical judgements. Where they are involved in this way it is again because of their advantage in separating facts from spin and in navigating through the complexities of the related empirical background. Even in such cases, the importance of the distinction between assessing the facts and applying values to the evidence remains intact.

Citizens who question

Because the new branch of government is overwhelmingly made up of those with expertise and specialised knowledge, it is easy to view it as nothing but institutionalised elitism and a threat to democracy. Such a tempting diagnosis misses the most important impact of the new branch. The new branch strengthens democracy because it provides a safer environment for people to benefit from expertise and the latest state of knowledge, to gather information that is reliable and relevant to themselves, to trust the information and to draw their own conclusions for their own actions. It helps citizens distinguish between the different components of public policy and the different responsibilities of different contributors to public policy. When citizens disagree with the way public policy is being formulated, their questions and criticisms can be more precisely informed and more sharply targeted.

A better-informed citizenry makes it much more difficult for elected politicians to play fast and loose with the facts or to claim privileged access to knowledge. This means that the rise of the new branch creates a radically different environment providing a new and effective check on the behaviour of the elected branches. The elected branches face a much more questioning attitude to what they say and do and a need to redefine their roles.

The more questioning attitude of informed citizens and the checks provided by the new branch are a challenge to which the elected branches of democratic systems of government currently respond with a great deal of confusion and even resentment. This book argues that, faced with the rise of the unelected, the role of the traditional elected bodies is not diminished but it does change its character. In the new separation of powers the traditional institutions of representative democracy need to change both what they are doing and the way they carry out their functions. Resentment against a more questioning public opinion is not the answer.

Reform

This book argues that the advantages of the new separation of powers can be captured, and the dangers to democracy can be avoided, by a clear understanding of what it is that gives unelected bodies their legitimacy and in what ways they can be held accountable. The standard answer does not distinguish between the two questions and gives the same response to both – unelected bodies derive their legitimacy from, and are accountable to, the elected bodies of democracies. By contrast, this book distinguishes between legitimacy and accountability and provides a different answer. It is that the new branch stands on its own claim to legitimacy. This claim is based on developing the principles and procedures appropriate to empirical inquiry analogous to those of the social and physical sciences. The framework of accountability is provided by the way in which the other branches of government reorient their functions in a new system of checks and balances.

According to this account, what distinguishes the new branch and provides the basis for its legitimacy is the greater rigour with which it approaches facts, seeks information, weighs the state of empirical knowledge and tries to draw evidence-based conclusions for public policy. This does not imply that there is some simple line connecting gathering the facts of a situation, empirical analysis of those facts and a public policy conclusion. If the making of public policy was that simple then elected politicians could do it. Unelected bodies have arisen for the opposite reason. The 'facts' are often estimates, the evidence usually incomplete, the science may be contested and the analysis needs to highlight uncertainties and probabilities. It is in steering through the difficulties of the empirical analysis and the uncertainties in the body of knowledge underlying public policy where unelected bodies have an overwhelming advantage over the politicians.

The new separation of powers and framework for accountability have a number of clear implications for the reform of democratic systems of government. These reform messages are important for national systems of government but, in addition, both for the European Union and for the world of international institutions, the reform implications are far-reaching too. Both have blurred the key distinctions in public policy-making and the basis for the new separation of powers. Both now face major overhaul.

The rise of the unelected

In recent years, most democracies around the world have seen a striking expansion in the number and role of bodies in society that exercise official authority but are not headed by elected politicians and have been deliberately set apart, or only loosely tied to the more familiar elected institutions of democracy – the parliaments, presidents and prime ministers. The world of the unelected is a hugely varied world. Unelected bodies include independent central banks, independent risk management bodies, independent economics and ethics regulators, regimes of inspection and audit and new types of appeal bodies. It is also a large and growing world. Around 200 unelected bodies now exist in the United States and around 250 in the United Kingdom. Other countries, even with different democratic traditions and structures, are following suit. In addition, the role of the judicial branch of government, in most democracies traditionally set apart from the jostle and scramble of democratic politics, has also grown.

Political scientists refer to such unelected bodies charged with official powers and authority as 'non-majoritarian institutions'.[1] This is a cumbersome and ungainly term and so this book uses the less precise but more informal term of 'unelected bodies' to refer to the same institutions.

At the same time that unelected bodies are playing a much larger role within states across the world, people have become aware of the important role that they play in the international arena outside the compass of state structures. At the global level the unelected bodies are the international institutions and organisations that are sometimes recognised for their words and sometimes for their deeds but most of all for their acronyms. There are about seventy international bodies that have universal or intercontinental memberships. Most people, even the well informed, would be hard pressed to define the precise role of individual institutions such as the OECD or the BIS in the world of international institutions, let alone associated bodies such as the FATF[2] or the FSF.[3] Nevertheless, there is a correct perception that, taken together and in conjunction with international networks of national unelected officials,

---

[1] Non-majoritarian institutions have been defined in formal terms as government entities possessing some grant of specialised public authority that are neither directly elected by the people nor directly managed by elected officials. See Thatcher and Stone Sweet (2002). The phrase has developed as a way to bring together a variety of terms for describing unelected bodies reflecting different forms in different countries.

[2] The Financial Action Task Force. A key body housed with the Organisation for Economic Cooperation and Development (OECD) bringing together national officials charged with combating money laundering and terrorist financing and instigator among other activities of a 'know your client' approach to banking and other relationship dealings.

[3] The Financial Stability Forum. A body housed with the Bank for International Settlements (BIS) that brings together central bankers, finance ministries and financial regulators to develop core standards relating to the stability of the international financial system and to help co-ordinate emergency actions if needed. Sector-specific international regulatory bodies involved with it include the Basel Committee on Banking Supervision (BCBS), the International Accounting Standards Board (IASB), the International Association of Insurance Supervisors (IAIS) and the International Organization of Securities Commissions (IOSCO).

they are more important than in the past. Equally to the point, they do not fall within the orbit of democratic politics.

For democracies in Europe, the European Union adds yet a further dimension. An unelected body – the Commission – sits at the centre of institutional arrangements and there are in addition over thirty other unelected bodies in the EU that have been created mainly in recent years.

The importance of the unelected

The combined effect of these developments is that bodies set apart from electoral politics now play a much larger role in the life of democratic regimes than in previous periods. In practice they may have greater impact on people's daily lives than the activities of elected politicians. The words of an independent central bank governor may carry more weight in financial markets than the words of a finance minister and the pronouncements of an independent inspector of schools may carry more clout with the public than those of an education minister. Public reaction to a food or medicine scare or a pension and savings scandal may direct criticism at an independent agency just as much as any minister or Cabinet member with nominal responsibility to the electorate.[4] A far-reaching change in the pensions expectations for an entire generation may be triggered as a result of an accounting change policy prompted by an international body of whose role people are quite unaware,[5] a tribunal attempts to suspend the elected Mayor of London and a court decides the outcome of a US presidential election.

The drama of a court that decides the outcome of a presidential election is, it is to be hoped, a rare occurrence. More typically, unelected bodies in national settings shun the limelight. With the exception of independent central bankers who are required to give their views on the general state of the economy, the unelected do not pontificate on matters of grand politics such as 'the state of the nation', or a nation's place and

---

[4] On 17 November 2004 two heads of independent agencies in the UK subject to public criticism resigned on the same day: the managing director of the National Assessment Agency in charge of national curriculum tests and the head of the Child Support Agency responsible for ensuring maintenance payments are made by parents who have separated.

[5] In 2000 the UK's Accounting Standards Board (an affiliate of the Financial Reporting Council) adopted FRS 17 a new standard that has effectively spelt the end of defined benefit pension arrangements. In adopting the new standard the Board noted the importance of coming into line with a revised standard of the International Accounting Standards Committee (IASC) that adopted a standard similar to a United States standard FAS 87. (See Financial Reporting Standard 17. Accounting Standards Board. London. Nov. 2000. Appendix III.) Other countries following international accounting or US standards confront the same consequences for pension schemes.

standing in the world outside, or on matters of war and peace. Their importance stems from a different source. They affect the fundamental fabric of people's lives in intimate and immediate ways.

First, their influence extends into most areas of daily life. The air we breathe, the water we drink, the food we eat, the electricity we use, the phone calls we make, the value of the coins and banknotes in our pockets, our access to media, the disputes we get involved in, are all influenced in basic ways by their activities. Secondly, unelected bodies have a crucial impact at key stages in a person's life-cycle. In the early stages of life they may influence the nutrition we receive, the quality of schools we attend and the value of the types of education diplomas we receive and our job prospects. At a later stage in life they may decide the information or financial structure that determines the benefits from a pension arrangement, and they may affect the choices we have of medicines or treatments to combat wear and tear in the final stage of our lives. Thirdly, the unelected affect the way we are able to deal with life's accidents and chances, fortunes and misfortunes. They may, for example, have a decisive say over the risks we take in using different forms of transport, or eating different foodstuffs. Thus, when all are added up, unelected bodies can be seen at the sharp end in most fields of public policy in which modern government is active – the bodies that in a myriad of ways affect the quality of our daily life, our life chances and our life prospects (see box 1).

While the unelected play a much larger role in the life of democracies, by contrast the stature of the traditional elected institutions seems severely diminished. Not only do ministers seem to exert less control over public policy but Members of Parliament also find themselves further removed from positions of influence and less equipped to be able to scrutinise what is going on effectively. Parliaments not only do not control governments but do not appear to control the unelected bodies either.

We experience this shift in the influence of traditional democratic institutions in diffused ways – when an unelected central banker warns a finance minister to 'keep off my turf'; or when a distant and unfamiliar body such as the FATF spreads a 'know your client' policy through the enforcement authorities of the world with the effect that people find themselves asked for personal information to carry out transactions such as selling an investment or transferring money that was once a purely private transaction; or when an unelected body from another country reaches across traditional 'sovereign' borders.

Sometimes the effect of the unelected on the 'feel' of our democracies may be entirely beneficial – for example in relation to those unelected bodies with a role in enforcing freedom of information or in opening up

---

Box 1: The influence of the unelected

INFLUENCING OUR DAILY LIFE

UK's Energywatch makes the first energy 'super-complaint'. *'Yesterday, Energywatch filed a 60 page dossier with OFGEM, the energy regulator, detailing a "myriad" of problems with energy billing which it said were causing debt and misery for consumers ... Last year 40,000 consumers called Energywatch to complain about their bills.' 'The complaint, which can lead to fines for businesses that fail consumers, is one of two that will be handed to the OFT (Office of Fair Trading) in the next few months.'* The Times, 7 April 2005.

The Australian Child Support Agency 'no stranger to controversy but claims greater success'. *'Compared with its overseas counterparts, it (the Australian Child Support Agency) has been a resounding success, according to Matt Miller, its general manager ... More than 90 per cent of separating couples with children are registered with the agency, which transferred A\$2.4bn (£1bn) in support to more than 1.1m children in the last financial year.'* Financial Times, 10 Feb. 2006.

AFFECTING KEY STAGES IN THE LIFE CYCLE

'Mothers got wrong advice for 40 years'. *'Breast feeding mothers have been given potentially harmful advice on infant nutrition for the past 40 years, the World Health Organisation (WHO) has admitted ... Health experts believe the growth charts [used] may have contributed to childhood obesity and associated problems such as diabetes and heart disease in later life.'* Sunday Times, 23 April 2006.

The UK Accounting Standards Board sets out the accounting treatment for retirement benefits such as pensions and medical care during retirement (FRS17). Nov. 2000. *'FTSE 100 companies alone are estimated to have deficits of almost £70bn. Several companies have sought to reduce liabilities by closing defined benefit schemes and by switching to career average rather than final salary arrangements.'* Financial Times, 8 Feb. 2006.

UK's NICE rules on treatment for Alzheimer's. *'Drugs should be funded for patients with moderate Alzheimer's but not those with mild or severe forms of the disease according to the body which advises the Government on drugs ... Between 290,000 and 380,000 people are estimated to suffer with Alzheimer's in England and Wales.'* Daily Telegraph, 23 Jan. 2006.

AFFECTING LIFE'S RISKS

WTO rules against Europe in GM food case. '*The World Trade Organisation ruled yesterday that European restrictions on the introduction of genetically modified foods violated international trade rules, finding there was no scientific justification for lengthy delays in approving new varieties of corn, soyabeans and cotton . . . The European Commission halted the approval of new GM varieties in 1996 but began limited approvals again in May 2004, after the US launched the WTO case . . . The WTO decision also found against separate national bans established by Austria, France, Germany, Greece, Italy and Luxembourg.*' Financial Times, 8 Feb. 2006.

New opening for biotechnology medicines. '*The European Medicines Agency yesterday threw open the door to a new generation of cheap biotechnology medicines . . . The decision by the agency removes a big obstacle in Europe to so-called bio-similar products – generic copies of bio-pharmaceuticals already on the market . . . The ruling also puts the EU ahead of the US, where the regulator is dithering over approval.*' Financial Times, 28/29 Jan. 2006.

Air safety and new pilots. '*The minimum number of flying hours for trainee pilots is to be halved under new rules . . . The changes are being supported by the International Civil Aviation Organisation (ICAO) which has come under pressure from Lufthansa, the German airline, to reform pilot licensing.*' The Times, 13 Feb. 2006.

new channels of redress. But the net effect of having so many decisions that affect the fabric of daily life being taken outside traditional democratic channels is that modern democracies now seem very far from providing for popular government. Nor is it clear how the new bodies fit within traditional notions of the rule of law. The rise of the unelected means, therefore, that there is a fundamental question to be answered about what role the traditional institutions of democracy such as popularly elected assemblies should now play (see box 2).

A challenge both to democratic practice and to democratic theory

The rise of the unelected is a challenge to democratic practice that goes far beyond the apparent diminution in the role of traditional institutions. Unelected bodies seem to reduce the scope for traditional political debate by treating issues as ones of technocratic problem-solving or as questions

---

Box 2: Affecting the 'feel' of democracy

UK Freedom of Information Commissioner 'Strikes blow for disclosure'. *'Government departments are likely to be forced to reveal minutes of top-level meetings after a landmark ruling by the freedom of information watchdog. Richard Thomas, the information commissioner, has ordered the Department for Education and Skills to comply with a request to disclose minutes of senior management meetings . . . He estimates more than 100,000 FOI requests were made last year.'* Financial Times, 13 Jan. 2006.

'Bundesbank "hawk" set to join board of ECB'. *'On fiscal policy, Mr Stark is a passionate defender of the EU's much abused "stability and growth pact" which is supposed to impose fiscal discipline on member states . . . That means he is unlikely to have much patience for eurozone finance ministers who try to resist interest rate moves.'* Financial Times, 14 Feb. 2006.

'Perceived infringements of sovereignty'. *'The Public Company Accounting Oversight Board . . . is putting auditors under the microscope . . . its mandate extends beyond the US, encompassing any auditor that works for companies traded on the US stock market . . . The inspections . . . have prompted grumblings in some quarters about perceived infringements of sovereignty.'* Financial Times, 20 Feb. 2006.

London's Elected Mayor reacts to suspension by the Adjudication Panel for England. *'Commenting on his four week suspension as Mayor of London the Mayor said, "This decision strikes at the heart of democracy. Elected politicians should only be able to be removed by the voters or for breaking the law. Three members of a body that no one has ever elected should not be allowed to overturn the votes of millions of Londoners."'* The Times, 25 Feb. 2006.

---

of good administration. Increasing reliance on experts also appears dangerously disconnected from the real world because it seems to rest on the view that public policy can be based on a narrow rationality when in practice so much that is involved in politics concerns emotion, strength of feeling and instinctive values and judgements. Politics as an arena for raw expression cannot just be cast aside.

The rise of the unelected is also a problem for the theory of democracy. When all is said and done and after all qualifications to majority rule necessary to protect minorities have been expressed, it remains the expectation of theorising about democratic forms of government that policy outcomes will pay attention to what the majority wants and respect also what it does not want. But the unelected bodies exercise power, influence and authority out of the reach of whatever majorities might want or might not want.

None of the current main approaches to democratic theory can accommodate easily what is happening. The growth of unelected institutions is troublesome for theories that emphasise the importance of democratic participation. Participation is meant to ensure that politics delivers what people want. Participation is also meant to help ensure that political power is not distorted by special interests, or misused by those holding office, or by those close to the seats of power. But when key functions are being taken out of the traditional democratic arena and when key interests switch their efforts to influence unelected bodies, political participation seems much less important. It seems to take a major cataclysm such as the Iraq war to stir the voter.

The rise of the unelected is also troublesome for accounts of democracy that emphasise its deliberative qualities. According to this approach to democratic theory, politics is not just about resolving clashes of interest in society but about transforming public opinion; debate, discussion and persuasion are seen as the means to do this in a civil and civilised way. Yet when so much is being taken away from the traditional institutions of democracy the role of political debate also seems much less important. Other, non-political channels for getting views across, provided by the unelected bodies, seem to have become more relevant. Moreover, dealing with conflicts of interest, even though they take a different form compared with the conflicts of the past, once again seems to have risen in importance. What is more, it is the unelected institutions that are better equipped to deal with conflicts of interest in their new form than the traditional democratic bodies.

Unelected bodies are troublesome in addition for concepts of democracy under the rule of law. The rules are intended to provide a framework for democratic rule. However, the unelected institutions occupy a new space between law and politics. Their procedures are different from both and present a challenge to what the rules should be and how relationships between the different branches should be formulated.

Together, these mainstream accounts of democratic politics offer active participation as a means of bargaining between different interests, discussion as a means of accommodating different opinions and beliefs, and rule-based behaviour as a means to find common norms in pluralist societies. But whichever approach is taken, unelected bodies sit like an unwelcome guest at a dinner party – part of the scene but not part of the company.

The new separation of powers

Initial attempts to reformulate democratic theory in ways that take account of the growth of unelected bodies have offered conflicting accounts. One account emphasises the continuation of a democratic 'overhead' that extends a form of democratic control from the traditional institutions over the new unelected bodies. Another regards the attempt to extend democratic controls as likely to be frustrated. But it emphasises instead the relevance of a new style of constitution-making and the need to replace old styles of political control with new methods of constitutional control. Still another approach rejects the formalism implied by constitutional controls and suggests instead that the growth of unelected bodies reflects a change in the focus of democratic politics. According to this account, democracies are turning away from ideologically oriented political debate in order to focus on pragmatic tasks for which the new institutions are peculiarly well suited. Yet, for different reasons, none of these approaches seems fully convincing and this book puts forward a different approach.

The theme laid out in this book is that the rise of the unelected bodies reflects the arrival of a new branch of government and a new kind of separation of powers in government. The classic separation of powers distinguished between an executive, a legislature and a judiciary. If the new separation simply reflected the arrival of a new class of executive organisation created mainly for administrative or managerial reasons, the new branch would not perhaps be too significant. But the new separation stands for something much more fundamental. What we are seeing separated out is a new branch within systems of government with a special responsibility for the handling and dissemination of information, the analysis of evidence and the deployment and use of the most up-to-date empirical knowledge. Democratic societies require a variety of forms of authority and the new separation of powers represents a major new dimension to decision-making in democracies.[6]

The radicalism of the new separation of powers

The emergence of unelected bodies as a new branch of government might be seen as a story in itself with no further implications for democratic

---

[6] See Dahl (1970).

behaviour and democratic institutions. However, one of the most important analytic qualities of the separation of powers is that it places a focus on the dynamic effects of political behaviour in the different branches of government. From this perspective the emergence of a new form of separation of powers is only the beginning of the story. The new separation presents two challenges to existing patterns of democratic government. The first centres on the implications for electorates. The second centres on the impact on the traditional elected institutions.

In order to examine the first of these questions the book goes back to the logic underlying the classic separation of powers. The thinking that lay behind the original separation of powers started life as an approach to try to improve the efficiency and acceptability of monarchical government. Yet it had an unexpectedly radical outcome. The system of checks and balances came to be perceived as providing a way of making the world safe for democratic government. Instead of more power to the monarch, it led to more power to the people.

The dynamics of the new separation of powers are similar. It too can be seen as starting from a desire to improve the efficiency and acceptability of the existing institutions of representative democracy. But it too has much more radical outcomes. This is because the new separation of powers overturns one of the key assumptions of representative democracy, that people are better off delegating judgements and decisions to their elected representatives on the grounds that elected representatives are better informed and have more knowledge at their command. With the new separation of powers, elected politicians can no longer claim privileged access to knowledge and information. People do not trust the information that governments provide and the new separation makes it possible for people to rely on sources of information untainted by the machinery of government. This safer environment in turn encourages them to defer much less to what politicians say, to seek out information for themselves and to make their own judgements and decisions. What is at stake with these new behaviour patterns thus is a challenge to the basic premises of representative democracy. Instead of politicians playing to deferential electorates they find themselves looking at a citizenry that is better able to inform itself on matters it considers important and more than ready to question the claims of politicians that they know better.

The new temper of an informed citizenry has been vividly illustrated by the reaction to the Madrid bombings in March 2004. In this case voters appear to have formed the view that the government of Prime Minister Aznar was not telling the facts and was placing a self-serving interpretation on who had been responsible for the bombing. The electorate took immediate retribution. Similarly both President Bush and Prime Minister Blair lost a large measure of public confidence in the handling of the Iraq war because of the way in which information was handled. It became apparent not only that the information and knowledge of Saddam Hussein's regime was deficient, but that professional assessments of the quality of that information also had become confused by the political interpretations placed on it. The new separation of powers involves a much clearer demarcation between professional judgements based on knowledge and its limits and political judgements that bring to bear outside values and principles on that knowledge.

The fact that an informed citizenry no longer takes at face value what politicians tell it and instead wants sources of information and guidance to the latest state of knowledge taken out of the hands of politicians can be taken as a sign of the maturing of democratic practice. From a historical perspective, democracies are relatively new for most countries in the world, including in Europe, and it is a good sign if people want to see the facts for themselves and to form their own judgements. At the same time, it also places the question of how to re-orient the functions of the traditional institutions of democratic government in the judgemental processes of democratic systems of government within a more radical setting.

Defining the new role for the traditional institutions

In order to see the implications for the traditional elected bodies of representative democracy this book distinguishes between two very different functions of the traditional institutions. First, there is the problem-solving role as people look to their government to respond to certain needs or perceived inequities. Secondly, there is a role as an arena for expressing values, principles and attitudes that contribute to the judgemental processes of society. It is tempting to elide or conflate these two different roles of democratic government. We expect governments to pay at least lip-service to underlying values and principles when they put forward problem-solving answers on matters of public policy. Nevertheless the two roles are distinct.

This book argues that with the new separation of powers both roles are changing. The problem-solving role will be transformed both because people want to make more decisions for themselves and because the unelected institutions will be better problem-solvers in new areas of importance to informed citizens. In a world where individuals make more judgements for themselves, the arena role will also need to change in order to contribute to the judgemental processes of society.

The legitimacy of the new branch of government

Alongside the more radical implications of the new separation of powers for traditional electorates and the traditional institutions of representative democracy ride two fundamental questions as to how the new branch of government is to receive its legitimacy and how it is to be held accountable within a democratic system of government. Conventional accounts of how the unelected bodies fit within democratic practice tend to treat these two questions as one. Because the new bodies operate under powers delegated by elected bodies and often with public funds, their legitimacy seems to flow from the elected bodies and it is to them that they also seem accountable. This book argues that this conventional account is implausible in practice and mistaken in theory. It is based on hope rather than reality. Yet if this conventional account is set aside, the new branch of government, belonging neither to the judiciary, the executive or the legislative branches, appears to be answerable to nobody.

The separation of powers helps to provide an answer to the democratic challenge because it makes a highly important analytic distinction between legitimacy and accountability. In the classic depiction, accountability flows from the system of checks and balances. Each branch has a role in holding the other in its place. With respect to legitimacy, as formulated by the founding fathers of the American system, each branch could be seen as resting on its own form of legitimacy. This book suggests that the legitimacy and accountability of the new branch should be approached in a similar way as being a part of a system of checks and balances and a branch that rests on its own form of legitimacy.

The argument developed in this book is that the legitimacy of the new branch should be viewed in a manner analogous to that of the judicial branch. An independent judiciary is important for a healthy democracy but its fundamental legitimacy does not rest on answering to the people. Similarly, the new branch is an important part of a democratic system of government but should not be seen as legitimated by answering to the people. Nor does an independent judiciary answer to the legislature or the executive. Their relationship is one of mutual respect for the core functions of each other. Equally, the relationship of the new branch to the traditional branches needs to be based on a mutual respect for core functions. In the final analysis the law has developed its own standards of legitimating behaviour that centre on the principles and procedures suited to the law itself. Its legitimacy hinges on the observance of these standards. Correspondingly, we need to look to the development of standards appropriate to the new branch as providing their own form of legitimation.

The new separation of powers also presents a major challenge to the supranational institutions of the European Union and to international bodies and networks operating at the global level. This is because the functions that are being separated out at the national level are mingled together within the EU and at the international level. Major changes are implied in the way in which they operate and claim legitimacy.

Organisation of the discussion

The book starts by measuring the dimensions of the phenomenon itself – by describing the world of unelected institutions. It is a diverse world and in order to characterise the distinctions the first chapter sets out functional categories according to whether the bodies can be seen primarily as service providers or risk managers or inspectors or perform other functions. It then looks behind the diversity in order to identify what features they share in common.

Chapter 2 looks at why the unelected bodies have risen so far in prominence. It examines two conventional economic and managerial explanations before identifying a different type of explanation. This involves the distinction in policy-making between the information and knowledge base that underlies public policy and the value judgements that are brought to bear on that information and knowledge.

The discussion continues in chapter 3 by looking at the special advantages unelected bodies possess over the traditional elected bodies of representative democracy as gatherers and processors of the information and latest knowledge needed in the formation of public policy and the public confidence that this generates. It tests the view that value judgements cannot be separated from the evidence base behind policy-making. It describes the further advantage to the public of unbundling the different elements in policy judgements as well as the different roles of different institutional actors.

In chapter 4, the discussion then steps back from the real world to discuss the difficulties encountered by different theories of democracy in incorporating the rise of unelected bodies within their framework. It explains why their growth cannot easily be accommodated either by theories of participatory democracy that place the emphasis on the right to vote or bargain, or by theories of deliberative democracy that place the emphasis on discussion, or by democracy expressed as the rule of law.

Having discussed the difficulties of traditional democratic theory in encompassing the rise of the unelected, chapter 5 moves on to discuss the more recent and conflicting approaches that try to integrate the world of unelected bodies within traditional democratic theory. It examines critically what is probably the most widely held view that the elected branches of government still provide a democratic 'overhead' and it gives briefer treatment to the rival ideas that the new bodies can be fitted within new styles of constitutionalism or that they can be seen as representing a new focus on pragmatism in politics. The chapter argues that, quite apart from offering conflicting accounts about how unelected bodies fit within democracies, these attempts to modify democratic theory also share a number of common weaknesses.

In chapter 6, the discussion then returns to examine the growth of unelected bodies as a new form of separation of powers and looks particularly at the dynamics involved. Classical accounts of the dynamics focussed on the conflicts of interest that arose when different functions were combined within the same branch of government. This approach is updated and the chapter explores the way in which the new separation of powers leads to a change in the behaviour of electorates. It describes the new setting in which an informed citizenry gather their own facts and make their own judgements rather than rely on politicians to spin the facts and make judgements for them.

The new separation of powers and a world of informed citizens raise fundamental questions about the role that traditional institutions now play. In order to explore their new role the discussion continues in chapter 7 by making a distinction between the problem-solving functions of governments and the function of democratic institutions in providing an arena that illuminates the values and principles held by society. It examines the changes to both of these functions.

Chapter 8 turns to the question of how the new branch of government is to derive its legitimacy. It sets out an analogy with the judicial branch. Based on this analogy, it describes the principles and procedures that legitimate its activities.

The scope of the analysis is widened in chapters 9 and 10 to look briefly outside the setting of the individual state to international organisations and the EU. International organisations do not fit easily within traditional accounts of democracy because they have only a remote connection with electorates. The EU also does not fit easily within traditional accounts because it has its own special and unconventional features. Separate chapters discuss whether there are insights to be gained from looking at them in the light of a new separation of powers.

Finally, chapter 11 concludes with a discussion of the framework of democratic accountability for the new branch. It also highlights the reforms needed in national settings and looks again at the special problems of the European Union and international organisations as they too face up to adapting to the new separation of powers.

1 The world of the unelected

The pervasiveness of unelected bodies wielding official powers in the structures of modern democratic societies comes as a surprise to many. Their growth has been gradual and justified largely on a case-by-case basis. The total number is rarely added up. In the UK, where a comprehensive list is now provided, it has been estimated that there were at the end of 2004 over 650 'public bodies' outside central government departments.[1] The majority of these (around 400) were in the business of providing advice to government departments and a further 20 were bodies involved in Britain's national health service. This still left about 250 bodies with executive responsibilities. Of these, it has been separately estimated that around 120 have regulatory functions.[2]

The rise of the unelected is an international phenomenon. In the United States two main waves of agency creation are usually identified – agencies created in the 1930s under the New Deal and agencies created in the 1960s and 1970s. A current tally lists over 1,000 federal agencies, of which the large majority were located within the executive branch, but around 200 were listed as independent or were more loosely attached.[3] In the case of Sweden there are over 100 official agencies (excluding temporary advisory committees) and in the Republic of Ireland over 60 agencies and statutory independent bodies.

Different terminology is used to describe the bodies. Many are called agencies but other terms are used including: quasi autonomous non-government organisations (QUANGOs), parastatals, indirect public administrative bodies, authorities, bureaus, commissions, centres, institutes and tribunals. They may operate with different degrees of autonomy

---

[1] Source: Cabinet Office.
[2] Better Regulation Task Force (2003). Independent Regulators. Annex A.
[3] Source: Louisiana State University Libraries and Federal Depository Library Program: Federal Agencies Directory.

and also take different legal forms, depending on the legal and adminis-trative traditions of different countries.[4]

The bewildering number of bodies and the complexity of the structures and terminology that have grown up can be illustrated in the UK by one single government department – the Department for the Environment, Food and Rural Affairs (DEFRA). In the case of DEFRA there were, at the beginning of 2006, 9 executive agencies, over 100 'non-departmental public bodies' (of which about 90 were advisory and the others executive or tribunals), 3 public corporations and 14 'other' public bodies, all outside the department but associated in some way with its work. Differences in terminology, form and the precise legal relationship with a central government department are highly confusing. They may also give a misleading impression about the relationship with bodies that appear under the umbrella of a central department but operate effectively outside the departmental structure. Concealed in the bureaucratic pano-ply lies a world-wide growth in reliance on unelected bodies.

Unelected bodies have become so pervasive that we take them for granted and rarely stop to think about how they all fit together and relate more broadly to the conventions of democratic government. We equate democracy with the traditional symbols of democratic life such as parlia-ments and overlook the fact that most of the work of keeping modern forms of government operational is really done by the unelected. We then fail to consider what this means for the elected institutions and for democracy more generally. This chapter therefore provides an overview of the world of unelected bodies and then asks what, if anything, is common to their world.

The illustrations in this chapter are drawn primarily from the UK where the process has favoured the creation of a multiplicity of function-ally specialised bodies. However, in order to capture the international flavour, the tables provide a selection of comparisons from countries outside the UK. Later chapters consider in greater detail examples for the EU and those drawn from the world of international organisations.

The diversity

The world of unelected bodies is hugely diverse. The core components comprise independent central banks and other independent service

---

[4] For an early discussion of the interplay between the functional forces leading to the devolving of powers from central government departments and national styles of admin-istration in Europe see Hood and Schuppert (1988). For a more recent discussion, including case examples, see Pollitt and Talbot (2004).

providers, independent risk assessors and risk managers, economic and other regulators, regimes of audit and inspection, and courts – both traditional and new. Discussion of their role is usually compartmentalised. The world of audit is not discussed in tandem with the world of independent central banks and the world of judicial review is also often treated on its own. Alternatively, discussion reflects statutory and legal categories that often flow from historical circumstance or legal tradition rather than more meaningful distinctions.[5] Therefore, in order to get a better overall sense of the space occupied by unelected institutions in modern democracies, this overview uses a simplified but more practical set of functional distinctions in order to describe the world within which they fit and one that reflects the way people may actually encounter them.

The distinctions are between five broad categories of institution deliberately set apart from democratically elected bodies:

- First, the service providers – bodies set up to provide a service such as central banking;
- Secondly, the risk assessors – bodies set up to monitor and manage risk whether it arises from the food we eat, or the medicines we take, or from the sporting activities we indulge in, or the risks from nuclear waste and environmental pollution;
- Thirdly, the boundary watchers – bodies set up to watch the most sensitive aspects of the boundary between state and market from the supply of basic utilities to privacy or to biomedical research;
- Fourthly, the inquisitors – bodies that audit and inspect and which are detached from politics so that their inspections may be seen to be free from political bias:
- Fifth and finally, the umpires and whistle-blowers – the new generation of tribunals, appeals bodies and ombudsmen that have expanded redress mechanisms beyond the traditional judicial branch of government.

These categories are not intended to be watertight. Many bodies fulfil more than one function. For example the UK's Financial Reporting Council provides a service (setting accounting standards for business) while it also acts as an umpire to enforce standards, investigate non-compliance and to discipline if non-compliance is proven. Similarly, the Child Support Agency provides an essential service in facilitating the actual transfer of child support payments between separated parents as well as having a key enforcement role. A different example of overlap is provided by the UK's National Patient Safety Agency that monitors safety aspects of healthcare but also provides a whistle-blowing service

---

[5] For a discussion of the untidiness of definitions in this area see Pollitt, Talbot, Caulfield and Smullen (2004: 7–11).

encouraging the reporting of incidents and 'near misses' when things go
wrong. Nevertheless, despite overlap, these main categories of activity
help depict the principal areas where unelected bodies have sprung up.

The service providers

Still probably the most widely known example in the UK of an unelected
body that provides a general service is the BBC – granted a royal charter
in 1927 in order to detach the power of broadcasting news from the power
of politics.

*Whereas in view of the widespread interest which is taken by Our Peoples in broadcasting
services and of the great value of such services as means of disseminating information,
education and entertainment, We believe it to be in the interests of Our Peoples ... that
there should be an independent corporation which should continue to provide broadcasting services ...* (BBC Royal Charter (1996 Renewal): Department of National
Heritage)

It is a task that remains difficult and controversial, as the challenge from the
British Government to the BBC during the Iraq war made clear. In retrospect, the creation of the BBC, as a response to tensions with politicians
over the reporting of the General Strike, can be seen as one of the first
landmarks on the way to a new separation of powers. Followed by other
countries only in a limited way as a model inside broadcasting, by establishing an independent body to separate the supply of information to the public
from governments and politics, it foreshadowed a line of thinking that was
to have a much wider influence outside the field of broadcasting.

For most countries the most prominent independent provider of a
service is the central bank in charge of the currency. The motivator
behind the creation of the BBC was the fear of government influence
over the media. It was a different kind of fear of government that became
the crucial institutional motivator behind central bank independence.
The fear was that a body of technical knowledge existed that could enable
a currency to be managed in a way that retained its value but that this
knowledge could not be deployed within democratic politics.

No central banker would claim anything like certainty in making the
kinds of technical judgement that are needed to keep currencies stable.
Judgement about the kind of rules to promulgate, when to deviate from
them and how best to manage market expectations is still required and
judgements are fallible. But what has been recognised in the move to
independent central banks is the fundamental difference between judgements based on the best knowledge available and judgements based on
political calculation. It came to be believed that political judgements about

what would be in the self-interest of politicians would systematically override the knowledge of how to achieve a stable currency. Thus by the 1990s, a combination of empirical analysis, about the way currencies lost their value when controlled by politicians, as well as theoretical analysis, of the consequences of 'time inconsistencies' suggesting that a rule-based approach to monetary policy would outperform any discretionary approach, led to a decisive shift towards independent central banking modelled mainly on the earlier example of the German Central Bank.[6]

Other types of service provided by independent bodies range from developing technical standards, to gathering statistics,[7] to the handling of research funding, to the provision of educational tests, exams and training and to the running of parks. Selected examples showing a variety of services are given in table 1 from the UK and other countries.

The risk assessors

As societies grow more prosperous, people seem more aware of risk in their lives. An increasingly important class of independent body (shown in table 2) is concerned precisely with the identification, measurement and management of risk. In principle, risk assessment (the gathering and weighing of evidence and the weighting of probabilities) can be separated from risk management (decisions about what to do based on the evidence and the probabilities). In turn, there is a distinction within risk management between the auditing, oversight and enforcement of the risk management practices of those with operating responsibilities and the direct responsibilities of the operators themselves. Lesson learning from safety accidents or near-accidents is another increasingly important aspect of the work of such bodies.

Some bodies reflect these distinctions. However, in practice, in the world of independent risk assessors, risk assessment is often coupled with risk management responsibilities and responsibility for overseeing or auditing the risk management practices of others.[8] Bodies in the health, safety and environmental area provide many examples. For example the UK's National Institute for Health and Clinical Excellence (NICE) provides both technology appraisals and clinical guidelines on appropriate care, as well as guidelines on the safety and effectiveness of medical intervention procedures.

---

[6] Kydland and Prescott (1977).
[7] Arrangements to ensure the independence of the Office of National Statistics (ONS) were announced by the UK Chancellor of the Exchequer on 28 November 2005.
[8] For a discussion of risk typologies see Hood, Rothstein and Baldwin (2001).

Table 1: *Selected independent service providers*

UK
Arts Council
Bank of England
British Broadcasting Corporation (BBC)
British Council
Child Support Agency
Dental Vocational Training Authority (DVTA)
Economic and Social Research Council (ESRC)
English Nature
Law Commission
Medical Research Council (MRC)
Office of National Statistics (ONS)
Qualifications and Curriculum Authority (QCA)
Training and Development Agency (formerly TTA)

USA
Federal Reserve System (FRS)
National Aeronautics and Space Administration (NASA)
National Railroad Passenger Corporation (AMTRAK)
National Science Foundation
Small Business Administration
US Postal Service

Australia
Australian Broadcasting Corporation (ABC)
Australian Bureau of Statistics (ABS)
Australian Research Council (ARC)
Child Support Agency (CSA)
Curriculum Corporation
Reserve Bank of Australia

EU member states
Centro de Investigaciones Sociologicas (CIS) (Spain)
Deutsche Bundesbank (Germany)
Federal Agency for Nature Conservation (BfN) (Germany)
National Council for Curriculum and Assessment (NCCA) (Ireland)
Royal Meteorological Office (Netherlands)
Swedish Forest Agency (SFA) (Sweden)

It is the complexity of risk analysis that seems to call in many cases for assessment by independent agencies. Four highly technical kinds of assessments need to be made. The first is scientific and technological. For example, is it technically possible to install smokehoods in aeroplanes to protect passengers against smoke inhalation in the event of fire? The second is the need to assess the probabilities and profile of the risk. In particular there is a need to distinguish between widespread, familiar and

Table 2: *Selected independent risk assessors*

UK
Adventure Activity Licensing Authority (AALA)
Council for Healthcare Regulatory Excellence (CHRE)
Environment Agency
Food Standards Agency
Football Licensing Authority (FLA)
Health and Safety Commission (HSC)
Health Protection Agency
National Institute for Health and Clinical Excellence (NICE)
National Patient Safety Agency (NPSA)

USA
Centers for Disease Control and Prevention (CDC)
Consumer Product Safety Commission
Environmental Protection Agency (EPA)
Food and Drug Administration (FDA)
National Transportation Safety Board
Nuclear Waste Technical Review Board (NWTRB)

Australia
Australian Safety and Cooperation Council (ASCC)
National Heritage Trust (NHT)
National Industrial Chemical Notification and Assessment Scheme (NICNAS)
National Institute of Clinical Studies (NICS)

EU member states
Federal Institute for Risk Assessment (BfR) (Germany)
Food Safety Authority of Ireland (FSAI)
French Agency for Food Sanitary Safety (AFSSA) (France)
Instituto Nacional de Investigacion y Tecnologia Agraria (INIA) (Spain)
Irish Water Safety
Medical Products Agency (MPA) (Sweden)
National Institute for Public Health and the Environment (RIVM) (Netherlands)
National Research and Safety Institution for the Prevention of Occupational Accidents
    and Diseases (INRS) (France)
The Swedish Environmental Protection Agency (EPA)

---

low-grade risk compared with unfamiliar risk and low probability but catastrophic risk. The third is the need to assess the reliability of data and the quality of the evidence. Science is not typically dealing with certainties and for many areas of potential risk the information is patchy or incomplete and involves contested science. The fourth is the need to assess one risk against another. The typical risk scenario does not involve comparing a situation of risk with a situation of safety but a situation where the reduction of one risk may lead to an increase in another. These are all areas of technical difficulty and sophistication that lend themselves to analysis by specialised bodies.

The boundary watchers

Another growing class of unelected bodies consists of those agencies charged with responsibility for watching the boundary between private sector activities and the public interest at points where there is a particular sensitivity for social, environmental or ethical reasons.

One type of body that falls into this category is the independent economic regulator. These have been created in the UK mainly following the privatisation of previously state-owned utilities starting in the 1980s. Privatisation by itself did not necessarily bring about competition in the market. The primary task of the economic regulator has been to bring about competitive markets in the sector or sectors they regulate, in the belief that competition will bring consumer and social benefits. The sensitivity arises partly because the sectors they cover are basic to modern living and it only takes an interruption in power supplies or a water shortage to remind people how dependent they are. It also arises because the paying for the provision of these services, or interruptions in supply because of difficulties in paying, can be particularly harsh for those on the margins of the economy. The overall task of these bodies is thus to develop competitive markets while watching the boundary between the behaviour of their market and selected public goals. They ask the question whether the market is producing the economic and social improvements expected, as well as security of supply, or whether regulatory intervention in the market is required.[9] The model of the independent economic regulator is now widespread across Europe.

Another type of boundary watcher is formed by an equally new generation of bodies that look at private activities in relation to the latest ethical concerns of society. These have sprung up not only in areas of social discrimination but also in the health and biomedical area, triggered by the fact that people are living longer and healthier lives and making ever greater demands on medical services, and by the growth in medical innovation including knowledge of the human genome.

Also of growing sensitivity are those bodies dealing with the handling of hitherto private information. Modern search engines can pull together

---

[9] For example in 2005, UK's OFGEM (the gas and electricity market regulator) undertook a review of supply licences with one of the main aims to give adequate protection to customers who are elderly, or disabled, suffering from long-term sickness or on low incomes. Source: OFGEM Press Office. 7 March 2006.

from public and private sources an enormous amount of personal data. The point at which this becomes intrusive or invasive is a boundary that has become increasingly important in the light of measures to combat terrorism and crime. Britain's Information Commissioner has to look on the one hand at the risk of over-intrusive 'big brother' government and on the other hand at the risk of a prying private sector where detailed personal information ends up in the hands of those an individual would never voluntarily release it to. Examples of these different types of boundary watcher are shown in table 3.

The boundary watchers now provide the main bridge between the public and private sector. There was a time, not so long ago, when the demarcation between public and private was defined by ownership – what was in the hands of the state and what was in the hands of private owners. That distinction has gone. It is not ownership that defines the boundaries of modern markets and the boundaries of the state, it is the new breed of appointed watchers.

The inquisitors

Shortly after William Duke of Normandy seized the English throne in 1066 he sent out a band of inspectors to tally exactly what he had acquired in his new realm. The compilation that resulted, the Domesday Book, laid the basis for effective government by the Normans. The modern inspector and auditor (shown in table 4) is also concerned with the effectiveness of government. This category includes traditional inspection bodies focussing on compliance in a narrow sense of following government regulations. But the category has expanded with the growth in the role of modern government to include new audit bodies with the task of inspecting and auditing many of the other unelected bodies as well as central government departments. They monitor and report on this new world and also themselves belong to it. They act on behalf of the traditional organs of democratic government, the executives and parliaments that have established the new institutions. At the same time they are independent of government and need that independence in order to be able to do their work without politicians telling them in advance what their findings should be. They are inquisitors but not adversaries. The unelected bodies themselves also need to know whether or not they are doing a good job from an independent source. An adversarial relationship would not assist the learning process.

It is not so much the number of auditors and inspectors that is important as the widening scope of their functions. Traditionally, audit focussed on expenditures in a narrow book-keeping sense – it looked at strictly financial processes and whether they could provide the assurance

Table 3: *Selected boundary watchers between state and market*

UK
Civil Aviation Authority (CAA)
Commission for Racial Equality (CRE)
Disability Rights Commission (DRC)
Equal Opportunities Commission (EOC)
Financial Services Authority (FSA)
Gambling Commission
Gangmasters Licensing Authority (GLA)
Human Fertilisation and Embryology Authority (HFEA)
Information Commissioner
National Consumer Council (NCC)
Office of Communications (OFCOM)
Office of Fair Trading (OFT)
Office of Gas and Electricity Markets (OFGEM)
Office of Rail Regulation (ORR)
Office of Water Services (OFWAT)
Reviewing Committee on the Export of Works of Art (RCEWA)

USA
Commodity Futures Trading Commission (CFTC)
Equal Employment Opportunity Commission (EEOC)
Federal Communications Commission (FCC)
Federal Trade Commission (FTC)
Office of the Comptroller of the Currency (OCC)
Pension Benefit Guaranty Corporation (PBGC)
Securities and Exchange Commission (SEC)

Australia
Australian Communications and Media Authority (ACMA)
Australian Competition and Consumer Commission (ACCC)
Australian Securities and Investments Commission (ASIC)
Human Rights and Equal Opportunities Commission
Office of the Gene Technology Regulator (OGTR)
Office of the Privacy Commissioner

EU member states
Equal Opportunities Commission (Sweden)
Federal Cartel Office (Germany)
Financial Markets Authority (FMA) (France)
German Financial Supervisory Authority (BaFiN) (Germany)
High Authority against Discrimination and for Equality (HALDE) (France)
Irish Human Rights Commission (IHRC)
National Institute for Consumer Protection (France)
The Swedish National Post and Telecom Agency (PTS)

Table 4: *Selected audit and inspection bodies*

UK
Adult Learning Inspectorate (ALI)
Audit Commission
Commission for Social Care Inspection (CSCI)
Council on Tribunals
English Heritage
National Audit Office (NAO)
National Lottery Commission (NLC)
The Health Commission

USA
Government Accountability Office (GAO)
National Institute of Justice (NIJ)
US Sentencing Commission

Australia
Aged Care Standards and Accreditation Office
Australian National Audit Office (ANAO)

EU member states
Court of Accounts (France)
Irish Social Services Inspectorate (ISSI.IE)
National Board of Health and Welfare (Sweden)
The Federal Court of Auditors (Germany)

---

that money had been spent on the purposes intended. This function is still important. But the role has expanded to include the concept of perform-ance audit. This is a much wider concept that involves tracking whether expenditure and regulatory programmes are yielding the results originally expected. It involves measuring outcomes against intentions and its scope ranges far wider than financial analysis.

The umpires and whistle-blowers

A final category of institution set apart from democratic politics are the new courts, commissions, tribunals, appeals bodies and extra-judicial disputes settlement bodies such as Ombudsmen (shown in table 5). They comprise the 'umpires' of the new system because they decide when powers have been misused or exceeded and processes violated. In the UK they comprise bodies such as the Competition Appeals Tribunal that provides a venue of final appeal against rulings of the Competition Commission that is itself a body to which the decisions of sector regu-lators can be appealed, and the Pensions Regulator who can intervene

Table 5: *Selected umpires and whistle-blowers*

UK
Care Standards Tribunal (CST)
Charity Commission
Competition Appeals Tribunal
Electoral Commission
Employment Appeal Tribunal
Family Health Services Appeal Authority (FHSAA)
Financial Reporting Council (FRC)
Independent Police Complaints Commission (IPCC)
Information Tribunal
Legal Services Complaints Commissioner (OLSCC)
Occupational Pensions Regulatory Authority (OPRA)
Office for the Commissioner for Public Appointments (OCPA)
Office of the Telecommunications Adjudicator (OFFTA)
Pensions Ombudsman
Standards Board for England

USA
Federal Election Commission
Financial Accounting Standards Board (FASB)
Merit Systems Protection Board (MSPB)
Office of Government Ethics (USOGE)
Office of Special Counsel (OSC)
US Commission on Civil Rights

Australia
Administrative Appeals Tribunal (AAT)
Administrative Review Council (ARC)
Australian Accounting Standards Board (AASB)
Australian Competition Tribunal
Commonwealth Ombudsman
Social Security Appeals Tribunal (SSAT)

EU member states
Alien Appeals Board (Sweden)
Children's Ombudsman (Sweden)
French Office for the Protection of Refugees and Stateless
Office of the Data Protection Ombudsman (Finland)
Office of the Pensions Ombudsman (Belgium)
Ombudsman for Children (OCO) (Ireland)

when occupational pensions appear under jeopardy from either corporate mismanagement or takeovers. The Independent Police Complaints Commission investigates charges against the police.

The new breed of tribunal and appeals body comes on top of an increasingly activist traditional judiciary as courts have adopted a more and more assertive role vis-à-vis the traditional political branches – both parliaments and governments. For the citizen, what counts, at the end of the day, is that increasingly they may turn to new complaints mechanisms and new dispute resolution procedures to supplement traditional avenues of political or legal redress.

Common features

It can be seen from the examples selected above that in the UK unelected bodies range from the obscure (the Gangmasters Licensing Authority set up to protect the lives of cockle pickers) to the publicly prominent (the Bank of England). Taken in their entirety, they cover a huge range of terrain of importance to people in their daily lives. In the modern world it would be possible to construct an imaginary day for an imaginary person where their every significant action, from making a cup of tea or coffee when they got up, to turning the light off when they went to bed, was in one way or another affected by them.

At first sight, the unelected bodies occupy very different worlds. There seems no obvious connection, for example, between the world of the central banker and the world of health and safety executives. There also seems to be a basic difference between those bodies that deal with subjects that are familiar to people, such as the education system, or child maintenance, and those bodies that deal with areas of scientific advance such as genetic engineering where many people will feel ignorant and lost.

There are, however, four fundamental features that unelected bodies share in common. First, most operate in technically sophisticated areas. Secondly, almost all rely on sources outside the government for information and knowledge. Thirdly, with this specialised information and knowledge they form their own communities. Finally, discussed in a later chapter, they also have their own disciplines.

A technical world

The unelected bodies, in their entirety, make decisions that affect everybody in their daily lives. However, behind these decisions about goods and services with which we are very familiar, often lies a technical world with its own highly specialised knowledge that is far from mundane. Concepts such as 'market dominance', that weigh the number of firms and type of behaviour in a market below which competition is likely to be diminished, may excite competition authorities. Similarly, 'local loop unbundling', that concerns the way in which fixed wire telecommunications operators may control access to the consumer at the final stage of delivery, may be of enormous interest to economic regulators. Moreover, the way in which these issues are approached ends up by having an impact on the general public. But these and similar topics are not the stuff of normal conversation, the standard fare of the popular media or even the daily bread of politicians. Similarly, central bankers may debate vigorously whether to target monetary indicators, or price indicators, or a broader set of economic activity indicators, but it is a debate that does not extend beyond a narrow range of practitioners and academics. Equally, accountants and auditors may be very insistent about what should be 'marked to market' and how to treat 'goodwill' on the balance sheet but the debates around the subject, even if they are of great importance to the public as shareholders or investors in pension funds, will rarely escape the bounds of the professions and the agencies involved in their interpretation and enforcement. The technicalities and specialist knowledge involved are equally evident in the world of health, safety and environmental regulation.

The gathering and processing of detailed first-hand information

A second feature common to the world of unelected bodies is that they rely for their information and knowledge largely on the world outside politics and in particular on the private sector. Economic regulators must be deeply conversant with the businesses they regulate, central bankers with financial markets, and health, safety and environmental regulators both with scientific thinking in academia and everyday management practices in the business world.

The information-gathering relationship is not a straightforward one. From the perspective of the private sector there are costs involved in supplying information. In addition, the information may be market sensitive or involve commercial confidentiality. The private sector may see advantage in keeping better informed than a regulator and therefore also deliberately withhold information. From the perspective of the unelected bodies themselves, the best possible information is needed on which to base their policies or their actions may be challenged as unreasonable. At the same time they have to devise their own tests to ensure that the information supplied is reliable and that they are not being misled, either deliberately by the source of the information, or by inaccurate data.[10] A large part of their work thus concerns checking the quality and reliability of data.

---

[10] In March 2006 one of Britain's water utilities (Seven Trent) was penalised in a landmark case for having 'provided regulatory data that was either deliberately miscalculated or poorly supported'. Source: OFWAT. PN 09/06. Dated 7 March 2006.

Epistemic communities

Finally, the inhabitants of the world of unelected bodies form a key part of what are known as 'epistemic communities'. What this means is that they acquire specialised knowledge and skill in exercising their functions and that this knowledge and skill is of particular interest to others exercising the same or similar functions.[11] When they talk, they talk to each other. Central bankers talk *at* financial markets but they talk *to* other central bankers; economic regulators talk to other economic regulators, competition authorities to other competition authorities and auditors talk to other auditors. The reason for this is that they see themselves operating in similar settings, facing similar problems and having similar experiences to share. They often share a common intellectual approach and procedural disciplines. When there are lessons to learn they are likely to be learnt from each other. Often, as mentioned later, the peer group will be international in character rather than national or local. The unelected are prime movers behind the formation of policy networks.[12]

The negative aspect of epistemic communities is that they can form closed worlds and insulate themselves from the broader public. They are often viewed as elitist. However, unelected bodies in a national context have a strong self-interest in keeping the public well informed about what they are doing and why. The reason for this is that they need public support and understanding for what they do. If interest rates have to be kept higher than people would like, or if the price of drinking water at the tap has to go up, or electricity prices rise, or environmental concerns are stirred by the construction of new power stations, the unelected bodies need public acquiescence. Public protest would mean not only a challenge to a particular decision but could threaten their status itself. It could stimulate politicians to seek to claw back their independence.

A self-effacing class

In the UK the regulators see themselves by and large as a 'self-effacing class'. Their actions affect our daily lives, our prospects at key stages in our lives and the kinds of hazard our lives are exposed to. Yet, they do not actively court the public limelight; in addition, unlike ambitious civil

---

[11] The term was introduced by Peter Haas using a stricter and more comprehensive definition (see Haas (1989)).

[12] Defined in minimal terms as informal, decentralised and horizontal relationships between largely autonomous actors. See Marin and Mayntz (1991). For a review of attempts at more ambitious accounts of the role of policy networks see Thatcher (1998).

servants that like to be close to their minister, they prefer their arm's-length relationship to politicians. Their temperament inclines them towards the judicial or the academic rather than the political. Respect from their own peer group is as important as any other form of recognition. But, however self-effacing they may be by temperament, the fact is that unelected bodies have become the operational and practical arm of systems of democratic government – the part that works rather than the part that attracts attention. Just how they have quietly grown into this role is discussed in the next chapter.

2 The driving forces

Conventional explanations for the growth in the numbers and variety of unelected bodies focus on the demanding external environment facing modern governments and the pressures for managerial reform that this created. Such managerial accounts offer important but insufficient explanations. They avoid talking about how public policy is formed. Public policy formation involves two elements – empirical judgements about the facts and political and ethical judgements about the values involved. This leads to a different type of rationale for the creation of unelected bodies – an institutional separation between bodies responsible for the two different types of judgement. Unelected bodies take on a special responsibility for empirical judgements in policy-making and elected bodies focus on value judgements.

The shift to a service economy

The most general explanation for the growth of unelected bodies lies with the forces of 'globalisation'. Globalisation opened up to a broader array of external influences previously sheltered activities, including government structures and government policy-making.[1] Change became inevitable.

Because it is such a broad term, 'globalisation' by itself is an unsatisfactory explanation in this area just as it is in others. A slightly more precise explanation is that the changes in the structure of government have paralleled broad changes in the structure of the economies of developed countries. The change of particular relevance has been the striking switch in recent decades away from output from manufacturing and industrial activity to output from the service economy. The reform of the public

---

[1] An OECD report notes, 'Shortly after a few countries undertook reforms ... there was a huge upsurge in interest in international comparisons ... there is no doubt that the way public administration was thought about had undergone a deep and permanent change. From long being "closed shops", governments opened up to new ideas on how to organise themselves.' Matheson and Kwon (2003).

sector across the world can be seen as belonging to this broader movement of a shift to services.

At the same time that consumers were turning to services in the private sector they may have increasingly been tempted to judge the public sector by the same demanding standards that they expected to encounter in the market. It set up a comparison that many government services were likely to fail – they produced the wrong products; they were slow to respond to demands and complaining was fruitless and unrewarding. For their part, politicians did not want to be associated with perceptions of failure and lack of receptivity. The response of the politicians therefore to a demand for higher service standards from the public sector has involved two actions. Within government there has been increasing use of a variety of indicators of performance, usually in the form of targets, to try to measure and improve delivery of government services. But in addition, there was motivation to look for what could be cast off and placed at arm's length.

The explanation that the rise of unelected bodies corresponds to the perception of government as part of the service economy helps explain why the service-focussed activities of both providers and boundary watchers figure prominently among the independent bodies. A concern about performance also helps explain the growth of the inspectors and the widening remit of audit and evaluation.

The strength of the general economic explanation about the shift to services is that it helps account for why both the public and existing government bodies would have either actively supported change or at least allowed it to happen. A major shift in the way in which government is organised needs, at the least, an accommodating attitude both from the public and from other political institutions.[2] The weakness of the explanation is that it remains very general.

Managerial explanations

A much more specific explanation for the growth of non-majoritarian institutions rests on the influence of 'the new public management'. This approach to the machinery of government came into vogue in the 1980s and quickly spread around the world. Under its guiding principles a large

---

[2] Pollitt and Bouckaert (2000: 185) list three requirements for public sector reform including, 'A degree of public acceptance, or at least acquiescence.' Similarly, Lynn (2001: 12) notes, 'Any particular governance arrangement . . . is embedded in a wider social, fiscal and political context.'

number of bodies were detached from previously centralised government departments.[3]

The new public management

The new public management placed an emphasis on achieving results through the means of more flexible organisation structures in government instead of through traditional, highly centralised and hierarchical government departments. Phrases such as 'competition between providers' introduced the thinking of the market into the heart of public administration. The vocabulary changed to talk about 'mission statements' rather than procedures to be followed.[4] The jargon of management consultants replaced the jargon of bureaucrats. Both forms of jargon share an equal facility to irritate and obfuscate.

At the centre of the new public management gospel lay a distinction between the service delivery functions of government and the policy functions. It was suggested that central government departments should focus their attention on 'policy management' for their political masters (the steering function) while many service delivery functions (the rowing function) could be delegated, or spun off, to specialised agencies. These were more appropriately placed at a distance from politics or even privatised. The new public managers were 'to steer and not row'.

A number of advantages were claimed for this approach. It distinguished between the skills needed for policy advice and the different skills of a manager of people or resources to deliver services. It suggested that the incentives to review and refresh policy would be stronger if the people in charge of policy were not at the same time managing the programmes that could be affected by policy change. It enabled different and more flexible recruitment policies to be adopted and more private sector management skills to be brought into public sector activities. It provided a different professional and career setting for scientists and other experts as well as professional managers. It enabled the new independent agencies to develop their own procedures and ethos.[5]

Critics suggest that the advantages claimed for the new public management were based on selective examples rather than hard analysis.[6] Notwithstanding their possibly shaky underpinnings, the various tenets

---

[3] For a useful overview of the new public management and its many variations see Pollitt and Bouckaert (2000).
[4] For a popular account see Osborne and Gaebler (1992).
[5] See Hood and Schuppert (1988: 246).
[6] Hood (1998). A later OECD report noted, 'Reforms have produced positive results but also some negative and perverse results.' OECD (2002).

of the new public management consolidated into a new orthodoxy and spread, with variations, around the world.[7] It undoubtedly encouraged the growth of independent agencies set at arm's length from government departments. Nevertheless, at the end of the day, the litany of reforms encouraged by 'new public management' has a hollow core.

The shortcomings of new public management

The hole at the centre stems from what the new public management said, and what it omitted to say, about public policy and how public policy gets formed.

First, the basic premise that a distinction can be made between 'policy management' and 'service delivery' is not convincing because the distinction is often a difficult one to draw.[8] For example, a rise in the incidence of self-harm among prison inmates may be seen by politicians as a question of failures in 'service delivery', and the responsibility of an independent prisons agency, but for prison managers it may be seen as a 'policy management' question to do with inadequate resource levels, as well as politically confused signals about the aims of incarceration. The crux of the matter is that policy failure may only become visible at the operational level and it may be easier to detect failure against operational indicators than at other stages in the process.[9]

Secondly, the basic underlying distinction between service delivery and policy 'management' does not pay enough attention to the way in which 'policy' is put together. The phrase 'policy management' leaves unanswered the question of what content goes into policy-making and how it gets there. The new public management tended to assume a top-down policy process, focussed on outcomes, and did not offer a coherent account of the processes of policy-making itself.[10]

There were reasons why policy processes were neglected and why 'policy' was presented mainly in terms of the management of something given from outside the system by politicians. Policy processes often seem too opaque and unpredictable to be systematically analysed. Governments, together with the policies they come up with, are notoriously the creatures of the pressures of outside 'events' rather than internal agendas. Their agendas are heavily weighted too by the burden of past

[7] See Bekke, Perry and Toonen (1996).
[8] The distinction is rejected by, among others, Hughes (1998).
[9] See Barberis (1998).
[10] For an account of policy-making as an after-the-event interpretation of government activity, see Lynn (1987). For the view that this leads to an incoherent treatment see Peters (1996).

legislation and experience. Thus, there does not seem to be a clear trail to follow between policy inception, the weighing of policy choices and the final policy decisions. The received wisdom was that the policy process was about 'muddling through' – a process in which policy-makers mixed goals, values and empirical data in a series of approximations.[11] Another influential metaphor was of the 'garbage can'.[12]

In the face of these difficulties, and in the face also of the emergence of several competing approaches as to how to better express the policy-making process, it was understandable that the new public management would prefer to take policy as a 'given'.[13] But this neglect of the policy process led to the neglect of a different and powerful factor also altering the way governments were going about their work – the way in which the components of public policy were being brought together was changing in a fundamental way.

The new separation of powers

A different perspective on the rise of unelected bodies is to see their growth not simply as part and parcel of a broad shift to the service economy, nor simply as a reflection of a new culture of management inside the public sector, but in addition as a response to a fundamental division emerging within the policy process itself – a division between the empirical judgements underlying a policy and the political judgements.

Two types of judgement: two types of institution

This division in policy-making distinguishes between two streams in the process that enter into the formation of public policy. The first stream involves empirical judgements on the facts of a case, analysis of those facts, the identification of possible causal connections and linkages to a body of knowledge. The second stream involves the interpretation that politics and politicians may place on those facts and the political and moral judgements that they may make about the analysis.[14]

---

[11] For a description see Lindblom (1959).

[12] 'The pure garbage can model is basically institution free, or structure is treated as exogenous. Decisions are produced to a large extent by the temporal linkages of problems, solutions, choice opportunities, and decision makers.' Olsen (2001: 193).

[13] For a summary description of different approaches to the policy process see Sabatier (1999: 3–18).

[14] Dahl (1989: 69) remarks, 'Because moral understanding and instrumental knowledge are always necessary for policy judgments, neither alone can ever be sufficient.'

The fundamental importance of this distinction for public policy-making can be seen from the example of the policy of 'zero tolerance' towards petty crime. This policy has been copied around the world. It has been justified in part because the evidence from its highly publicised use in New York seemed to suggest that a crackdown on petty crime would lead to subsequent reductions in more serious crime. But, at the same time, the adoption of the policy in many different jurisdictions across the world has also owed as much to the judgement of politicians that the public wanted stronger policies against crime. 'Zero tolerance' was there for the picking.

In this example there are the facts about what happened on the streets of New York and empirical judgements to be made about the chain of possible causality between petty crime and serious crime. There were also analytic judgements to be made about whether the conditions in other urban centres were sufficiently 'similar' to New York that policy lessons could be transferred to other settings. In addition, there were the values introduced by the politicians. The public wanted action and it was 'good' for politicians to be seen to be 'tough' on crime. Even if there were questions about the causality, or about the appropriateness of the transposition of a policy from one urban and social setting to other possibly different settings, politicians saw a value to be attached to 'law and order' that justified the adoption of the policy despite any uncertainties in empirical judgements.

What this example shows is that, typically, public 'Policy' involves both evidence and value judgement.[15] There are the facts, evidence and analysis about the causalities involved in crime. There are also the value judgements to be made that the rise in crime should be tackled in a particular way as a social and political priority. The distinction between the two types of judgement is crucial over most areas of public policy, from whether to launch a pre-emptive military strike to whether to allow certain types of genetic engineering.

It is precisely this question of how to handle evidence and empirical knowledge in relation to political values in policy-making that provides a much more fundamental explanation for the growth of unelected bodies around the world. Their growth can be seen as a way to institutionalise within democracies the distinction between the two types of reasoning and judgement, between knowledge-based judgement and political judgement. Unelected bodies concentrate on gathering facts, doing the

---

[15] 'Whereas drawing a lesson is about getting to grips with technicalities of programmes in two different countries, the adoption of a lesson is an exercise in political judgement' Rose (2005: 90).

analysis and making knowledge-based judgements; the traditional elective branches of democratic governments make the political judgements.

The distinction between judgements based on evidence and judgements reflecting political values applied to the evidence does not imply a hierarchy between the two streams of judgement. It cannot be assumed that knowledge-based judgements are superior to judgements reflecting political values, for example that the interpretation that politicians may place on facts, or the judgements that they may make in order to introduce political or other values, are necessarily misplaced or wrong or inferior. Nor can the contrary be assumed – that the political valuation is necessarily superior. The evidence may point to a flaw or inconsistency in the valuation process.

Both types of judgement have their place, both may be rational in their own terms, and the stress may be placed on either depending on the nature of the decision. But the distinction between the different types of judgement is vital.[16] The facts about whether or not Iraq possessed weapons of mass destruction (WMD) prior to the outbreak of the Second Gulf War may have appeared uncertain to those analysing them; their professional judgements on how to interpret the uncertainties may have led the UN analysts to judge that it was unlikely that Sadam Hussein did actually possess WMD. Nevertheless, even though the evidence was less than clear, it was a different type of political judgement that the leaders of the USA, the UK and other allies had to make in assessing whether the stakes involved in getting rid of a dangerous and unethical regime justified outside military intervention.

Externalising empirical judgements

The traditional view of the relationship between empirical judgements (for example those of scientists, economists and technical analysts) and the judgement of politicians was that these two streams of judgement could be internalised within central departments of government. There was a long-standing debate about how this relationship could best be expressed.

One view was that those with expert knowledge should just present their analysis and leave all further elements in policy formation to the politicians – the drawback being that politicians might not understand the implications of the analysis. A second view therefore was that the expert should also present the politician with a range of choices coming out of

[16] For one discussion of the interrelationship between evidence-based processes and the ethical context see Gillroy and Maurice (1992).

the analysis but leave the politician to decide between the choices. The drawback to this position was that the politician might want to know which choice the expert preferred and why. This led to a third view that experts should also indicate their preferred alternative. Finally, there were those who believed that the politicians could provide the expert with the relevant value judgements that could then be integrated into the analysis.[17]

These distinctions remain relevant but they now apply to decisions on the terms of reference of independent bodies outside the machinery of central government. At one end of the spectrum there are agencies, such as those in the European Union, that are essentially confined to fact gathering. At the other end of the spectrum there are bodies such as the UK's Information Commissioner (set up to oversee the Data Protection Act and the Freedom of Information Act) and the Human Fertilisation and Embryology Authority (set up to license and monitor human embryo research) that are charged with deploying and assessing empirical knowledge in order to safeguard values stipulated by the politicians. The next chapter looks in greater detail at the reasons for this development.

---

[17] For a discussion of these distinctions see Hammond and Adelman (1986).

3 The advantages of the new separation of powers

The separation of powers identified in the last chapter involves an institutional separation between those unelected institutions primarily concerned with mobilising the facts, evidence and empirical knowledge in public policy-making and those elected bodies primarily concerned with the value judgements that enter into public policy-making. This chapter looks further at the reasons for this separation and at the advantages to the public of entrusting unelected institutions with mobilising facts and making empirical judgements.

At a very general level, the provision of information and knowledge is a service in society and the advantages to the public of the unelected bodies in this area can be seen as part of the general move to more service-oriented economies. But there are two much more compelling reasons examined in this chapter why the public is likely to have seen benefits in the institutional separation of the two streams of judgement. The first relates to public confidence in the empirical information and analysis they are provided with. The second involves the advantages to the public from unbundling different institutional roles and responsibilities for the two streams of judgement. This chapter also examines the objections of those who suggest that such a separation is impossible.

Independent information gatherers

What has transformed the traditional debate from one about how to organise the gathering of information and the mobilisation of empirical knowledge within government, to one about how to organise it outside and independent of government, are the advantages that independent bodies possess as fact gatherers and sources of expert knowledge and judgement.

When it comes to gathering information and mobilising empirical knowledge in modern societies, the information and knowledge required to form and to implement policy comes, as mentioned in the previous chapter, increasingly from the private sector rather than from a government's own sources. In obtaining this information governments have one significant advantage. That advantage flows from the ability of governments to require people, institutions and companies to divulge information by law. But in other respects the traditional institutions of democratic government are not well equipped to handle information and knowledge. Elected politicians are unlikely to have the technical knowledge to gather, process and appraise information since many will be professional politicians and lack the relevant experience and qualifications.

By contrast, independent institutions have a number of advantages as information and knowledge gatherers and assessors:

First, they have the advantages of specialisation – they know what they are looking for and where the information might be found. In this they also hold an advantage not only over politicians or political appointees but also over the traditional civil service departments of central government where job rotation may also curtail the growth of specialised knowledge.

Secondly, they can develop their own procedures calculated to elucidate and sift the facts. They are neither tied to parliamentary procedures nor to government procedures. Neither do they have to follow procedures identical to the way courts have developed their procedures for sifting facts and evidence. Compared with the consultations organised by a government department, unelected bodies can be more systematic and organised in gathering information; compared with a parliament they can be more focussed on evidence gathering rather than on the more general canvassing of public attitudes; compared with courts they can act in advance of specific cases being brought and can also aim for non-adversarial procedures in establishing the facts.

Thirdly, because independent bodies are freer to hire according to specialist needs, they can bring their own expertise to bear on fact gathering and assessment and are likely to be better at evaluating the information. Providers of information may offer partial information, may offer information intended to further self-interest, or to mislead or manipulate or as a bargaining chip. Everything requires evaluation and assessment.

Fourthly, they derive advantages as part of a peer group of people and institutions involved in similar activities. This provides advantages in lesson learning and through the exchange of experience on related issues.

Fifthly, because of both their independence and expertise they can speak with greater authority on the facts and their assessment of them. Becoming authoritative, and being seen to be authoritative in their field, is an important aim for many. An independent central bank seeks credibility in financial markets; a finance minister seeks re-election.

Finally, they are likely to be more motivated to diffuse the facts they gather and the assessments they make. They want to be well regarded by their professional peers for the quality of their assessments and they want acceptance by the public for the conclusions they reach. They do not want to be challenged in the courts for un-investigated claims or for arbitrary or unsupported decisions. Equally important, an economic regulator does not want to catch either the firms it regulates or the public by surprise and, similarly, an independent central bank does not want to catch financial markets by surprise.

Assessing facts and weighing evidence

Independent bodies not only offer advantages in gathering information but also in exercising professional judgement on it. Evidence, whether it is based on the physical sciences or on the social sciences, rarely allows for one unequivocal interpretation. Interpretation of evidence in the real world is not usually about establishing certainty but about making judgements based on the balance of probabilities, on the weight of evidence and in the light of missing evidence. Thus the ability to assess evidence critically, to make evidence-based judgements and to recognise the limitations of the evidence is crucial.

One practical example of the kinds of judgements involved concerns official statistics of the type used over most of the range of public policy-making. Attitudes towards such statistics, according to folklore, tend to hover between two extremes. At one extreme are those who regard all statistics as sophisticated lies. At the other extreme are those who regard them as unquestionable facts. In most cases they are neither – they are best estimates.[1] Even the production of the driest form of data requires judgement.

The assessment of 'facts' requires judgement, so too does the assessment of 'evidence'. A practical example of the kind of assessments involved in looking at evidence is provided by efforts to reduce public exposure to airborne pollutants in the form of fine particulate matter. In this case it is possibly important from a public health perspective that the fine particles put out by power stations are chemically quite different from those put out by vehicles and other industrial sources. Public policy

---

[1] See Statistics Commission. Report No. 24 (2005: 6). 'The aim of statistical work is generally to produce usable information from incomplete data. Sampling, imputation and estimation are the essence of statistics, not totting up scores in a cricket match. So official statistics are mostly the best estimates that can be made at the time they are produced, no more or less.'

will also be affected by forecasts about the prevalence of pollution in this form.

Judgements about the evidence in this area involve weighing three types of uncertainty. There is uncertainty about the forecasts about the future prevalence of airborne pollutants of different types. In addition, there is uncertainty about differential effect estimates by different particle types and uncertainty too surrounding the several potential biological mechanisms that might associate inhalation of fine particles at standard concentrations with a risk of premature death.[2]

The qualities of judgement required in such situations are unlikely to be found among professional politicians in traditional democratic institutions. This is not a slur on their capabilities, which may be great, but rather a reflection of the fact that the professional qualities and skills that make for a successful politician are not the same as the professional skills that come into play in weighing evidence and assessing its limits and uncertainties. Nor do the incentives within politics work in the direction of encouraging the exercise of this kind of judgement. An ability to capture the headlines, to score debating points, to act opportunistically and to rally partisan supporters and to catch a fleeting public mood may all be valuable attributes in a politician – but they are not the attributes needed in judging the quality of 'facts' or in mobilising and assessing the weight of evidence and in recognising its limitations.

As mentioned earlier, the institutional separation between unelected bodies with a special responsibility for assessing the empirical evidence in public policy and elected bodies with a special responsibility for bringing social and ethical considerations to bear on the formation of policy is not absolute. The unelected bodies include those with an ethical responsibility in new fields, such as an embryology authority, as well as those with a social responsibility in traditional fields such as health and safety. But in such cases separation still hinges on the need for mastery of the empirical evidence and the latest state of scientific and empirical knowledge.

Confidence in public information

The rise of unelected bodies as gatherers and assessors of facts and evidence has required public acquiescence. The first reason why the public may have acquiesced in the development of entrusting the mobilisation of information and expert knowledge to independent bodies

---

[2] This example has been drawn from Office of Management and Budget (2004: 10–11).

relates to public confidence in the information they provide and the judgements they make.

The 'least bad' alternative

Independent assessors do not offer perfectly reliable sources of untainted information and analysis. Nevertheless, from the perspective of having confidence and trust in respect of gathering the evidence, in assessing the evidence and in passing judgement on the evidence in public policy, the unelected bodies appear to offer the 'least bad' solution for the public. Independent agencies are largely free from any suspected bias that manufacturers or service providers may have, for example to suppress risk information; they are free from the bias that politicians may have either to downplay or exaggerate facts, and they offer an informed guide through the disputes about the evidence within the scientific community itself. The former chairman of the UK's Food Standards Agency has said, 'If you are independent, that means being objective and impartial about the evidence and not succumbing to pressure from interest groups, whether they are the food industry, consumer groups, green groups, or politicians.'[3]

Independent agencies are not themselves free from suspicion – for example that they might be captured by powerful interests, or bend to a government's will, or simply be biased by a pursuit of their own self-interest. Independence from governments and parliaments is not a complete defence against suspicion of bias. Experts and expert bodies may also have their own personal or 'house' biases. Personal biases may range from the bias of 'hired guns' employed to provide 'expert' evidence in courts of law, to the bias of social and physical scientists with an interest in presenting their findings in a manner not to inform but to get funding or publicity. In-house institutional biases arise from internal habits of mind or cultural dispositions that become entrenched. Defences against both kinds of bias are discussed at a later point. However, independence remains a good starting point and the 'least bad' solution compared with the alternatives.

The point is illustrated by the recent decision of the British Government to make the Office of National Statistics clearly independent of government. Earlier controversies about changes to the way in which employment was being measured, inflation indices constructed, immigration figures recorded, the way privatised but subsidised bodies were to

---

[3] Sir John Krebs, quoted in the *Financial Times* (10 Feb. 2005).

be recorded as belonging to the public or private sector, and improvements in the way health indicators were measured, all pointed to the suspicion about the way data services are handled when produced within a government department. Independence is seen as a way of removing these suspicions and creating public confidence in statistics on which much public policy is based.

Sources of authority

Another way of viewing the issue of 'confidence' is to see it as related to the fact that democratic societies need more than one type of basis for taking decisions and that unelected bodies can be viewed as the most reliable vehicle for taking decisions that are based on 'competence'.[4] 'Competence', however, suggests decisions based on the type of technical expertise required in knowing how to do something (such as how to fly an aeroplane or to carry out a surgical procedure). Unelected bodies indeed need to be competent in what they do. However, they address a broader and more fundamental dimension – how to mobilise information and knowledge authoritatively in societies – including the judgement needed to evaluate conflicting information and competing claims about the state of knowledge. The unelected will make errors but the authority of political bodies in this area is weak by comparison. The unelected bring a major new dimension to the way in which decision-making is approached in democracies.

Economists summarise the advantages of authority in terms of savings in 'transaction costs'. They arise from each of the two sources identified – the savings that come from having bodies with institutional advantages in gathering and analysing information and the savings that come from people having greater confidence in using that information.

The fundamental limitation to unelected bodies as sources of authority is that while independent bodies have advantages in gathering information and assessing evidence, they have no inherent advantage when it comes to making value judgements about what should be done when all the evidence is weighed. They are equipped to make professional judgements based on the balance of evidence, but they are not necessarily equipped to make value judgements drawing on non-scientific values and principles.[5] Here the politician comes back in.

---

[4] Dahl (1970) suggests that there are three bases for decision-taking: personal choice, competence and efficiency.
[5] Dahl (1989: 69) makes the point that experts are specialists and thus often ignorant of matters outside their field of speciality.

This boundary line between unelected bodies with an advantage in making empirical judgements and elected bodies with an advantage in making social judgements is crossed over in those cases where the unelected body has ethical responsibilities. Such cases are likely to arise in technically sophisticated areas. In these situations the unelected body still possesses an advantage in distinguishing between the empirical evidence that informs its decisions and the social or ethical judgements it makes. Institutional lines are crossed but the two types of logic – the empirical and the normative – are clarified.

The second major area of benefit to the public arises because of these institutional distinctions. The public derives practical benefits from being able to distinguish institutionally between the role of unelected bodies clarifying the empirical bases of public policies and the role of elected bodies focussing on the normative. It is not just a question of confidence but, equally important, the wider advantages of knowing which kind of body is responsible for what kind of judgement.

Before considering the nature of this further benefit to the public there is a crucial objection to consider. The objection strikes at the root of the new separation of powers by denying that evidence-based judgements of the unelected bodies and the value-based judgements of the elected institutions can in fact be prised apart – the two are simply inseparable.

The inseparability of value judgements?

The idea that professional assessments of information, evidence and judgements on the evidence can be usefully separated in policy-making from the kind of value judgements that are typically made by politicians is open to two types of challenge – the first is philosophical; the second practical.

The twin challenge

At a philosophical level there are those who contend that facts and values are entwined and that knowledge judgements cannot be distinguished from value judgements. They stress the influence of social and cultural context in shaping claims about what we 'know', the predispositions or the bias of the observer and the limitations and conventions of language. The pertinence of this theoretical position to the new separation of powers is discussed in a later chapter. This is because it is particularly relevant to questions relating to the legitimacy of the new branch.

The related challenge revolves around the charge that attempts to distinguish between empirical judgements and value judgements cannot be successful as a practical matter because the empirical analysis smuggles in and disguises ethical or political judgements under the cover of empirical analysis.[6]

At a practical level, the attempt to distinguish between the two different streams of judgement does not necessarily involve taking a position on the philosophical distinction. Even those who hold that facts and values are entwined could, in practice, benefit from attempts in the real world to distinguish between claims about values and claims about empirical knowledge because they too might find themselves better able to substantiate (or not) their perception of any bias or predispositions. If such biases are established they can also propose alternative approaches to policy-making.

Relevance and acceptability

The key issues in this practical debate revolve around empirical analysis at two crucial points – in the initial decision and selection as to what it is that involves 'relevant' information and knowledge and in the end decision as to what involves an 'acceptable' conclusion – for example about the 'acceptable' level of risk. Those who contend that empirical judgement is inevitably entangled with value judgement focus on what is happening at these two points.[7] If the critics are right, the promise that independent bodies can help the public distinguish between the different types of judgement and to be more confident about information and professional analysis is deceptive.

There are two types of response to this kind of criticism. One response is to accept that the starting point of fact gathering and analysis is value-laden and also that the end point, of deciding what is 'acceptable', is value-laden too. However, between these two points, the contention is that the methodology can be value-free.[8] According to this view it is this 'in-between' ground that provides the territory on which unelected bodies can base their activities.

An alternative response allows for a more expansive role for unelected bodies, one that corresponds much more closely to what they actually do and takes into account that in some cases they are charged with implementing social values. It involves looking further into both the starting point of the analysis and the end point of what is 'acceptable' or not.

---

[6] For this line of argument and a guide to the debate see Owens, Raynor and Bina (2004).
[7] For a critical view of what is involved in judgements on what is acceptable see Douglas (2002).
[8] See Hollis (1994: 208–9).

The suggestion is that the two types of judgement can still be distinguished in practice at these two crucial points and that unelected bodies can help people in making the distinction.

The beginning judgements

The key issue at the starting point of any empirical analysis is one of 'translation'. This means that a normative question, for example whether or not a group of patients should receive a new medicine, is translated into an empirical question – whether or not the new medicine will be effective and at what cost. An analogous 'translation' is made by many unelected bodies in terms reflecting their own field. The language of 'cost' is pervasive.

The criticism of this methodology is that the reframing of the question results in a loss of some of the normative aspects contained in the original normative question while substituting its own normative standard – the standard of the market.[9]

However, this criticism does not stand up to inspection. In the example given, the empirical question of whether or not a new medicine is effective can be empirically measured against the standards used in clinical trials and its cost can also be ascertained. Empirical conclusions can be drawn.

What cannot be drawn is a normative conclusion. The effectiveness of the medicine may be unclear and the costs may turn out to be high. Nevertheless, it would still be possible for a normative conclusion to be drawn that, despite uncertain evidence of effectiveness and despite high costs, the medicine should be introduced because the denial of treatment would be unethical. The original normative question has not been lost but the empirical part of the question has been clarified.

What has happened to the original normative question is that it is carried forward to the end point. There it is reintroduced alongside the empirical judgements about cost and effectiveness. This turns the question towards whether the normative and the empirical can still be distinguished at the end point in the overall judgement of what is 'acceptable'.

Ending judgements

One way of examining the end point in order to see whether or not the empirical can be distinguished from the normative is to look at the way in which some of the boundary watchers make their end judgements on

---

[9] See Morgan (2003).

social or normative issues. In such situations it can be seen that their empirical and value judgements remain distinguishable. For example, an independent water regulator can explain why a particular level of water purity designed to meet the value placed on the environment by politicians will result in the need for a particular level of investment and water charges. Similarly, a power regulator can make clear when a billing policy is being introduced to implement a duty to protect the elderly in harsh winters.

It remains the case that the end judgements of many economic regulations and boundary watchers involve an acceptance of the worth of a competitive market. This judgement is not, however, an implicit or concealed judgement. Typically, an economic regulator is likely to have to justify any end judgement that results in market intervention in terms of 'market failure'. This requirement to present evidence of market failure forces an empirical analysis to be made about how the market is working. In turn this empirical analysis will illuminate the end value judgement about what kinds of correction may be required on normative grounds, such as consumer protection, or whether the market should be left alone. The idea that there has been a loss in normative content is unfounded. On the contrary, the need to analyse market failure means that normative judgements are made overt and explicit.

Hard cases

The hard cases are those that combine scientific uncertainty with matters of great ethical concern. Such a situation is illustrated by the controversy in Europe about the introduction of genetically modified (GM) foodstuffs. In 2004 a six-year moratorium on their introduction came to an end as a GM sweetcorn was approved for introduction into the food chain. In this case the European Food Safety Authority (EFSA) concluded that the weight of evidence suggested that the particular GM sweetcorn in question did not pose additional risks compared with 'traditional' crops. The conclusion that the risk of introduction was 'acceptable' was not opposed by the Council of Ministers and the release was authorised by the Commission.

The differences about what is 'acceptable' in this situation and many others crystallise around what standards of proof to look for and where the burden of proof should be placed. These are value judgements against which the empirical evidence can be assessed. In this particular example the normative benchmarks about what was acceptable rested in the hands of the Commission and the Council. The politicians could have insisted that the EFSA applied a higher base-line standard of proof of safety than a comparison with traditional crops (a benchmark based on experience). The further judgement was about the burden of proof. The evidence suggested an absence of additional risk. Ministers could have insisted on a positive assurance of safety on such matters as the possible impact on the environment or, for example, on allergenicity or the long-term effects of consumption.

What has been achieved in the final decision about the 'acceptability' of risk in this case is that the different types of judgement can indeed be distinguished – the knowledge-based judgements of the agencies about the nature of the evidence can be distinguished from the value judgements about the standard of proof to apply and about where the burden of proof should lie. Those who object to the end conclusion about 'acceptability' thus know whether to object to the evidence or to the standards applied to the evidence.

In the case of GM foods, Europe's politicians reserved the final word to themselves about what values to apply in judging what is acceptable or not. In many cases the terms of reference of the unelected bodies will specify in advance the normative standards of proof to apply and where the burden of proof should lie. What matters is the possibility of distinguishing between the normative standards being applied as a benchmark and the empirical evidence.

There remain other cases, in addition to novel foods and crops, where the relationship of empirical knowledge to value judgements becomes extremely contentious and feelings run very high.[10] The UK's Human Fertilisation and Embryology Authority is the body regulating in the highly emotive area of so-called 'designer babies' where new scientific embryology techniques constantly raise new ethical questions. In such cases the Authority has not only to keep abreast of the latest scientific advances in a complex field but also to make ethical judgements about what is in the public interest (rather than in the interest of scientists or doctors) and what is 'suitable' in a particular context. What is 'suitable' is a value judgement as well as an empirical judgement. In such circumstances the decisions of the Authority will inevitably sometimes be contentious and challenged in the courts. Nevertheless, as recent cases have shown, the science involved remains distinguishable from the ethical judgements made by the Authority.[11] In this area public confidence

---

[10] Feeling very strongly about an issue is not necessarily to be seen as acting irrationally in the face of evidence, although it may be. The relationship between strong feelings and rationality is more complex. See Elster (1999: 283–331).

[11] See, for example, House of Lords: *Quintavalle* v. *Human Fertilisation and Embryology Authority*. 28 April 2005.

rests both on the ability of the Authority to marshall the evidence and also on its composition. Precisely because the Authority is charged with making ethical judgements, it was established with a majority of lay members so that it would not become the creature of the medical profession or the scientific community.

Unbundling institutional responsibility for policy

Unelected bodies that help distinguish between knowledge-based judgements and value-based judgements provide two major benefits to the public. The first great practical benefit to the public from the separation of evidence from political judgements is the one already mentioned that the public can have greater confidence in the evidence on which a public policy was based. In the case of Iraq, where the evidence provided by the intelligence services was handled inside the machinery of central government (in No. 10 in the case of the UK), the public had no means at the time to judge whether the politicians had 'sexed up' the evidence or not.

The second benefit for the public occurs because the separation of institutional roles enables the public to better distinguish between the different actors in public policy-making and to react to them in different ways. If the public disagrees with the judgement of an independent agency a court case may be an appropriate form of reaction; the ballot-box may be the right venue to protest against a politician; a cancelled membership subscription may be the message bearer to a campaigning NGO.

In the example of GM foods, the institutional setting of the EU is particularly difficult for the public to navigate because the Commission is interposed between the body making the scientific judgement (EFSA) and the body making a political judgement (the Council of Ministers), while the Commission itself is both a political and a technical body. However, a different example also illustrates the point. In the case of treatment for Alzheimer's there has been controversy in the UK about withholding the use of anti-cholinesterase drugs for treatment depending on the severity of the condition. The controversy is partly about the science involved – the reliability of the cognitive tests used to determine the severity of the condition and the effectiveness of the drugs. It is also partly about the ethics of denying patients access to a class of drugs that might possibly offer some hope of delaying the progression of the disease.

The science debate focusses on the scientific reliability of the analysis by the unelected body making the decision (NICE). Those faulting the science have the opportunity to contest its findings about costs and to challenge the reliability of the cognitive measures used to measure efficacy. Those who are concerned about the ethics support the NGOs urging treatment for all patients and, with their help, they lobby politicians to stop what they see as 'cruel and unethical' drug restrictions. From the politicians' perspective, costs and effectiveness need to be established empirically because their decision about what is ethically acceptable may hinge on the allocation of resources. In a resource-constrained environment they may have to decide between the claims of a patient group to receive costly treatment of doubtful efficacy against the claims of other groups of patients to cheaper medicines that are more effective for their medical condition.

In principle, therefore, the new separation of powers potentially offers the public a better way of sorting out the different elements of even the most contentious public policy decisions, the role played by different actors in it and clearer signposts as to how to react and who and what to react to.

Separation as the driving force

It turns out therefore that general economic explanations to do with the service economy do not seem to get to the heart of what is driving the creation of the world of unelected bodies. A demand for a more service-oriented government sector of the economy does not identify what it is about information and knowledge that argues in favour of separation from government. Similarly managerial explanations also fall short. The distinction between 'policy management' and 'service delivery' does not dig beneath what goes into 'policy'. The development of this new separation of powers is taking place for reasons that go far beyond questions of managerial or business efficiency in the public sector.

Instead, what lies at the heart of the rise of the unelected are the advantages that independent bodies have in gathering and presenting information, analysing evidence and linking them to the current state of knowledge. In turn, the benefits of a more systematic and authoritative mobilisation of knowledge in society flow through to the public in terms of more reliable and trustworthy information on the components of public policy and a much better possibility to distinguish evidence-based judgements from value judgements. This applies even in cases where the unelected body is making social judgements. Furthermore the institutional separation provides the public with more targeted ways of responding to the different actors. Yet despite the benefits to the public of this major new dimension to decision-taking in democracies, the rise of the unelected to positions of power and influence presents an enormous challenge to traditional democratic theory. The next chapter explains why.

4   The challenge to conventional democratic theory

At first sight the development of a new form of separation of powers within democratic structures of government would not appear to offer any great challenge to democratic theory and practice. The development is taking place within a democratic context and for reasons that are about improving the quality of information, knowledge and judgements within democratic societies. The people themselves are the ultimate beneficiaries. Yet the new separation of powers does indeed challenge conventional ways of looking at democracy and is giving rise to new adaptations to traditional accounts of democracy. This chapter examines why conventional accounts of democracy are challenged by the growth in importance of the unelected bodies. For this purpose it looks at three currently fashionable accounts of democracy – participatory democracy, democracy expressed as the rule of law and deliberative democracy. None can deal with the rise of the unelected.

The erosion of participatory democracy

The rise of the unelected is a challenge first of all to theories of democracy that stress the fundamental importance of participation in politics. Widespread and compelling evidence of disinterest and disinvolvement in established democratic politics has re-established the relevance of the tradition in democratic thought that stresses the importance of participation in government by the people.[1] People power has had some striking successes in recent years – from the former East Germany to Georgia, the Ukraine and to the Lebanon. Participation is clearly valued when democracy is new. Yet, by contrast, among the most prominent features of established democracies at the end of the twentieth century were voter apathy, low voter turn-out at elections and a distancing by social and

---

[1] Although the importance of participation figured strongly in early accounts of democracy, its importance was downplayed for a time in the post-war world partly as a reaction to the abuses of techniques of mobilisation such as referenda in the 1930s. See Pateman (1970).

political activists away from affiliation with political parties towards identification with single-issue causes.[2] These symptoms should not be confused with a general civic apathy since citizen activism might take different forms.[3] Nevertheless, each is witness to a turning away from traditional democratic politics. Neither is a lack of democratic participation just a feature of large-scale political associations where individual voters might feel that their voice did not count. Abstention and the rise of single-issue groups is indeed a feature of large political units such as the USA and the EU, but it is a striking feature also of smaller units.[4] It seems to take major catastrophes such as the attack on the Twin Towers or the Madrid bombings and the Iraq war to stir electorates.

The virtues of participation

The core message of participatory democracy is that democratic politics hinges on people actually exercising their right to vote. Participation is important as a means of contesting what is in the collective interest of a democratic society.[5] In addition, if people do not bother to vote, then politicians will equally not bother to take account of what the electorate is concerned about. In the ensuing vacuum, political power can be captured by unrepresentative minorities for their own purposes, or by politicians for theirs.[6] The essence of the message about participation is thus that the presence of representative institutions does not by itself guarantee democracy. Democracy is a 'use it or lose it' choice.

The very simple message of participatory democracy does not seem to get across. This has led theorists to look more closely at the conditions under which people are motivated to participate actively in politics. This search has generated a significant volume of writing emphasising the importance of civic attitudes, or extolling the virtues of 'civil society' organisations such as NGOs said to encourage the development of civic involvement, or that stresses the importance of community involvement

---

[2] For discussion of the evidence for 'a general erosion' in support for politicians and government in most advanced industrial democracies, see Dalton (2004). See also Mair and von Biezen (2001).
[3] For a cross-country comparison of the evidence on voter turn-out and a warning against exaggerating trends, see Norris (2002).
[4] It has been noted in the case of the UK that in the 2005 general election the victorious Labour Party polled 9.5 million votes while 17 million registered voters did not vote. See The Power Inquiry (2006: 33).
[5] For an expression of this view see Pettit (2001).
[6] For various 'minimalist' accounts of what democracy is about see Shapiro and Hacker-Cordon (1999a).

or 'social capital' that breed habits of co-operation.[7] Features of social organisation such as norms and networks that make up 'social capital' are claimed to improve the efficiency of society by facilitating co-ordinated actions with the happy outcome that the more civic a society the more effective its government.[8]

Alongside this diagnosis of democratic fundamentals go purported remedies to counter the defects. Measures range from encouraging education in the virtues of active citizenship or civic responsibility, to finding new ways to encourage voting – for example through electronic or postal voting – to exploring improved ways of funding political parties and possibly a greater use of the methods of direct democracy such as referenda and popular initiatives, to the construction of better physical neighbourhoods.[9] There also has been an attempt to extend the notion of democratic participation to include notions of 'stakeholder democracy'. In addition, governments and international organisations are encouraged to bring NGOs into partnerships.[10]

Meanwhile, the growth of unelected bodies has taken place in what appears to have been a total disconnection with this concern about the underlying health of democracies and the revival of interest in participatory democracy. Far from featuring on any list of remedies to help revive participation, the growth of unelected bodies seems to run in a completely opposite direction.

Unelected bodies as a disincentive to participate

The growth of unelected bodies presents a challenge for theories of participatory democracy for four main reasons:

First, unelected bodies seem to remove part of the agenda of politics and thus demotivate people from actively participating in traditional politics. For example, if the role of an independent central bank is defined in terms of achieving price stability, then subsequent political debate about how much attention to pay to inflationary pressures in an economy in relation to other goals such as full employment seems much less relevant because the conclusion in favour of price stability has already been pre-empted. Judgements on any trade-offs, if indeed they exist, are made outside democratic political channels. Central bank independence

---

[7] See Barber (1984).   [8] See Putnam, Leonardi and Nanetti (1993: 167).
[9] Putnam (2002).
[10] The evidence for an association between social capital and democratic participation is mixed. For example, Krishna (2002) finds a positive link based on Indian data, but Norris (2002: 166–7) discusses the difficulty of finding empirical evidence associating social capital with democratic participation.

may well provide a good instance of defending democracy against itself, but at the cost of reducing the scope of the democratic agenda.

Secondly, by moving functions away from the ambit of democratically elected politicians they demotivate even more. It is not only the content of politics that is whittled down but the importance of politicians is also downgraded. In the case of the United States, the head of the Federal Reserve is now seen to be just as important as the Treasury Secretary (even more so in the eyes of the financial markets) and yet cannot be called to account through the democratic process. The growth of unelected bodies seems to take the care of the public interest back to pre-democratic days. Instead of the care of the public interest being delegated by citizens to politicians whose credentials rest on electoral legitimacy, it seems as though the function has been delegated to the non-elected whose claim to legitimacy rests on their expertise.[11]

Thirdly, the rise of the unelected identifies a complete failure of theories of participatory democracy to grapple with the content of modern policy-making. The issue can be presented as a question of the relationship between the rise of the unelected bodies 'nurturing competence' and the role of traditional elected institutions that depend on the 'nurturing of participation'. There may be no conflict between the two.[12] But, as already discussed, the role of the unelected extends beyond mere competence. By failing to look at the nature of modern policy-making, theories of participatory democracy have also failed to consider what the rise of unelected bodies means for the tasks of the traditional elected bodies and what in turn this implies for electoral involvement in politics.

Finally, theories of participatory democracy seem to have overlooked the declining relevance of politics as a means to vent grievance and discontent. Voters can still vote against governments or presidents or parties but, at the same time, across a range of questions of day-to-day importance, new non-political channels to hear views and to redress grievances have opened up. The new umpires may seem more effective, more certain and more immediate. Politics again seems less relevant.

Repoliticise?

One response to this situation is to suggest that the growth of unelected bodies has gone too far and that certain functions should be clawed back into the political realm. For example some argue that the creation of the

---

[11] Dahl (1998: 69) refers to the idea that government should be turned over to experts as 'the major rival' to democratic ideas.
[12] See Braithwaite (1999).

independent central bank for the Eurozone has created an imbalance between disempowered elected finance ministers and fully empowered but unelected central bankers. Similarly, others argue that services of 'general economic interest' should be removed from the reach of competition law and competition authorities and be subject to political oversight so as to ensure that the providers of public services such as utilities or banks perform in the public interest.

The difficulty with 'claw-back' is that it has to deal with the original reasons why it seemed desirable to set certain activities at a distance from politics in the first place. Despite the complaints that can be made, and are indeed made, about the functioning of unelected bodies, there are few who would wish to turn the clock back to the days when their tasks were internalised within the machinery of central government and electoral politics. The compelling reasons discussed in the last chapter why certain functions should be separated from electoral politics remain valid.

The reasons for disconnection

In looking for reasons why there has arisen this disconnection between the world of participatory democracy and the world of unelected bodies, the first challenge that theories of participatory democracy have to confront is that the greater volume of more reliable information and analysis provided by independent institutions, together with the unbundling of the different streams of judgement that enter into policy-making, do not necessarily lead people to wish to participate more actively in traditional democratic politics. The missing step is to go from the better-informed citizen to the more politically actively involved citizen. The relationship cannot be taken for granted as running from better information and more reliable knowledge to more active participation.[13]

A second reason for the disconnection is that unelected bodies may encourage the rise of single-issue politics rather than engagement in traditional political activism built around broad party affiliations. The disaggregating of information, knowledge gathering and risk management into specialised agencies may encourage the disaggregating of political issues. Groups concerned with human embryology, for example, may look to influence directly the activities of an embryology authority and to address the politics of the specific issue rather than maintain allegiances

---

[13] The difficulty of making a link between information and political engagement is discussed in Scheufele and Shah (2000).

within a broad political party. When Nancy Reagan spoke in favour of stem-cell research and against the Republican party stance on the issue, she illustrated how party loyalties may be decomposed by specific issues. This tendency towards a single-issue focus to public debate is likely to be more generally encouraged when there is confidence in the way that sensitive knowledge-based issues are handled outside politics. It weakens traditional broad-based political parties as vehicles for participation and reduces reliance on politicians and political processes.

Thirdly and more fundamentally, it is argued later that, armed with better information and confidence in independent unelected bodies, citizens may be more inclined to make judgements on the information for themselves and decide for themselves what is best rather than to turn to politics at all. For example, confidence in a regulatory regime for pensions and insurance provided by an unelected regulator might lead people to prefer to make their own private pension and insurance arrangements rather than rely on the state. Collective arrangements that depend on how politicians interpret the information may be less attractive. Indeed the state may be seen as an unwelcome, uncertain and disruptive source of interference in decisions which people feel more confident about making for themselves. Instead of political participation being encouraged, people may instead turn away from politics.

What this means is that theories of participatory democracy have yet to absorb the implications for the political activism of citizens of the growth in importance of unelected bodies. The basic premise of participatory democracy – that people must be ready to be politically active in order to keep democracy alive – is at some level true and important, but the rise of the unelected makes the case for participation, particularly through traditional vehicles, much more difficult to make.

Gaps in the rule of law

The rise of the unelected is a challenge also to theories of democracy that rest on notions of the rule of law with which the idea of the democratic state has long been coupled. At its simplest, the rule of law means that in democratic states no person in a position of power will be 'above the law', or able to flout laws that apply to every other citizen, or able to make laws simply of their own choosing. It stands too for the idea that the law constrains what those with political power can do, and that ordinary citizens should be defended against arbitrary or capricious actions by governments. In addition it stands for the idea that there should exist conformity between the law on the books and law in the real world and that laws should be publicly accessible and inapplicable retroactively.[14] The rule of law also provides a connection between democracy as the organising principle for political life and the market as the organising principle for economic life because both rely on enforceable rules.

In order for the rule of law to apply there must be some benchmark, or set of principles, derived outside politics, that stands above the action of rulers and against which their actions can be measured. These standards developed in pre-democratic days based on principles derived from common law or from theories of natural rights.[15] Since the days of the Founding Fathers of the American Constitution it has also been accepted that principles contained in a constitution can serve this purpose. This does not mean that constitutions are synonymous with the rule of law – the rule of law can exist without a constitution and constitutions vary widely in quality. If there is a constitution in place, it itself has to be legitimate. Constitutions may, however, express what the rule of law is about.

Extending the concept of the rule of law?

In certain ways the rise in importance of unelected bodies is helpful to the concept of the rule of law. In particular by circumscribing the role of politicians they help reduce the risk that politicians will abuse their lawmaking or executive roles. For example, when a government sets up an independent body to monitor privacy issues it reduces the possibility that it might itself abuse private and personal information from levels that might prevail in the absence of such a body. This does not mean that the government cannot still be a major invader of private and personal space, but it may reduce somewhat the chances of abuse in this area. Thus, in the case of the UK where the government has decided in favour of introducing ID cards, it has had to cast a wary eye at the views of the independent Information Commissioner. In this and in other functional areas the unelected bodies can be seen to help the rule of law.

The unelected bodies also help extend the practice of the rule of law because, as a result of their own information- and evidence-gathering activities, they place greater pressure on governments to produce the reasons behind any law-making initiative. In itself, a need to produce reasons provides a check on arbitrary government. In addition, an

---

[14] For a discussion see, for example, Sunstein (1996).
[15] Theories of natural rights hold that there exist some normative standards that are intrinsic and which stand prior to their being chosen by individuals or collective groupings.

exposure of reasons and reasoning may increase the potential for judicial review to hold an act of government as unlawful on grounds that the measure is disproportionate, or arbitrary, or that incorrect procedures were followed in formulating the measure.

Unelected bodies help the concept of the rule of law more directly in the sense that they themselves often adopt quasi-judicial rules of procedure in their own activities. In addition, as already mentioned, they provide citizens with an expanded possibility of using the system of justice to obtain redress in cases of grievance rather than having to turn to politicians for political redress. The unelected bodies too can be hauled before courts for following incorrect procedures or for acting outside their terms of reference.

Unelected bodies and weaknesses in the rule of law

Despite the case that can be made for saying that the growth of unelected bodies expands the scope and practice of democratic notions of the rule of law, there is another side to the story. The other side concerns the way in which their rise touches on the most vulnerable areas of accounts of the rule of law.

There are three long-standing sources of difficulty with the application of the principle of the rule of law. The first is that government is itself the source of much law. This makes it possible for law to become an instrument of government rather than a check on government. It is for this reason that a judiciary independent of government, not involved in law-making itself and detached from any political agenda, seems a basic requirement for democracies to flourish. The idea of an independent judiciary also involves an underlying argument that the fundamental legitimacy of the law itself does not rest on closeness to government, or on the fact that it can call on the power of the state for enforcement.

The rise of unelected bodies is a challenge to how the law and politics are to be kept apart because they themselves occupy a new space between politics and the law. They have taken over some of the functions of the elected branch. The new bodies have also in many ways replaced the traditional role of courts as the main interpreter of statutory law and in updating and particularising law.[16] Defining the new space being occupied and the change in roles is therefore important in order to uphold the independent status of the law.

[16] See Sunstein (1999: 227).

The second traditional source of difficulty in the concept of the rule of law lies in specifying what should be treated as constitutional, determining the rules under which political power is exercised, and what should be treated within the rules as political – that is to say, what can be left to be determined through democratic debate. The idea of the independent judiciary is that it should uphold the rules but not interfere with decisions taken within the rules.

The activities of unelected bodies enlarge this area of difficulty because their constitutional placement is itself uncertain. Their growth expands the area of ambiguity of what rightly belongs in the constitutional field and what rightly remains in the political field. It is this issue that underlies the argument about the relative powers of finance ministers compared with central bank governors. The growth of the unelected is relatively recent and tends not to be reflected in any consistent way within modern constitutional frameworks. Some independent central banks have constitutional recognition; others do not. Some other unelected bodies may also have constitutional recognition but most do not. They represent a new separation of powers, but that separation is not yet constitutionally recognised or defined. As a result it may be difficult for the judiciary to know when its intervention is justified or when it amounts to interference.

The third traditional source of difficulty for concepts of the rule of law concerns the role of judicial review in interpreting the rules. When the principles of interpretation are unclear or disputed, or constitutions do not specify clearly the limits on powers, then judicial review is on uncertain ground. If there were to be constant conflict between unelected bodies and the traditional judiciary, it is not only the new bodies that would find their authority challenged. The authority of the law could also be undermined.

The rise of unelected bodies poses questions for judicial review because the principles of interpretation to be applied by judges in looking at any abuses of power are difficult to formulate. When the principles and procedures that form the basis of holding the new bodies to account or underpin their legitimacy are themselves unclear, courts will either hold back or become venturesome. Neither approach helps the application of the rule of law. The procedural and factual grounds warranting judicial review of the acts of the new bodies is still an evolving and uncertain area.[17]

Traditional approaches to the rule of law are therefore challenged by how to recognise the new separation of powers and how to place the new

---

[17] For a discussion of US case law see Breyer, Stewart, Sunstein and Spitzer (1998: 33–144).

institutions. The fundamental issue underlying each of these specific areas of difficulty is that the way in which the unelected bodies themselves can be said to be held accountable and legitimate has to be agreed in order for the role of the law in that process to be fully defined.

It is tempting to say that none of this matters too much. Notions of the rule of law are fairly abstract and, as a practical matter, precisely because the new bodies operate in a space between the law and politics, it is possible to argue that they will be held to account in one way or another, partly by law and partly by politics. Thus their precise position should not matter too much either to notions of the rule of law or to traditional elected branches of government.

However, insouciance seems difficult to justify in the face of the everyday influence of unelected bodies in contemporary democracies. In undertaking much of the practical work that enables democracies to function effectively, in watching the boundaries between market and state and in affecting daily lives, they can overstep the limits on their powers. They can also exercise their powers in capricious ways. The precise way in which they are to be held accountable and the precise way in which they can claim legitimacy thus matter. The fact that both politics and the law can claim a role means that there is a danger that methods of holding unelected bodies to account will stand on ambiguous and uncertain ground between judicial review on the one hand and political oversight on the other. Moreover, as discussed later, it may be that the fundamental legitimacy of the new bodies depends neither on the law nor on politics but is rooted instead in their own principles and procedures. If so, the relationship to the principles and procedures embodied in the rule of law also needs to be clear.

Undermining deliberative democracy

Another currently fashionable account of democracy whose shortcomings are exposed by the growth of unelected bodies is the body of theory that emphasises the importance of the deliberative qualities of democracy. Rather than placing the emphasis on bargaining between interests or on voting as a method to settle disputes, instead, this account of democracy places the emphasis on arguing.[18] According to this account, what gives democracy its special quality is the possibility it offers for discussion and the changing of minds on matters of public importance through

---

[18] Jon Elster (1998: 5) suggests that there are only three ways in which democratic societies can go about resolving differences, either through arguing, voting or bargaining – 'I believe that for modern societies this is an exhaustive list.'

exchanges of view. Deliberation provides people with the chance to move away from a perspective of the democratic process based on the pursuit of narrow self-interest, or competition between the interests of narrow groups, to a perspective that holds out the possibility of harmony and the development of a sense of common interest based on discussion with those of other views. The hallmark of democratic politics and a test for democratic legitimacy is thus the possibility of transformation of attitudes through discussion and debate.[19]

Transformation by public discussion

The appeal of deliberation as the essence of democratic practice is that it ties in with other key qualities of democratic societies. It ties in with a belief in the virtues of achieving social change through peaceful and non-coercive means. It links to the idea that democracies encourage civil behaviour where people look to persuade others through the reasonableness of argument rather than by hurling bricks. It grapples with the pluralism of modern societies and suggests, even where people hold very different beliefs and values, that by explaining what they are or why they are held it may be possible to reach an accommodation that satisfies everyone. It ties in also with the idea of respect for persons since it gives space for each person to express their reasons for what they do or what they believe.

Although, deliberative democracy requires people to wish to behave 'reasonably', it does not require unrealistic standards of rationality. It hinges on communicating what people regard as good reasons in everyday discussion. It does not insist on the kind of stringent ordering of personal preferences that economists need for their abstract models, or on the kind of consistency and coherence that philosophers might look for in their account of rational thinking. Writers in this tradition have tended therefore to focus on what are, in their views, other necessary preconditions for deliberation to take place, such as agreement on the norms of social justice or equality among the deliberators.[20]

At first sight, the growth of unelected bodies with advantages as gatherers of information and mobilisers of empirical knowledge and judgement seems supportive of this view of the democratic process. Discussion can be better informed. Greater knowledge, both about what the issues are and what the evidence is, can lead to more facts being brought to bear in democratic discussion and more relevant values being identified. The

[19] For one presentation of this view see Bohman (1996).
[20] See the discussion in Bohman and Rehg (1997).

arguments of special interests can be exposed to daylight, bias can be more easily identified and greater pressure is placed on those with political power to give reasons for the way in which they propose to exercise their power. However, something is missing.

The willingness to communicate

There are two main problems in squaring the deliberative account of democracy with the growth of unelected bodies. The first is that there must exist an initial willingness to communicate among the voting population. As mentioned earlier, the new bodies themselves possess a built-in tendency to want to communicate with the public and to get information out into the public sphere. But deliberative democracy requires more than information being made available. It depends on the willingness of people to use the information and evidence in political debate in order to exchange views or to consult or to swap notes with those of different views. It presupposes the mechanisms to do so and counts on a willingness to have one's views or actions transformed through the interchange. Participants in deliberative debate must recognise that they can influence outcomes and they must expect that their reasonable views will in some way be incorporated into decisions.[21] The provision of better information and the ability to point to more facts and relevant values does not in itself provide for this kind of exchange.

In theories of both participatory democracy and theories of deliberative democracy there is a missing step in the connection with the activities of unelected bodies. Just as more trustworthy information does not necessarily translate into more active participation in democratic politics nor does better information necessarily translate into greater willingness to deliberate through democratic channels. In fact a disinterest in traditional politics is a feature of contemporary democracy. In the UK a survey in 2005 showed that 44 per cent were not much or not at all interested in politics, and the proportion was still higher for younger age groups (below thirty-four years).[22]

One way in which the unelected bodies may feed this disinterest is that the provision of better information may expose inadequate justifications for policy action by politicians. This can lead to a more general questioning of the claims of politicians to act in the general interest, a more general disenchantment with politics and a disinclination to engage in debate. In

---

[21] See Bohman (1996: 33).
[22] Source: Goddard (2005: 17). Similar results are reported in Pattie, Seyd and Whiteley (2004: 92) and in the Electoral Commission and Hansard Society report (March 2006).

addition, citizens may just seek out information of relevance only to themselves and their own concerns and are possibly more likely to look for exchange with the like-minded or those with similar interests than with those of opposing views.[23]

The second way in which unelected bodies may encourage disinterest in deliberative debate revolves around what theorists refer to as the 'sincerity' of communication. If the assumptions of deliberative democracy are to hold water, then communication must be 'sincere'. What this means is that the communicator must actually be seen to believe in what they are trying to endorse. Putting this requirement in the negative means that they must not be engineering reasons, inventing facts, or being deceptive with reasons, or economical with the truth, or trying to manipulate. The reason for this requirement is that once trust in the worth of deliberation has been destroyed, then the process no longer works. If the sincerity of one side of an exchange is doubted then the benefits of reciprocity and the exchange of views is destroyed.[24]

The separation of powers and the development of unelected bodies with a focus on information and knowledge helps to improve the underlying quality of information and thereby to reveal insincere communication. This, however, is a two-edged sword. It illuminates a potential gulf between the sincere communication of the unelected bodies and the possibly insincere communication of politicians. If politicians are revealed as sources of spin, deception and manipulation, this in turn may result in more people being turned away from politics and political channels of communication. Therefore, even if the potential for sincere communication is expanded in democratic societies by the activities of the unelected bodies, there is no necessary boost to deliberative politics. On the contrary, the impact may be to depoliticise.

What deliberative democracy misses, therefore, is an account of the way in which public deliberation is triggered or altered as a result of more and better-quality information provided by unelected bodies and the way in which this feeds into democratic politics. It does not consider what people may do with better information or how better information in people's hands from non-political sources will feed back into democratic processes revolving around the traditional institutions. In order to see how the growth of unelected bodies fits into democratic practice, a different account has to be provided of the democratic arena and the way it is altered by the advent of the new separation of powers.

[23] The prevalence of 'Confirmation bias' is discussed by Mele (2004).
[24] For a discussion of 'sincerity' and other assumptions underlying deliberative democracy see Pettit and Smith (2004).

The need to adapt traditional approaches

What this discussion has shown is that, for different reasons, traditional accounts of democracy are undermined by the new separation of powers. One or more of their basic assumptions is thrown into question. Theories of participatory democracy are undermined because the new institutions reduce the role of the traditional institutions of democracy, reduce the motivation to pay attention to what politicians say and do and correspondingly diminish the value of participating in democratic mechanisms.

Traditional accounts of the rule of law also seem to lag behind the new separation of powers. There is a damaging lack of clarity about where the new bodies fit within constitutional arrangements supporting the rule of law, what normative standards underpin their accountability and legitimacy and how these in turn relate to the normative standards of the rule of law. In addition, theories of deliberative democracy are also weakened. People may be better informed as a result of the new separation of powers but, at the same time, the way in which that additional information is deployed and the way in which that deployment affects the traditional institutions of democracy are not captured by theories of deliberation.

Because the relevance and credibility of mainstream approaches to democracy seem to be greatly reduced by the rise of unelected bodies, a number of attempts are being made to update them in ways that preserve their basic tenets. These are discussed next.

5   Adapting traditional approaches

Conventional accounts of democracy are severely challenged by the new separation of powers, but there are three recent adaptations to the leading accounts of democracy that offer a way of placing the rise of the unelected within mainstream theory.

The first, and most widely accepted, account emphasises the continuation of a 'democratic overhead' that links the new institutions with the old through what is known as 'principal–agent theory'.[1] This account is consistent with the theories of participatory democracy. The proposed link between the old institutions and the new gives a continued function and meaning to participating in traditional forms of democracy relying on the old elected institutions.

A second account adapts traditional approaches to the rule of law by emphasising the relevance of a new type of constitutionalism. This new style of constitutionalism attempts to bring the unelected bodies within the scope and definitions of the rule of law by extending the coverage of constitutions.

A third account argues that the content of democratic politics is changing and that the rise of the new institutions taps into a shift in what people want out of systems of government. This shift is away from political ideology towards pragmatic solutions to practical problems. Unelected bodies, including courts, are a beneficiary of this shift in the subject matter of democracies, but at the same time they retain and encourage the essential deliberative qualities of reason and civility. This account of 'pragmatism' can therefore be seen as a way to update and to modify theories of deliberative democracy. This chapter discusses these adaptations and explores why they fail to rescue traditional accounts of democracy.

---

[1] 'Principal–agent (PA) has been the dominant theoretical approach, exploring politicians' delegation of powers to non-majoritarian institutions in terms of insulation from political pressures and performing functions for elected politicians.' Coen and Thatcher (2005: 332).

The democratic 'overhead'

According to the theory of the democratic overhead, functions can be delegated to the new institutions without a democratic loss because the unelected bodies function as agents for a democratic principal. The democratic principal can be defined either as a democratically elected minister in a government acting on behalf of the electorate, or as a legislature, or as the electorate itself.

If the idea of the democratic overhead actually works in practice, participation in traditional democratic politics remains worthwhile and important, despite the shift of functions to the unelected, because voters decide on governments whose ministers control the new institutions. Legislative assemblies also remain relevant because they have a role in setting the terms of reference of the new bodies and also can hold ministers to account for their oversight of them too. Assemblies, in addition, can examine for themselves how the non-elected bodies actually perform.

The idea of the democratic overhead offers an approach both to the accountability of the unelected bodies and to their democratic legitimacy. They are accountable in the last resort to ministers and to governments. Their legitimacy is a derived legitimacy. It is bestowed by the traditional institutions of democracy – the elected governments and parliaments.

Contracting with a democratic principal

The idea that the unelected bodies are still covered by some kind of democratic means of control hinges on the applicability of principal–agent theory.[2] Principal–agent theory has many different applications because an agency relationship exists whenever one individual or body depends on the action of another individual or body.[3] In this particular application to unelected bodies, the theory depends on three related elements: a straightforward principal–agent relationship, a clear contract setting out the terms of that relationship and an ultimate political sanction – the power to hire and fire.[4] In order to express clarity about who exactly is the principal, most versions of the democratic overhead stress

[2] For a classic account, see Arrow (1985). For a recent analysis of democratic institutions deploying a principal–agent framework for analysis, see Strøm, Müller and Bergman (2005).
[3] See Pratt and Zeckhauser (1985a).
[4] Other possible instruments of on-going control may include budget sanctions, monitoring, audit and the threat of statutory reorganisation. For a view that these, together with the power to hire, are decisive, see Calvert, McCubbins and Weingast (1989).

the importance of a minister in parliamentary systems and Congress and the President in presidential systems.

The classic problem of government as viewed by principal–agent theory is the tendency for the supposed agent to slip the leash of the intended principal – in other words for the institution to break free from ministerial oversight. Agents have incentives to pursue their own agendas – particularly those that expand their own powers. In addition, where the function being exercised is highly technical, as is often the case with the unelected bodies, the principal may not have sufficient knowledge to exercise effective control or supervision.

Contracts are intended to take care of this problem. The contract sets out the statutory definitions of the duties of the body, its goals and its mission. The definitions of duties will define where the agent has discretion, where its responsibilities begin and where those of the political masters end. Clarity of contract between principal and agent is therefore pivotal.

A further attraction of contract as a means to define the relationship between a democratic principal and an unelected agent is that it can fit within a broader vision of democratic politics as a series of contracts. The overarching contract is between the populace as a whole and their form of government. Within this overarching scheme other contracts can fit.

The 'hire and fire' component of the democratic overhead introduces a means of ultimate political control in case the agent transgresses the terms of the contract. It involves the political principal retaining the possibility to appoint and get rid of the heads or executive boards of agencies. The power to fire is the most draconian in a range of instruments that appear to offer democratic principals the possibility of on-going controls to buttress the initial means of control offered by the definitions of statutory duties.[5]

The idea that there is some kind of democratic overhead that extends over the new world of unelected bodies is a comforting one for politicians to believe in. It leaves traditional institutions intact in their supremacy within a democratic system of government and in their belief that they are 'in control' on behalf of the electorate. Nevertheless, this belief is a delusion. The attempt to establish a clear relationship between a principal such as a democratically elected minister and an agent, the unelected body, is flawed.

---

[5] Epstein and O'Halloran (1994).

The conflict between contract and independence

The first problem encountered by the theory of the democratic overhead is that there is an irreducible internal conflict between the independence of the unelected bodies and the instruments whereby the political principal controls the agent – the contract that is supposed to define the terms of that independence and the hiring and firing link.

The difficulties are illustrated by the different approaches taken to central bank independence. In the case of the New Zealand contractual model of central bank independence (followed also by the UK), the Central Bank has statutory independence in order to achieve price stability, but it is the finance minister that defines the actual price stability goal set for the Central Bank. In the case of the New Zealand model, therefore, a link with the democratic chain is maintained because price stability goals are set by political principals. By contrast, the 1992 Maastricht Treaty that established the European Central Bank specifically forbids the ECB or any member of its decision-making bodies to take instructions from any government or EU institution precisely because it is feared that goals set by elected ministers will compromise the price stability objective of central bank independence. The only nod in the direction of what ministers or governments are doing is the requirement for the ECB to support the general economic policies of the EU.[6] The difference between the two is that the New Zealand approach offers a clear political overhead but not so clear independence, while the ECB model offers clear independence but an apparent absence of any political overhead.

Terms of reference set out in a contract do not give a complete picture of a contract. In many cases the question of independence boils down to the hiring-and-firing provisions in the contract. When ministers have the power to hire they can look for candidates to head agencies who they think will be compliant and sensitive to the government's political situation and policies. They may place in charge members of their own political party. The power to fire means that they can get rid of them if they feel they are not compliant. In the case of the New Zealand model of central bank independence, the governor of the Central Bank has a duty to explain to the Board if the goal set by the finance minister has been missed and may find his or her job on the line if the explanation is not good enough. By contrast, in the case of the ECB, the firing of the president by ministers for poor performance is not allowed, except in

---

[6] Treaty Establishing the European Community Art. 105.

cases of malfeasance. The possibility of political control lies in the appointment process where ministers may look for a head of the ECB who is sensitive to their wishes.[7]

In whatever way it is defined, the hiring-and-firing link means that the exact relationship between principal and agent is often less clear than it seems. It introduces an essential ambiguity into the relationship. An ability to hire can lead to politically compliant agencies. Equally, if the threat to fire is constantly dangled above the heads or the boards of agencies then their ability to carry out their terms of reference in an independent fashion is compromised. Even if the power to fire is held as a reserve power to be exercised only when things go wrong, it is still likely to exert an influence on the behaviour of the agent. In practice, therefore, the power to hire and fire that seems to provide the essential link between elected politician and the unelected agent leads in practice to a half-way house where the unelected body may be neither fully independent nor fully under control.

One way of viewing this internal conflict between independence and control is to see it in terms of 'durability'. A democratic principal wants to put in place a contract for the agency that offers it independence and freedom from interference from future legislatures or governments with possibly different political agendas.[8] But in establishing this durable independence the principal also gives up the means of control. Another way of looking at the conflict is in terms of 'discretion'. Contracts provide agencies with discretion, but discretion only makes sense if at the same time there is a means of control.[9] There is a tension between the independence of an agency and forging and maintaining a link with elected politicians that can never wholly be resolved.[10] Recognising this tension, some political scientists argue that politicians may simply decide it is better not to try to use the controls theoretically available to them.[11]

[7] 'At the ECB the process of making appointments to the governing council has always been highly politicised ... Senior appointments remain one of the few sources of influence individual countries feel they have.' Brione (2005).

[8] Horn (1995).

[9] Dworkin (1997: 31) notes 'Discretion, like the hole in a donut, does not exist except as an area left open by a surrounding belt of restriction.'

[10] In their study of the statutory control of bureaucratic behaviour, Huber and Shipan conclude that control is 'non-trivial' but 'We must also admit that we cannot say anything about the absolute control over bureaucrats or about what, in fact, bureaucrats do after legislation is adopted.' Huber and Shipan (2002: 224).

[11] See Thatcher (2005).

Multiple principals and chains of agents

The second problem encountered by the theory of the democratic over-head focusses on the situation where there is more than one principal. Principal–agent relations can be difficult even when there is one principal and one agent. The plausibility of a clear relationship is much diminished when there are either multiple principals or extended chains of delega-tion. In practice, multiple principals and extended chains are common-place and this weakens the likelihood of any effective democratic control.

Such a situation arises whenever the theory of the democratic overhead is reformulated to stress control by parliaments or assemblies rather than by a minister. Parliamentary control can be exerted mainly in three ways. The first is through the setting by parliaments of the initial terms of reference of the agency or by adjusting them subsequently,[12] the second is through the ability of parliaments to hold inquiries into the way the terms of reference are being carried out and the third is to threaten budget sanctions.

The weakness in this version of the democratic overhead is that parlia-ments and their committees are likely to contain a variety of conflicting views. In particular, party divisions are likely to spill over into the relation-ship with any agent. Effectively therefore the agent will be dealing with multiple principals. If the relationship between a single principal and a single agent is likely in practice to be much less transparent and much more ambiguous than the theory of the democratic overhead maintains, the difficulties are even more marked where democratic control is spread between several principals. The existence of multiple principals weakens the principal–agent relationship because terms of reference are more likely to contain overlapping or conflicting objectives; agents can play off different political forces against each other, and firing decisions become more difficult to make. Other 'transactions' costs, such as the uncertain effect of any parliamentary intervention and other inefficien-cies, also come into play.[13]

In the real world many unelected bodies operate in a setting with multiple principals. Economic or health and safety regulators, for exam-ple, are likely to answer on paper to several different ministers – ministries with responsibilities for particular sectors, such as power or telecom-munications, and ministries with cross-sectoral responsibilities, such as

---

[12] For the argument that delegation is 'self-regulating' because legislatures can always adjust the agency terms of reference, see Epstein (1999).
[13] Huber and Shipan (2000). See also Epstein and O'Halloran (1999) and Steunenberg (1996).

industry or the environment. Whenever this happens the agent is likely to escape any clear control from a political principal. In the United States an analogous situation arises. It is very doubtful whether an agency can be seen to answer to any single point, such as the President or Congress, because in practice its terms of reference are likely to reflect bargaining between Congressional committees, the two Houses of Congress and the President, and it can play off the different relationships.[14]

A similar type of problem arises when there is a chain of principals. This occurs, for example, when a minister is several steps removed from an agent. In such situations clarity of tasks are likely to be lost and the greater the distance between the ultimate agent and the original principal, the greater the likelihood that the agent will slip the leash of intended controls.

The problems involved in chain relationships expose a basic weakness in the theory of the democratic overhead because it shows up the weakness of any purported connection between the ultimate principal in democracies – the people themselves – and the unelected bodies contracted by ministers or legislators. The government has to be modelled both as an agent responsive to the electorate (the principals) and as a principal giving direction to agents (the unelected bodies).[15] Yet the initial contract between people and a party that enters government, let alone the policies pursued by a particular minister, is already likely to be vague and it is most unlikely that the chain of causality will flow through in any meaningful way from the people to the agent.[16]

Between politics and the law

A third weakness of the theory of the democratic overhead is that it gives too much weight to just one channel of accountability – the political. Even if there were robust ways of reconciling the independence of unelected bodies with ultimate control by a political principal through contracts, and, if contracts could in turn maintain clear principal–agent relationships through extended chains of command or with multiple principals, there would still remain problems with the idea of the democratic overhead for reasons unconnected with principal–agent theory. This is because democratically elected politicians provide only part of the setting within which the new bodies operate. In practice the unelected bodies occupy a space between politics and the law. Most of them also have to

---

[14] See Bawm (1995). See also Huber and Pfahler (2001).
[15] See Lane (2005: 30).
[16] See the discussion in Bergman, Müller and Strøm (2000).

consider the possibilities of judicial review by courts or, if they themselves are a court or a tribunal, by superior courts to which there is a right of appeal. Any attempt to situate the unelected bodies within a democratic system of government has to consider the role of the courts as well as the role of politicians. If there is an 'overhead' that covers them, it is a judicial as well as political overhead. Any theory of accountability has to take account of both law and politics and cannot rest on one alone.

It is possible to argue that the new breed of unelected body is indeed accountable to both the political branches of democratic systems of government and to the judiciary – a hybrid form of accountability. But this diminishes the idea that there is any straightforward relationship to the institutions of democracy, elected parliaments and governments.[17] The precise relationship between unelected bodies and the other branches of government – the political and the judicial – has also to be established. The nature of that relationship with other branches is discussed later in this book where it is argued that the relationship can best be formulated not in terms of an 'overhead' but in terms of 'mutual respect' in a separation of powers.

Own procedures

A fourth and final weakness of the theory of the democratic overhead is that the theory does not recognise the possibility that the unelected bodies may have their own independent source of legitimacy outside politics that is derived from their own approach to information, evidence and knowledge-based judgements. Many of the new bodies have had their original incarnation within the machinery of elective politics. But it does not follow from this history that they should still come under the control of the traditional elected bodies.

This fundamental criticism of the idea of a democratic overhead is that it fails to recognise that the procedures and operating standards of unelected institutions are not the same as those of elected institutions. The procedures are primarily those needed for the gathering of facts or evidence or knowledge and for steering through the inherent gaps in information and uncertainties in knowledge. They have nothing to do with political consent or even political consensus between divergent factions. By contrast politics has to look for compromise and to deal with value judgements related to the evidence as well as opinions that may be unfounded but are nevertheless real to those that hold them.

---

[17] The difficulty in formulating a hybrid theory is discussed in West (1995).

Politics also has to deal with intensity of feelings and with irrational prejudice. Different standards apply to these different worlds.

These procedural differences suggest, in turn, that in looking for an approach to holding the new branch of government to account, or to provide a basis for its legitimacy, there is a need to look for an approach that recognises the standards and principles that the unelected bodies follow in their own activities. The analogy, discussed in a later chapter, is with the judiciary. In just the same way that politicians usually understand that they should stand back from the processes of the law and distinguish the different realm of legal judgements from the realm of political judgements, so too procedural differences suggest that politicians may have to learn to stand back from the unelected bodies and to distinguish their judgements from political judgements. The idea that a democratic overhead survives as a way to retain the values of participatory democracy is implausible as a practical matter and inappropriate in a much more fundamental way.

Constitutionalism

If unelected bodies cannot plausibly be said to answer to democratic politics, then there is a strong case for saying that their position needs to be justified within the rules of a democratic constitution. In other words it is to a constitution that we should look for definitions of their role, their procedures and for their legitimacy. The constitution should also provide the method for calling them to account. In so far as constitutions can be regarded as a kind of higher law, this constitutionalist approach to the new institutions brings them within the tradition of the rule of law.

What the constitutional approach aims to achieve is to reconcile the need of the unelected bodies for protection against political interference with a mechanism to make sure that their existence and role is grounded in assent. What this approach argues is that as long as the constitution, or amendments to it, are democratically founded through approval by the people, then there is a democratic basis for the way in which it specifies the role of institutions – including in those cases where the constitution specifies independence from politicians. It also brings the unelected bodies clearly within the scope of constitutional and judicial review. It thus combines a form of democratic legitimacy with judicial accountability.

Constitutions are often regarded as somewhat abstract documents, particularly in the British context. But in theory they have one important democratic advantage compared with the political means of control embodied (unsuccessfully) in the theory of the democratic overhead.

The advantage is that a constitution can attempt to express the way in which power flows directly from popular assent. Constitutional control makes it possible to remove any intermediate agent between the public and the institution in the form of a minister or a parliament. By contrast, the politics of the democratic overhead essentially rests on power flowing down from purported ministerial or parliamentary control.

The constitutional perspective not only offers an alternative to the idea of a democratic overhead but also provides an update of the notion of the rule of law. The traditional definitions of the rule of law failed because they did not address the particular problems raised by the growth of this new body of institutions poised between politics and the law but having at the same time their own special characteristics. The new type of constitutionalism tries to escape from these limitations by offering rules with a broader compass that are applicable to many of the new institutions and that try to take account of their special features. The new constitutionalism also seems particularly apposite because insights gained from it have been partly responsible for the intellectual justification of some of the new institutions themselves.

The relevance of the new constitutional perspective

The new constitutionalism has been developed over the last fifty years by those who look at political institutions through the lens of economics. Its contribution to updating concepts of the rule of law essentially consists of three elements: the justification of new types of rules, the need to look at the way in which incentives work on institutional behaviour and the nature of the discovery process in politics and the law.[18] Each of these three elements is important to the world of unelected bodies. The new rules apply particularly to their world, the wrong incentives can destroy their world and if they themselves are to carry out their special responsibility for information and knowledge, they need constitutional support that encourages the discovery process.

The first area of insight about the need for new types of rules concerns the importance of rules of pre-commitment to good behaviour. Constitutional economics looks further at the pressures on those with power in society to err. Rules that act as a defence against temptation to stray from the narrow path are seen as an essential extension of the notion of the rule of law. They are highly relevant both to the new unelected bodies as well as to the traditional elected institutions. For example, fiscal rules can

---

[18] The theoretical approach is outlined in Buchanan (1990).

help discipline elected politicians; monetary or price stability rules can help discipline the activities of independent central banks; audit rules can help discipline those with spending or regulatory responsibilities, and rules of pre-commitment to impact analysis can help discipline regulatory bodies.

Secondly, constitutional economics has placed particular emphasis on the role of incentives on institutional behaviour. Classical constitutions defined the role of the traditional institutions of democracies – parliaments and executives – and essentially left them to check each other's behaviour through a separation of powers. Constitutional economics looks further into the incentives driving institutional behaviour. It looks at such questions as whether the new institutions will respond to the needs for information and knowledge, or become the victims of powerful interests, or simply be driven by their own internal agendas. It offers intended institutional or procedural safeguards against such possibilities. These safeguards cover such matters as definitions of duties, methods of appointment and dismissal, limits on terms of office and other restrictions.

A third area emphasised by constitutional economics is the importance of entrenching a discovery process about what works and what does not work in democratic politics. The reason for this new approach is that classical constitutional approaches were based on being able to align public policies with political territories and to allocate different policies to different territories. This kind of classical federalism allowed for experiment in public policy within the same political system. Since the boundaries of public policy in the modern world do not respect territorial boundaries there have to be other approaches to safeguarding the discovery process in the formation of public policy.

This new look at the constitutional requirements for a discovery process in democratic politics emphasises the importance of maintaining the integrity of different tax jurisdictions, the importance of allowing choice between different regulatory approaches and the importance of treating claims about rights, not as unquestionable claims, but as guides to right reason in circumstances where there are many possible interpretations about what is 'reasonable' and benefits from allowing for different interpretations.[19]

These provisions in a constitution about the discovery process may seem somewhat remote from the world of unelected bodies. However, if unelected bodies are to mobilise relevant information and knowledge from wherever it is outside government, reflect best practice, learn lessons

---

[19] See the discussion in Vibert (2001: chap. 5).

where they can and spread those lessons to others, they need a supporting constitutional environment and there have also to be defences against collusion between the different institutions.

Problems

Despite the relevance of the new constitutionalism to updating the rule of law to the world of the unelected, there remain both theoretical and practical problems with this approach.

One class of question concerns the old problem of what it is that should be constitutionalised and put in the formal framework of systems of government and what should be left to politics within constitutions. It is not clear, for example, which of the new institutions deserve constitutional status and protection and which of their procedures should be constitutionalised. The growth of unelected bodies has occurred quite rapidly and hitherto with little formal constitutional recognition. The question is whether the issues are now sufficiently clear that it makes sense to crystallise them in a rather rigid form. For example, in the USA, support for a balanced budget amendment seems to have declined because of the concern that such a rule might be over-rigid. Similarly in the case of the EU the quasi-constitutional provisions in the treaties addressed to attaining fiscal stability have quickly been called into question as over-rigid and their application revised.[20] In practice, constitutionalism in its new form has had little impact in the real world. This may simply reflect an inevitable time lag between theory and practice. It may also reflect uncertainties in what to constitutionalise.

A second question about constitutions concerns the process of constitutional change itself and the idea that the new unelected bodies can derive their legitimacy through the processes that legitimise a constitution. The dilemma is a long-standing one. If change is made too easy then a constitution loses its purpose of providing a long-lasting framework of rules. If, on the contrary, it is made too difficult, then popular consent becomes impractical and change takes place not through popular control but through other processes such as interpretation by courts. Thus the idea that people can be reconnected to the world of the unelected, not through the politics of the democratic overhead, but instead through the legitimising processes of popular approval of constitutional change encounters a different kind of implausibility.

---

[20] Treaty Establishing the European Community Art. 104.

Thirdly, the question of the rigidity of constitutions raises a more general issue about formalism. The issue is that the kinds of procedures and rule-based procedures which constitutions might require of the unelected bodies could encourage a kind of empty procedural formalism. The procedures would be followed but would have no meaning or could even be deceiving as to what is really going on. Regulators would undertake cost–benefit analysis but justify their preconceptions anyway; auditors would evaluate performance but nothing would change as a consequence; courts and tribunals would follow procedures for gathering evidence but their minds would have been made up ahead of time; independent central banks would operate under the outward appearance of making their own minds up on monetary policy but in practice would take 'under the table' instructions from finance ministers. At their worst, formalities can conceal rather than illuminate, offer the appearance of action rather than results; the pursuit of procedure becomes an end in itself, and the boundaries defined by formal rules become an obstacle to real-world success where boundaries are often shifting and opaque.[21]

It is fears such as these that suggest a different approach to the growth of unelected bodies – one that does not yet attempt to formalise their world, but one which encourages their growth as a pragmatic response to changes in what democratic societies want out of their systems of government.

Pragmatism

The perception that there has been a shift towards pragmatism in democratic systems of government is in large part a response to the collapse of socialism and the resulting sense that much ideological content has vanished from public debate. Democracy seems widely accepted as the 'least bad' way of organising systems of government and the market order as the least bad way of organising economic activity. With fundamental ideological challenges removed from political debate it seems that what is important in modern systems of government is practical problem-solving.

In this pragmatic world the unelected bodies enjoy a natural rise to pre-eminence because they, above all others, are the pragmatic problem-solvers. They are dealing with the practical world, not the world of ideologies, and their actions focus on detailed decisions that affect daily lives. They seek a reasoned way through disputes about the evidence or about the balance of scientific probabilities or through differences of

---

[21] For various kinds of formalism see Sunstein (1996: 24–5).

opinion in the scientific community. They have the knowledge, the expertise, the approach and a practical mindset.

The theoretical roots of pragmatism are diverse. One strand seems to be related to legal pragmatism that looks at the way law is actually practised and derives principles from that practice rather than from external norms.[22] Another strand looks at what is of practical importance in people's lives and sees that in modern life many of our life chances are affected by decision-takers who stand outside the traditional domain of politics or the market.[23] A further strand comes from those who look at bureaucratic behaviour, see the danger in procedures being followed for the sake of procedure itself, while recognising the virtues of a pragmatic 'muddling through'.[24] At a more philosophical level pragmatism represents a somewhat defensive reaction to so-called 'post-modernist' criticism that the ways in which we try to ground our beliefs are suspect and suggests that philosophers should turn instead to deal with real problems for real people.[25]

Pragmatism and deliberation

Because pragmatism rejects ideological approaches to problem-solving it is sometimes presented in opposition to theories of deliberative democracy or as an antidote to 'too much democracy'.[26] Deliberative democracy seems particularly germane to societies where there is a need and desire to discuss and resolve differences over fundamental values. Practical problem-solving does not seem to value either the abstract discussion highlighted by deliberative democracy or the abstract rules of constitutionalism.[27] The experts who inhabit the world of unelected bodies are said to offer quality assurances and certifications that must be taken on trust rather than providing information for communication and dialogue.[28]

Pragmatism, however, also shares a number of characteristics with deliberative democracy. The first is a belief in the importance of being reasonable and trying to settle problems through reason and evidence. The second is the importance of standards of civility in settling public

---

[22] For one theoretical presentation of this view see Coleman (2001).
[23] See, for example, Elster (1992).
[24] For a discussion of formalism versus reality in the context of audit see Power (1997).
[25] Diggins (1994).
[26] For this view of the role of unelected elites see Zakaria (2003).
[27] For an account of pragmatism that sets it apart from deliberative democracy and situates it within elitist theories of politics see Posner (2003).
[28] See Power (1997: 28).

disputes. The third is the importance of finding reasoned accommodation between opposing viewpoints. Thus, rather than standing in opposition to deliberative democracy, it seems more appropriate to see pragmatism as representing an updating of the goals of deliberative democracy. The content of what is being deliberated on has changed – from high values or ideology to practical issues. The venue has also been extended to include courts and regulatory and other unelected bodies as well as elected assemblies. But, at the same time, the goals of reason, civility and accommodation remain the same. Thus, in the same way that the constitutional approach can be interpreted as updating concepts of the rule of law, so 'pragmatism' can be seen as an attempt to update accounts and capture the virtues of deliberative democracy.[29]

What is important about this updating and extension of the concept of deliberative democracy is, first, the concern with a new type of politics that focusses on the critical choices that people have to make in their lives and, secondly, the suggestion that traditional accounts of deliberation have failed to give proper attention to the interaction between politics and the law. It highlights the importance of not focussing too exclusively on politics as the means through which democratic societies engage in reasoned problem-solving by looking more widely to include the law and a wider set of institutions.

Weaknesses

The idea of a shift in the nature of modern political debate seems to accord with the decline of fundamental ideological disputes. The claim of a new pragmatism also seems to fit in well with the world of the unelected. Nevertheless, this account of what is going on in modern democracies and the attempt to define where the new institutions fit in still suffers from fundamental shortcomings.

First, the pragmatic account accepts a diminution in the role of traditional politics at face value. It does not ask, as theories of participatory democracy ask, whether or not a diminution of the agenda of democratic politics is healthy for democratic societies. On the contrary it assumes that it is healthy because the shift in focus to pragmatism is said to correspond to what people actually want. It also offers no account of what is left for democratic politics if ideology has vanished and pragmatic problem-solving has been removed from the democratic arena. Nor does it question whether it matters if the locus of problem-solving in

---

[29] For the argument that judicial pragmatism is closely tied to the conventions of democratic deliberation see Sunstein (1999).

democratic societies has shifted. Efficiency gains from the new arrangements seem to provide their own sufficient justification for the change. Thus, we should all be content to leave pragmatic problem-solving to the experts or lawyers.

Secondly, along with an unquestioning acquiescence to changes in democratic practices that cannot be taken at face value, the pragmatic account gives a one-sided view of what democratic politics is all about. In this context, constitutional economists make a useful distinction between the 'expressive' purposes of politics and the 'instrumental'. 'Expressive' refers to the role of political systems in allowing for the ventilating of views about the values and principles held in society and the 'instrumental' refers to the ways in which democratic societies get things done.[30] Essentially, the pragmatic account focusses on getting things done and downplays the expressive side of politics. It may indeed be the case that ideology in its old form of a clash between the market order and socialism has vanished, but there are many other disputes about principles and values that take place within any society and that need a democratic outlet. The two sides of politics need to be looked at together.

Thirdly, the pragmatic account implies that the unelected problem-solvers can be held accountable between politics and the law. It gives too little consideration to the possibility that they have their own procedures and standards independent of, and different from, both those of the law and those of politics.

Contradictory diagnosis

These different attempts to adapt mainstream accounts of the democratic process to the rise of the unelected thus offer conflicting diagnoses and conflicting prescriptions. The idea of the democratic overhead attempts to work within the assumptions of participatory democracy by suggesting that the traditional institutions can retain effective control over the unelected bodies. The prescriptions revolve around well-defined contracts. By contrast, the new constitutionalism rejects the attempt to fit the unelected bodies within the framework of participatory politics. On the contrary, in order to remove the ambiguities and contradictions between independence and political control, the means of control need to be constitutional rather than political. This approach is rejected in turn by the pragmatic account of modern democracy because it objects to the formalism of rules-based approaches. The pragmatic approach suggests

---

[30] Brennan and Hamlin (2002).

that unelected bodies can be seen as problem-solving institutions poised between politics and the law and justified by the practical success and acceptability of what they do. But it accepts far too readily and without further investigation a vastly diminished world of democratic politics.

The shortcomings of each these adaptations to democratic theory lie not so much in the fact that they offer contradictory diagnoses and prescriptions but in a fundamental defect they share in common. The defect is that each of these approaches, unless much further adapted, attempts to rationalise a distancing of people from information and knowledge. The idea that there is a continuing democratic overhead assumes that a lengthening chain of agency will be acceptable to the principal – the people. Constitutionalism assumes equally that people will be content to have a control mechanism removed from the everyday thrust of political debate to the remoter reaches of constitutional choice. Viewing unelected bodies as non-ideological 'problem-solvers' distances people in a different way. It suggests that problem-solving is best left to the experts and in throwing out 'ideology' it is throwing out much else besides. This distancing alone weakens the claim of these adaptations to provide a viable update of democratic processes.

They have two other defects in common. First, they fail to look at the behaviour of democratic electorates that accompanies the new separation of powers. Secondly, they fail to give a plausible account of what is left in the world of traditional democratic politics after the rise of the unelected. A different approach has therefore to be taken to see how democratic practice and theory can adapt to the rise of the unelected. This involves looking again at the separation of powers identified earlier and examining in more detail its underlying logic and its impact on democratic processes. Before looking at the impact on elected institutions, such as parliaments, the discussion considers first the impact on electorates.

6 The new separation of powers and the advent of the informed citizen

In order to see what the new separation of powers means for the behaviour of electorates, this chapter looks at the logic underlying the classical doctrine and applies it to the new separation of powers. The implications of the classical doctrine of the separation of powers were revolutionary – the foundation for democratic government itself. The implications of the new separation of powers are also radical. They involve recognising that the new separation of powers makes possible a new style of democratic behaviour that implies in turn a recasting of the role of traditional democratic institutions and thinking afresh about the framing of national and international systems of government.

Conflicts of interest and the separation of powers

What is of enduring importance in the classic doctrine of the separation of powers is an underlying logic about identifying conflicts of interest within systems of government. This means identifying where institutional incentives work to the detriment of a system of government and conversely seeing where incentives can be harnessed to positive effect. The conflict can be presented in the negative or the positive. The negative aspect is the argument that when two functions are merged it is to the detriment of each. The positive aspect is the argument that if the two functions are separated there are gains for each and gains as well to the system as a whole.

The new separation of powers can be viewed from exactly this same perspective. In the negative it recognises conflicts of interest in the supply of information in the public sphere and the importance of ensuring that the incentives to inform are aligned with institutional tasks. In the positive it creates a new environment in which citizens can have much better access to reliable information and by acting as informed citizens can take a different approach to politics. This change in the environment has far-reaching implications for the way in which democracies work.

The classic doctrine

The classic doctrine of the separation of powers evolved in pre-democratic times and involved a well-known distinction between the executive, the legislature and the judiciary. In today's world these terms have to be used with a good deal of care. Even at the time when the classical theory was being developed, it was recognised that these terms were broadbrush and imprecise. Locke (1632–1704), for example, recognised that more than one class of function was covered by the term 'executive'. What, however, remains unchanged is the logic behind the distinctions.

The negative aspects of conflicts of interest had been stressed by Jean Bodin (1529–96) in terms that are now known as 'blame avoidance'. He argued in favour of the king relinquishing judicial functions by stating that the king's ability to make laws was damaged if the king had at the same time to be responsible for interpreting and implementing those laws. That unpopular task was better left to the courts and the judges. In this way the king would escape criticism and his authority to make the laws would remain intact.[1]

The positive aspect was emphasised by Locke and Montesquieu in arguing that the separation of powers could help hold each power in its place because it would give them the incentive to check and balance each other's activities. It was this presentation of the issue that was carried into the American constitution in its great leap into the experiment with democratic government.

There are many qualifications that can be made to the classic doctrine in considering its relevance to modern forms of government. The different branches in the American system of government, where the separation of powers was adopted, have never been completely separate in practice. The doctrine was about respecting core competences and the founders of the American system of government in fact established a very subtle interplay between the branches (discussed in a later chapter).[2] By contrast, most forms of democratic government in Europe have evolved in practice with a fusion of powers between the executive branch and the legislative, rather than a separation, although the ideal of an independent

---

[1] 'A state cannot fail to prosper where the sovereign retains those rights proper to his majesty, the senate preserves its authority, the magistrates exercise their legitimate powers, and justice runs its ordinary course. Otherwise, if those who have sovereign power attempt to invade the sphere of the senate or the magistrate, they only risk the loss of their own authority.' Bodin (1955 [1576], Book 4: 138).
[2] For example, the US Supreme Court is not in charge of all areas of US constitutional law; by tradition, courts will not review findings of the House of Representatives and Senate about impeachable behaviour. See Greenawalt (2002).

judiciary is observed in theory if not always in practice. Nowadays, the theory of checks and balances also tends to be approached through different methods of analysis, including, for example, through the identification of 'veto points'.[3] Nevertheless conflicts of interest within systems of government remain of fundamental importance and their resolution can have a far-reaching impact. In the classic doctrine an approach to government that started as 'blame avoidance' and a means to uphold a monarchical system of government turned out instead to undermine monarchy by making democratic government seem safe.

In the case of the new separation of powers the relevant conflicts of interest and the relevant incentives centre on the way information, evidence and empirical analysis is provided in the public arena. The traditional institutions can avoid blame by handing the gathering of information, analysis and the bringing to bear of the latest state of knowledge to the new unelected bodies. At the same time the new separation of powers has a positive effect on the way in which the public gets its information. This is not just because of the advantages identified earlier of unbundling the different elements in judgements on matters of public policy. It is also because separation puts in place new incentives that help reduce what are called 'information asymmetries'. Furthermore, this is not the end of the story any more than it was with the classical separation of powers. Access to more reliable, less politicised sources of information and analysis in turn provides a much safer platform for a different type of citizen behaviour in democracies that challenges the standard conventions of representative government.

The public and information asymmetries in politics

A contemporary way of looking at what the new separation of powers means for conflicts of interest and incentives in the provision of information for the public is to look at what economists call 'information asymmetries'. These refer to a situation where one party to a contract knows more about the contract than the other. They exist in the marketplace and they exist in politics.

Situations of information asymmetry are commonplace in the market where buyers quite often find themselves knowing less about the product or service they are interested in buying than the seller. Generally speaking, people do not like such situations. There is always the fear that one might be 'ripped off' or sold a lemon. In most cases the costs of making a

---

[3] See Tsebelis (2002).

mistake are small and people learn through their mistakes how to avoid them in future at relatively low cost. But sometimes a market in lemons persists. Moreover when it comes to making a major and infrequent purchase – for example of a house or a pension or a health insurance scheme – the costs of getting it wrong can be high and the chances of correcting a wrong decision may be limited.

In the case of traditional representative democracy, people also face the possibility of being sold a lemon by politicians on matters of public policy of importance to their life. They are promised a certain level of state retirement or pension benefits and then find the conditions are altered; or, they are promised a high quality of state education and then find that their educational qualifications are not worth what they had been led to believe. Behaviour which would land an entrepreneur in jail for engaging in misleading and deceptive practices is practised by politicians with impunity.

The market has responded to situations of information asymmetry in a variety of ways. The most common way is for companies to build a brand or corporate image as a way of certifying that a product or service is good. The brand aims to provide assurance to buyers and to convey information about the product or service without the purchaser having to make further detailed investigation. Another technique is through the provision of specialised information services. For example, before making a long-term commitment to the purchase of a pension product it may pay someone to take specialist advice from an independent financial adviser that does not have an interest in selling that product. It is also the case that, when things go wrong, a variety of forms of redress are open to dissatisfied customers – from returning a product to filing a law suit. The relative ease or difficulty in obtaining redress and the nature of redress available can also help people make decisions in situations where they do not have complete information on what they are getting.

The difficulty about such situations in politics, where we do not know quite what we are getting in matters of public policy, is that none of the remedies available in the market are quite so readily available in politics. The incentives in politics are towards the suppression of information. Politicians do not like to be embarrassed or contradicted by awkward facts. Politicians want to be re-elected and facts may stand in the way. Nor can politicians be seen as impartial sources of advice about products in which they have no self-interest. Politicians are out to sell their wares and not to offer dispassionate advice. In addition, party labels are not the kind of branding devices that enable people to know what they are getting with any great assurance. Neither do they contain mandated health and safety warnings. Means of redress are also much more cumbersome.

Voters get to the polls only once every four or five years, their options are very general and the relationship between a vote and policy outcomes is uncertain and unpredictable.

Changing incentives to inform

The analogy with the market suggests that the new separation of powers can be seen as a way to help redress situations of information asymmetry in matters of public policy. It changes the incentive structures that affect the flow of information and knowledge in a political system.

From the perspective of the traditional institutions the story is one of blame avoidance – the fear of being carriers of bad news and 'getting it wrong'.[4] The art of blame avoidance takes many forms and it influences governments and legislatures in different ways. It can take the form of rash legislation to avoid blame for 'doing nothing' when there is public outcry for action – for example when the US Congress rushed to pass the Sarbanes–Oxley legislation on corporate governance following public outcry over the fraud at Enron. It can also take the completely opposite form of 'doing nothing' when governments fear the consequences of a misstep.[5] But at the root of blame avoidance, whichever form it takes, is the difficulty governments and legislatures face in mobilising facts and analysis, in convincing the public that the facts and evidence are indeed what they are and in avoiding missteps because of inadequate information. Blame avoidance highlights also the fragility and waywardness of judgemental processes in politics. Faced with uncertainty over information and analysis, the uncertain practical effects of any action, as well as uncertainty about how the public may react to it all, politicians are less likely to want to set out all these uncertainties in front of the public and more likely to want to cover their tracks.

In cases such as Enron when governments face a politically irresistible compulsion to do something, the absence of facts and analysis is not a deterrent to government action. Governments will plunge ahead with costly and complex responses such as embodied in the Sarbanes–Oxley Act. But the base-line case is what to do in normal times when governments do not face one-way pressures for immediate action and where any action will do. In normal times, if the gathering of information and its

---

[4] 'Blame avoidance' fits within a stream of democratic theory that suggests that voters will mainly decide on their choice of a party to vote for on a minimal judgement about whether a government is performing well or not rather than on an 'enlightened understanding' of all the issues. It can be traced back to the identification of 'resentment' as a crucial factor in voting patterns. See Key (1948: 584–614).

[5] For a discussion of the varieties of blame avoidance see Weaver (1986).

interpretation is done within the machinery of government (the traditional executive branch), then governments run the risk of being blamed for bad news, for the inevitable gaps in information, or for differences between the experts over the interpretation of facts and the treatment of uncertainties and probabilities, or for failure to bring to bear the latest state of knowledge. Governments, from their perspective of wanting to retain public approval, are better off by putting all this at arm's length. In this way somebody else catches the blame for bad news or for faulty or inconvenient facts or analysis. Left within the government machine the incentives run in the direction of the suppression of awkward facts.

In contrast to politicians seeking re-election, the unelected bodies have, as mentioned earlier, a self-interest to release rather than to withhold information. This is because public understanding helps them get support for what they do and not only helps them in dealing with the interests they regulate or look after, but also helps protect them from intervention by their former masters – the politicians. At the same time, although the unelected bodies have an interest in persuading the public that the course of action they propose is the right one and avoiding being blamed for unwelcome information, the information they put out is seen as less susceptible to 'spin'. This is because they have a professional reputation to protect rather than an office to run for. For the many reasons discussed earlier, they speak with greater authority about the facts and the evidence and the judgements they are making on the evidence.[6]

In addition, as also mentioned earlier, the operation of the unelected bodies has changed the incentives applying to methods of redress. In the case of political means of redress, a minister may feel obliged to support a departmental position in cases where information or professional judgements have been developed within their own bureaucracy and thus be predisposed to deny any application for redress. By contrast, the unelected bodies may be in business for the express purpose of providing for redress or may offer much greater possibilities for judicial review. Unelected bodies will be well aware that if the procedures they have followed in obtaining facts and evidence have been deficient, or if inferences have been drawn that are not supported by the facts, then their judgements may be overturned in judicial review. Moreover, this review may be of a quite different order of effectiveness compared with any political review of deficiencies within the traditional machinery of

---

[6] Empirical research on the extent to which unelected bodies also engage in blame avoidance themselves is not available. Observation suggests that it happens but is counteracted by the other behavioural incentives mentioned.

government. Courts have no special interest in upholding the decisions of unelected bodies.

What citizens therefore have gained from the new separation of powers is an arrangement where the institutional incentives work in the direction of reducing information asymmetries in matters of public policy and favour more effective ways of protecting against being disadvantaged by them. The new separation of powers can thus be seen as a way of recognising conflicts of interest in the supply of information in the public sphere and as a way of ensuring that the incentives to inform are aligned with institutional tasks.

The radicalism of the new separation of powers

As mentioned above, when the classical doctrine of the separation of powers was first developed it was to support the powers of an absolute monarch. Bodin was concerned to buttress the powers of kingship by shielding the monarch from unnecessary blame. It evolved in a completely different direction to undermine the powers of absolute monarchy. This revolutionary outcome was a result of viewing the separation of powers as a system of checks and balances. The checks and balances were conceived as a check against absolute monarchs, but the genius of the American Founding Fathers was to see that they could equally well act as checks against misrule by popularly elected assemblies. In other words they made it safe for America to move to a democratic form of government.

The new separation of powers also has radical implications. It too may have started life as a result of governments wanting to avoid blame and to buttress their position with the public. But it too has radical implications for traditional models of representative democracy. This is because when information is more plentifully available and dissociated from political spin, the world is made safer for a different type of democratic behaviour.

Traditional models of representative democracy were built on the assertion that people would want to delegate politics to the politicians. Two assumptions were critical in justifying delegation. The first assumption was that the politician would have better sources of information and superior knowledge about what to do and how to react. The second assumption was that people would be content to leave judgements and decisions on the facts to politicians.

Neither assumption seems tenable any longer. The new branch removes from the traditional branches of representative democracy any automatic claim that 'they know best' on information known only to them. Deferring willingly to authority figures is also not what people do in other walks of life. There seems to be no compelling reason why people should want to act differently when it comes to making political judgements on matters that they regard as salient to themselves. People now have access to information and knowledge from a new branch independent from the traditional political branches and can much more safely use that information to make their own judgements and decisions. The two assumptions of the traditional model of representative democracy are therefore fundamentally weakened.

Encouraging the 'informed citizen'

The new style of democracy that is recognised and encouraged by the new separation of powers can be described in terms of the 'informed citizen'. The rise of the informed citizen can be seen in all walks of life. Today, people inform themselves directly about products and services they want – including in those areas where, in past generations, people were prepared simply to take on trust the advice or views of those who were conventionally given authority to speak – priests, doctors, teachers or scientists.[7] Today, informed citizens do not rely on conventional sources of authority but search out information for themselves and are more than ready to question those in traditional positions of authority if information or views are in conflict. People want to know about the sources of information, they want to see the information for themselves, they want to know what judgements the professionals make and, while they may want to know the interpretation and judgements of those in traditional positions of authority, they also want to form their own judgements.

The idea of the 'informed citizen' extends this behaviour to politics and matters of public policy. It holds that people no longer rely on the words and authority of politicians.[8] Informed citizens do not want politicians to say that they know best on the basis of information that is known only to themselves. Instead people want to see for themselves the information and knowledge on which politicians claim to act. They demand that the information and expert analysis should be made known to all and should

---

[7] The change in the relationship between doctors and patients from one of unquestioning acquiescence by the patient and 'the doctor knows best' has been dated to 22 Oct. 1957 and the 'informed consent' decision of Justice Absalom F. Bray of the California Court of Appeals. Justice Bray wrote that, 'In discussing the element of risk a certain amount of discretion must be employed consistent with the full disclosure of facts necessary to an informed consent.' See Gigerenzer (2002: 96).

[8] A recent inquiry into the state of British democracy referred to 'the creation of a large section of British society which is now better educated, more affluent, expects greater control and choice over many aspects of life, feels no deference towards those in positions of authority'. Power Inquiry (2006: 18).

no longer be privileged within the traditional branches of government. It must also be seen as untainted by political interference.

The new separation of powers encourages this behaviour. A better-informed public and a public with more reliable information and analysis at its fingertips will be more questioning of political authority, make its own judgements on the facts and wish to make its own informed decisions and interpretation of those facts in ever-increasing areas. Informed citizens do not wish to delegate.

Rescuing the conventions of representative democracy

In the face of this challenge from informed citizens there are essentially three grounds on which to rescue the conventions of representative democracy.

The first basis on which delegation to elected politicians can be defended centres on 'trust'. It is asserted that what is missing in political life is 'trust' and once this is restored then people will once again be prepared to defer to their representatives. The second relies on propositions from what is known as 'cognitive theory' that suggest that the public will not be capable, nor particularly wanting, to make judgements for itself and therefore will continue to happily delegate decisions to politicians. The third centres on what is known as 'the blame culture'. The assertion is that while people may be more willing to take judgements and decision for themselves they will not live easily with the consequences of decisions that turn out badly. They will turn instead to traditional politics as a means of blaming others and seeking compensation. Blame thus runs in a never-ending cycle of blame shifting from politicians to citizens and back again. Each of these attempts to rescue traditional democratic behaviour fails.

A question of trust?

Any unwillingness to delegate judgements and decisions to politicians is seen by some observers simply as a sign of lack of 'trust' and thus to be remedied by attempts to restore confidence in politics and politicians.[9] Theories of trust are closely related to the view that a healthy civil society and deeply rooted social capital will generate trust.[10] They also show a scepticism towards science and experts. Politicians may not be trusted by informed citizens but neither are scientists and experts. Thus, if trust in

[9] For a review of various approaches to trust see Misztal (1996).
[10] For a populist account see Fukuyama (1995).

politicians can be restored then the conventions of representative democracy can be retained and unelected experts can be put back in their box.
Arguments based on trust, however, have first to address the question
of the consistency of public attitudes towards traditional sources of
authority. If it is indeed the case that in other walks of life and areas of
judgement people are increasingly inclined to question traditional
authority figures about their information and judgement, for example to
question doctors about their treatments or church leaders about their
precepts, then the onus is to explain why this questioning would not also
extend to authority figures in politics. The evidence points in a different
direction – to a lack of trust. People may not trust scientists but they trust
politicians even less. Recent surveys in the UK about trust in politicians in
two specific and very different areas (official statistics and state pensions)
both showed a remarkable degree of distrust. In the case of official
statistics only 17 per cent of respondents agreed that official figures
were produced without political interference whereas 54 per cent disagreed.[11] In the case of state pensions a survey showed even greater
distrust. Only 23 per cent trusted the government in relation to the
state pension while 71 per cent did not.[12] These surveys about trust in
specific areas support the findings in other surveys comparing trust in
politicians with trust in other institutions where relative distrust of elected
representatives is again a striking feature.[13]

Secondly, arguments based on trust also have to ask whether the
preconditions for trust are likely to be met in modern political arenas.
From the perspective of economists, 'trust' allows parties to a relationship
to economise on the costs of that relationship. If there is trust there does
not need to be a costly mechanism for investigating whether one or other
party is telling the truth or not. Similarly, there is no need for costly legal
mechanisms for enforcing agreements or contracts, because each can rely
on the other to perform according to their understanding of the obligation. If disputes do arise it should be possible to settle them through
informal and non-adversarial means.

The viewpoint of the economist helps specify the conditions under
which trust flourishes. Trust is possible where each side is likely to
share the same appreciation of the same facts, is in close and repeated
contact and where the historical record of past interactions is positive.

---

[11] Of the 54 per cent who disagreed, 'About three-quarters of those asked gave answers
which either stated directly, or implied, that they thought there was likely to be deliberate
interference with the figures.' Source: Goddard (2005: 5).
[12] Source: Association of British Insurers. The State of the Nation's Savings 2005.
[13] See Pattie, Seyd and Whiteley (2004, table 2.3, p. 38 and table 6.5, p. 170); and Dalton
(2006: 254–7).

Modern democratic systems of government do not offer this setting. They offer large, anonymous arenas, distant and remote contacts, an adversarial setting and chequered interactions. 'Trust' therefore does not seem to provide a means of rescuing the conventions of representative democracy. Moreover, in another, more general sense, a desire for everyone to place their trust in politicians is misjudged. It is healthy in a democracy for the public to view those in power with a certain degree of mistrust – there is always the risk that they will abuse their power. If a politician cries, 'Trust me, I'm a politician', people are likely to head for the safety exits – and rightly so.

A question of limited judgement?

An alternative basis for believing that people will still want to rely on politicians to take decisions and make judgements on their behalf centres around well-established propositions in cognitive theory about the limits on the ability or interest of people to weigh their choices in a prudent and consistent manner. This is known as 'bounded rationality' where people do not want to examine exhaustively all their options.[14]

Theories of bounded rationality can be adapted to rescue the conventions of representative democracy because they suggest that people will want to limit the time and effort they spend on complicated decisions involving, for example, the acceptable level of risks in their lives. Instead, they will remain willing to delegate judgements and decisions to those who can think about them all the time – in other words to the politician. The politician, having been divorced from fact gathering and the making of empirical analysis, is now back on centre stage to tell people that they know best how to evaluate those facts and analyses and how best to take decisions on their behalf. In a recent survey 54 per cent of respondents strongly agreed or agreed with the statement, 'Sometimes politics and government seem so complicated that a person like me cannot really understand what is going on.'[15]

This defence draws on the many shortcomings in the way people make judgements for themselves highlighted by cognitive science. For example, strong desires or aversions may distort perceptions, the short-cut methods people use for convenience may be unreliable and people may prefer to make quick and dirty judgements rather than those slower methods that

---

[14] The components of 'bounded rationality' are set out by Simon (1986).

[15] Pattie, Seyd and Whiteley (2004: 67). Similarly, in the Electoral Commission and Hansard Society audit (2006), 51 per cent of those surveyed felt that they did not know very much about politics.

would yield better results. Above all, people are extremely poor at assessing probabilities and hugely influenced by the way in which a question involving probabilities is framed. Yet it is probability analysis that is key in any scientific or mathematic assessment of risk and uncertainty. By extension, people can be assumed to be very poor at countering the risks and uncertainties in their own lives. At the same time, theories of bounded rationality also suggest that people do not need to know very much in order to make a reasonable choice in politics; normal democratic mechanisms will work sufficiently well to provide people with all that in practice they need to know.[16] In these circumstances therefore they will continue to delegate in the traditional way.

The weakness in this defence of the traditional politician is that it gives a far too selective interpretation to the propositions of cognitive theory. It is not correct to move in any quick way from the technical weaknesses in the way that people approach problem-solving to conclude that what they do is 'unreasonable' or 'irrational' and requires 'correction' by the superior judgement of politicians. We do not 'normally' demand people to be expert in branches of mathematics or decision theory to judge whether they behave reasonably or not. Other standards of evaluation may be more appropriate.[17] On most definitions of rationality people have reasons for their choices even if they do not satisfy the demands of games theorists or economists.[18] It has been argued that their reasons only need to be good and sufficient in order to be both rational and morally justified.[19]

Moreover, the picture from cognitive science is not all gloom. There are other findings of cognitive science that emphasise the positive such as adaptability. In addition, while theory has emphasised that people do not want to exhaustively weigh all their options all the time, it also provides a guide to what they are prepared to do. For example, they may make judgements on matters that they consider salient by limiting the set of options they consider.

Theories of bounded rationality are also open to misinterpretation. They do not imply that people do not in some sense 'maximise' their options, but rather that people will take into account the costs of gathering information and decision-making in their choices. This places the emphasis on other highly important aspects of decision-taking that help

[16] See Lupia and McCubbins (1998).
[17] 'The psychologist is not necessarily authoritative on what the correct normative principles are.' Goldman (1986: 307).
[18] For an attempt to introduce a more 'modest' version of what would be rational in judgements involving probability see Kaplan (2002: 434–62).
[19] See Slote (1989).

people gather information.[20] First is the social setting in which individuals make many judgements. We can listen to what other people say and pool or multiply ideas on what is concerning us, even if we do not want to carry this interaction into politics or to listen to conventional figures of authority. Secondly, we can, and often do, turn to the market as a source of information. We may not be able ourselves to calculate the probabilities of living to a certain age but others can. When relevant, for example in financial planning for old age, independent advice can be bought.

What this means is that, far from rescuing the conventions of representative democracy, theories of bounded rationality are entirely consistent with the idea of the 'informed citizen'. When people take charge of their own decisions, their judgements do not have to be exhaustive or what is theoretically 'the best' after having examined all the available options from all points of view or after having weighed all the probabilities. All that a decision needs to be is sufficient for the purpose – including a decision to seek advice from others or from the market or to rely on their own judgement.

Thus, appeals to people to trust politicians, or appeals to the image of voters happy to defer on the basis of limited knowledge to elected representatives about what is in their best interest, do not offer an easy way to restore the traditional assumptions underlying the conventions of representative government. Once electorates can see the facts for themselves without spin from the politicians and have access to a more reliable source of information and facts, without intervening or superimposed judgements from politicians about how to interpret those facts, there is likely to be an accompanying lack of willingness to continue to delegate decisions to politicians. The traditional assumptions of representative democracy no longer square with public behaviour. The informed citizen is a 'dissatisfied democrat'.[21]

The politics of blame?

A third and final way to try to salvage the conventions of representative democracy is to accept the premise that, provided with a safer environment in which to seek and find reliable information and the most up-to-date empirical knowledge, people will make more judgements for themselves, but draw different conclusions. It is suggested that people will be unwilling to accept any adverse outcomes of their own judgements, engage in

---

[20] See the discussion in Lupia, McCubbins and Popkin (2000).
[21] Russell Dalton (2006: 257) refers to 'A new style of "dissatisfied democrats" ... citizens who are dissatisfied with political institutions but supportive of democratic principles.'

blame displacement behaviour and blame others instead. Politics becomes the chief means of seeking compensation. In other words, if individuals make decisions that damage their health they will look to government-supported health schemes to bail them out of the conse-quences, and, if they make poor decisions on retirement or pensions, they will similarly look to governments to provide them with support. Once again the representative politician rides to the rescue, this time to rescue people from any damaging consequences of their own decisions.[22]

Hard evidence about whether a blame culture is emerging as the under-side of the behaviour of informed citizens seems to be lacking but some believe that such a culture is indeed emerging.[23] If such a blame culture is emerging then it suggests that the political economy of blame leads in a complete circle. The blame game never stops. As a first step, politicians try to shed blame, but at the final step citizens turn once again to politicians – in order to blame anyone other than themselves – and seek compensation.

This cycle of blame does not necessarily salvage representative politics. Other channels of redress may be preferred. For example, anecdotal evidence suggests a greater willingness to litigate. The unelected bodies themselves may encourage such behaviour by opening up new avenues of redress and appeal.[24]

More important, the politics of blame concedes not only the premise that behaviour in democracies is changing as a result of the rise of the unelected but also accepts the consequence – that accounts of what functions are left to the traditional elected institutions also change as a result. But its particular depiction of the consequences, involving a rather unattractive scenario where the implications for the institutions of repre-sentative democracy are encapsulated by a shift to the politics of blame and compensation, does not necessarily have to be accepted.

The pivotal question for the traditional institutions is thus how to define their changed role in the new separation of powers. The disadvantages of having fingers pointed at them for poor information or uncertainties in

---

[22] Two different types of behaviour can be distinguished. One is blame 'reversion' where people turn again to blame politicians for adverse events even where unelected bodies hold responsibility. The other is blame 'displacement' where people blame politicians for their own personal shortcomings in making judgements. See Hood (2002).

[23] 'Of the different types of blaming system that we can find in tribal society, the one we are in now is almost ready to treat every death as chargeable to someone's account, every accident as caused by someone's criminal negligence, every sickness a threatened pro-secution. Whose fault? is the first question.' Douglas (2002: 15–16).

[24] The possibility that institutional arrangements may themselves encourage 'negativity bias' where people are more alert to adverse outcomes rather than to positive outcomes is an area where there is an absence of hard evidence. See Weaver (1986).

knowledge and for political missteps are avoided or reduced. But the advantages are unclear. They appear to be in danger of losing all relevance in modern democracies squeezed between unelected bodies on the one hand and impatient, uninvolved and unforgiving electorates making their own judgements for themselves on the other. If their chief remaining role is to act as conduits for blame and compensation, their future seems unappealing indeed.

7 Informed citizens and the changing role of traditional institutions

The key to seeing what the advent of informed citizens and the new separation of powers means for the traditional institutions lies in distinguishing between two roles. One role that traditional institutions can play is that of problem-solving. The other role is of providing an arena for the discussion of values and principles. When a government sets out its role as problem-solver it asks people to believe that it has the answers to questions such as how to provide comfortable retirement for ageing populations, or the answer to providing better healthcare or education. When assemblies provide an arena for discussion of values and principles, it is such terms as 'solidarity' or the 'social market' or 'family values', or 'the precautionary principle' or 'ethical' foreign policies, that colour the discussion.

Very often the discussion of values is thoroughly entwined with particular approaches to problem-solving. European politicians often talk about the 'social partners' or the 'social market' in the context of problem-solving, for example when talking about labour market reforms. When they do this, they are linking their approach to a particular problem to background values about the nature of the market, when it is justified for governments to intervene and how that intervention should be orchestrated. Similarly, when they talk about 'sustainable development' the aim is to link economic policy-making with environmental values. However, the fact that, in practice, policy discussion often joins both a proposed solution to a problem together with background values does not invalidate the distinction between the two functions.

The advent of informed citizens conjoined with the rise of the new branch of government changes the nature of both these two functions. The problem-solving function is influenced both by the greater willingness of people to make judgements and take decisions for themselves and also by the rise of the unelected bodies as problem-solving institutions themselves. At the same time the arena function is also altered. The concentration of evidence and knowledge-based judgements in the unelected institutions leaves it to the representative bodies to express ethical and political values through the judgemental processes of politics and to bring the two streams of judgement together. The rise of unelected bodies does not therefore mean that there is no role left for the traditional, elected institutions of representative democracy, or even that their role is of diminished importance. However, what they do and the way in which they go about their functions do change.

Outside observers were taken aback when voters in the 2004 US presidential elections referred to the decisive importance of moral values in determining their votes. The observers seemed surprised that issues such as abortion, stem-cell research and same-sex marriages were dominating over traditional concerns such as jobs or social security. They should not have been taken aback. When technocratic functions are carried out elsewhere, it is increasingly the role of representative bodies to illuminate values held in democratic societies.

The changing nature of problem-solving

The change in the problem-solving role of the traditional institutions is in the first instance an automatic consequence of people doing more to inform themselves and having a safer environment in which to make judgements and decisions for themselves. Even in cases such as national security where traditionally governments have had a free hand to interpret the public good, people now demand to know the facts or professional assessments unvarnished by political spin. The situation is well illustrated by the case of the difficulties of the British Government in justifying its engagement in the Iraq conflict. In this case the assessment of the professionals about the uncertainties of the information on WMD seems to have been overridden by a political imperative to find reasons for regime change in Iraq. Political intervention from the Prime Minister's office meant that the caveats that ought to have been applied to the information were swept aside. Subsequently, adverse reaction to suspected political tampering with professional judgements made public support for the war much more precarious. Thus, even in areas such as security and foreign policy, where the problem-solving role of governments seems most entrenched, the tide has swung. People want to see the evidence for themselves and make up their own minds for themselves. This means that governments have to define and approach their problem-solving role in a different light.

The change to the problem-solving role of governments arises secondly because some of the key problems facing modern societies are much more amenable to action by the unelected bodies than by the traditional institutions of representative democracy. This is not simply because they have a better command of the facts in complex situations but because the nature of the problems facing modern democratic societies is also changing.

The unelected bodies as problem-solvers

The rise of unelected bodies as problem-solvers reflects first a change in the nature of disputes within democratic societies about the allocation of resources and distributive issues. The old disputes centred around the divisions of rewards between social classes or between capital and labour. These were disputes where traditional democratic institutions could claim with some justification to be able to act in a problem-solving role because elected representatives and political parties reflected these same economic and social interests.

By contrast, allocation disputes in contemporary democracies revolve around claims about 'rights'. Most, if not all, rights claims can be viewed as claims about allocation, whether expressed in terms of the resources needed to provide a right to university education for disadvantaged groups, or the rights of access to buildings and transport for the disabled. The new kinds of dispute put traditional institutions at a disadvantage and play to the strengths of the unelected institutions instead.[1] The important feature of these types of claims about the allocation of resources is that many will start and end in the courts – the original bodies set apart from democratic politics – others will end up with the new bodies set up to monitor some of these specific concerns. In addition, political attitudes to them cut across traditional party lines and therefore it becomes more difficult for the mechanisms of representative bodies to mediate disputes. Political institutions still play an important role in such disputes but it is a shared role and not always the decisive one.

A second reason for the rise of unelected bodies as problem-solvers concerns the changing nature of clashes of interest in society. The old type was characterised in terms of clashes between different vested interests – labour or management, for example. Traditional political parties tapped into these constituencies and could again claim a role in mediating their differences. These types of clashes of interest are becoming less important and giving way to a different type of clash of interests important in the world of the informed citizen.

These new conflicts are the clashes of interest and incentives within the world of the information needed for private decision-taking. For example,

---

[1] The declining salience of class is discussed in Crouch (2004: 53–69).

individuals making a decision on where to place their savings, or how to fund their retirement in the private market, will need disinterested advice from an independent source. They will not want to rely on advice from analysts with a self-interest in supporting particular issuers of shares or with an interest in gaining commissions from the sale of particular investments. Similarly, patients may require second or third opinions from doctors so that they do not accept advice unquestioningly from one that may have a pecuniary or budgetary interest in offering or denying an expensive test. These types of conflict are the bread and butter of the boundary watchers among the new breed of unelected body. They are much more difficult for the traditional institutions to handle because they require knowledge of how information is provided in financial and other markets that politicians often do not possess or misunderstand. In the 2005 British general election, the Prime Minister was caught completely unawares of the conflict created for doctors as to how to treat patients on waiting lists because of their desire to meet government targets.

A third reason for the growth of the problem-solving role of unelected bodies concerns the context of decision-taking by informed electorates. In the world of informed citizens the way in which the market handles information becomes all-important. The issues do not just revolve around conflicts of interest in the provision of information but involve the operation of information markets more generally, including the market asymmetries mentioned earlier. For example, if market mechanisms do not encourage auditors to give a fair view of company financial statements or rating agencies to give an objective assessment of company prospects, then it is the regulator that steps in to adjust requirements for corporate reporting. Once again the unelected bodies are the key actors. The old politics of the marketplace was about excluding the market so that the state provided education or pensions or health services; the new politics of the market is about ensuring the flow and quality of information that people need in order to make decisions on pensions, education or health for themselves.

What these new problem-solving tasks have in common is that the traditional elective institutions have neither the specialised knowledge nor the special skills for dealing with them. On the contrary it is the bodies in the new branch where the relevant problem-solving skills are located. In addition the traditional aggregative methods of representative democracy are not as relevant. The new interests do not line up along historical party lines or affiliations.

In this situation the traditional problem-solving role of government seems squeezed within a pincer movement – on the one flank by people solving problems for themselves and on the other flank by the unelected bodies better equipped to take on the new kind of problem-solving. It would therefore be tempting to conclude that the problem-solving function of elected governments is simply less important than in the past. This, however, is not the case. Instead, the problem-solving activity of elected institutions has changed in two important respects. First, the issues that appear on the public agenda are no longer those picked by a dominant state but those forced to public attention by the implications of private decision-taking. Secondly, the capacity of elected institutions to adjust the basic framework for private choices has risen greatly in importance.

The changing dynamics of the public policy agenda

The first of these changes involves the shift taking place in the way the public policy agenda is set. The shift can be crudely summarised as a shift from a situation where the public agenda drives private decision-taking to one where private decision-taking drives the public agenda. What has happened is that the arrival of the informed citizen blurs traditional distinctions and practices about what is private and what is public and changes the dynamics of the way in which the public policy agenda is set.

Political theorists and economists have long tried to provide clear demarcation lines between what is public and belongs within the rightful domain of government action or provision and what is private and rightly belongs to the individual sphere where the government should not tread. For example, political theorists have drawn a distinction based on whether individual actions could possibly cause harm to others as one demarcation line. Similarly, economists, since the time of Adam Smith, have drawn distinctions between public goods and private goods.

The problem with these and other demarcation lines is that they do not provide clear boundaries. Economists have come to discover that most goods are neither clearly private nor public but mixed (private goods having public characteristics and public goods having private goods features). Similarly, political theorists have come to accept that many individual actions have spill-over features ('externalities' in the language of economists) and thus belong both to the private realm and the public.

The arrival of the informed citizen or elector adds to this blurring of lines. On the one hand, it is likely increasingly to lead individuals to want to make their own choices in areas that in Europe have, over the last fifty years, been dominated by state provision and public policy such as pensions, education and health. On the other hand, the public realm is likely to find itself increasingly dealing with the consequences of private decision-making. Thus the contemporary agenda finds itself increasingly treating such questions as the use of private off-road vehicles that disturb public spaces or destroy wilderness areas, or with the public health consequences of smoking, alcoholism or obesity. Subjects concerning private behaviour that once were an important part of public debate may now reappear – subjects such as frugality and the willingness to save for rainy days or the individual's work ethic compared with preferences for leisure. It is in this context where informed citizens make more judgements and decisions for themselves that such issues as taking personal responsibility rather than blaming others and seeking compensation for adverse consequences become much more important.

Updating the framework for private decision-taking

The second change that alters the problem-solving role of governments is that in this new environment where individual decision-taking is increasingly the driver of the public agenda, governments have to focus more on the general context or framework within which people can make their own judgements and decisions. More specifically, governments have to provide a framework based on facilitating private decision-taking rather than providing a framework that makes judgements on behalf of others.

The basic framework within which people make their lifetime choices is often taken for granted as part of the social and political wallpaper. Its importance becomes visible only when democracies make step-changes such as occurred in Europe first with the introduction of the post-war welfare states and subsequently with the Thatcher revolution. In the USA the New Deal was one and the Reagan revolution another. The growth of private problem-solving means that Europe is now in the situation of needing step-change as it looks to change the post-war social economy model that involved the state taking over many basic choices. The old driver of framework change was the politics of the external shock (usually war or the aftermath of war); the new driver of framework change is the politics of private decision-taking over much longer, healthier lifespans.

Economists and political scientists refer to such situations as 'punctured equilibrium'. This can be defined as involving long periods of slow gradual change punctuated by short periods of dramatic change.[2] Normal politics is about slow change or even gridlock.[3] Step-change is when gridlock is broken or forced open by external or internal pressures. The

[2] Denzou and North (2000). See also True, Jones and Baumgartner (1999: 97–115).
[3] 'The benefit of gridlock ... is that many actors outside of government ... nevertheless prefer a known and stable policy regime to frequent and often unpredictable changes.' Krehbiel (1998: 230).

emergence of informed citizens re-emphasises the importance of the overall framework and the need for elected institutions to be able to bring about step-changes.

In democracies with informed citizens, therefore, the problem-solving role of politics has not disappeared. It has, however, changed its focus. Elected institutions no longer have the capacity to intervene effectively in what economists call micro-decisions. These are best left to the new institutions and to people themselves. Elected institutions do, however, have an important remaining role in taking what economists call the macro-decisions – those decisions that alter the framework for private decisions.[4] Similarly, for elected bodies the arena role also has not disappeared. But again it has changed its nature.

The arena function

The earlier discussion argued that the new separation of powers involved a distinction between judgements based on information and empirical knowledge and political judgements that introduced values and principles that might enrich the knowledge-based judgements of democratic societies and add to, modify or even overrule them. The arena function is about harnessing relevant values and principles within the judgemental processes of politics and linking evidence-based processes to political processes.

The context of value differences

The end of the ideological contest between socialism and capitalism has led some observers to speculate prematurely about the end of disputes about fundamental values or principles and led others to emphasise different types of cultural dispute characterised as 'clashes of civilisation'. However, in the highly diverse societies of Europe and the United States, deep-seated and strongly held differences of opinion abound. Even if there is agreement at a general and abstract level about the rule of law, democracy and fundamental human rights, there are different views about the relevance of particular values, about their interpretation, about how to weigh different values together and about how to apply them. Even if one excludes different religious and belief systems from the equation, arguably it is accommodating the diversity of values and opinions in modern societies that is the central problem facing democratic

---

[4] Kolm (1996) makes an analogous distinction between questions of macro-justice, involving the overall allocation of resources, and the specific issues of micro-justice.

108 The Rise of the Unelected

practice. Pluralism, whether and how to accommodate plural values, has become an issue in and of itself.

This diversity within modern societies presents the institutions of representative democracy with a fundamental problem about how to bring ethical and political values into the judgemental processes of politics and what weight to give them alongside empirical and evidence-based judgements.

One way of looking for guidance about the treatment of relevant values in public debate is to look at what is said in a constitution. In this context the distinction that constitutional economists make between the instrumental purposes of a constitution (for example the parts that define the tasks of the institutions) and the 'expressive' (the parts that express values and principles) is again a useful one.[5] In the case of the current proposal for a European constitution, expressions of value include such principles as 'sustainable development', 'social inclusion', 'non-discrimination' in a range of guises and many more. In the United States the expressive part of the constitution is very much shorter but nevertheless continues to serve as the backdrop to important contemporary debates such as access to education, or the protection of privacy or the legality of same-sex marriages.

The constitutional context is, however, much less helpful than it might appear. If expressions of value are kept to a minimum, as in the case of the United States, many issues will arise on which the constitution will be silent or the link very tenuous. If, on the other hand, the constitution is filled to overflowing with expressions of value, as with the case of the constitution proposed for the European Union, its practical usefulness will diminish for different reasons. The values will be in conflict with each other, or need to be weighed against each other, and on such matters the constitution is silent once again.[6] In other words, in both situations the constitution does not provide the guidance needed. Either some of the most important and difficult issues faced by a society have to be left to judges to decide or, alternatively, the institutions of representative democracy and the voter come marching back into the frame. One interpretation of the importance that voters in recent US elections have placed on ethical questions is that the electorate wants to express its own views on how important values should be interpreted and not leave them to judges.

---

[5] For a further discussion of the importance of moral considerations in political settings see Brennan and Hamlin (2000).
[6] Art. I-3 of the proposed Treaty Establishing a Constitution for Europe defining the Union's objectives refers to over thirty values.

Defining the arena

Among the early writers on democracy, Rousseau saw the task of mediating values as the defining attribute of democratic government rather than the carrying out of particular functional tasks. He discussed it both through his writings on the importance of education and through his concept of the general will.

The aspect of the general will that has drawn most attention is the idea that the will of the majority stands behind the legislative programme in democracies. Formulated in this way it has long been criticised as opening the way for the tyranny of majorities over minority interests. But Rousseau also discussed the general will in a different way and not just in order to justify majority decision-taking as a decision rule for democracies. He used it also to discuss the nature of the key problems he saw in bringing values into the judgemental processes of democratic societies. First, he highlighted the importance of identifying potential conflicts between the values individuals hold themselves with the values espoused by society as a whole. Secondly, he emphasised the importance of 'backsliding' in individual behaviour – the difference between what we say we value and what we actually do.

Both problems involve potential conflicts in the way values are expressed in society but the sources of the difference are not the same. In the first case the conflict arises between the values an individual holds and the values that are assumed to be shared by all in society, and in the second case the conflict is one concerning the internal consistency of individual behaviour. This takes the focus of Rousseau's theory of the general will away from mechanical voting rules to the more important issue of how we identify and weigh relevant values in democratic politics.

When the contemporary role of elected representatives in weighing different values is considered there are two obstacles to overcome right at the outset. The first is the perception that the venality, sleaziness and lack of moral fibre of many elected politicians make them appear singularly disqualified to have any role in the value judgements of democratic societies. The distinction, however, is between the office and the person – a distinction exemplified in recent history by President Clinton. The second is the susceptibility of politicians to sound off and grandstand on what is politically correct – a tendency illustrated by the European Parliament in its handling of the confirmation of Rocco Buttiglione as a member of the Barroso Commission. Leaving the superficialities of politics to one side, the nub of the issue lies elsewhere in the two areas identified by Rousseau.

The mirror

In a contemporary context Rousseau's distinctions can be loosely interpreted to serve, not as a decision rule, but as a guide to what the traditional institutions of democracies, both governments and representative assemblies, should be looking at when they are incorporating values into judgemental processes. Following Rousseau's distinctions, the first task of democratic institutions is to illuminate the interaction between individual choices and the values assumed to be espoused by society as a whole. For example, European politicians like to proclaim that European societies favour a 'social' market and sustainable development. Applied to public policy in the transport area, such assumed values might be interpreted to mean that people want abundant public transport services running on environmentally friendly fuels. But at the same time people may in practice solve their personal need for transportation for the family by buying two cars and using them for commuting, for shopping and for most social purposes. The individual choices people make thus contribute to the loss of public transportation, difficulties for those who cannot rely on cars, issues of congestion, pollution and reliance on fuel imports. They are at variance with the values that are assumed to be espoused by society.[7]

The second task for democratic institutions is to focus on any disparity between what people say they believe in and what they actually practise. We often say that a particular objective is good and that we would like to see a certain type of society but then act in quite inconsistent ways. For example, people say that they would like to see more energy produced from renewable sources such as wind power but, when called upon to pay for it through higher electricity prices or called upon to accept unsightly and noisy wind farms in rural areas, may protest vigorously. Or they might say that they like pedestrian-friendly and unpolluted city centres but then protest strongly against congestion charging and high parking costs.[8]

There are a number of reasons why what we say and what we do may differ. It is usually blamed on a 'not in my backyard' syndrome. However,

---

[7] The importance of the interplay between the image we have of our own values and those of society is discussed in Boulding (1956).

[8] A 'Populous' poll for *The Times* (8 Nov. 2006) reported the following discrepancies between what Britons say on green issues and what they actually do. Sixty-five per cent say they buy only energy-saving lightbulbs against less than 20 per cent actually sold; 76 per cent say they recycle everything they can, while only 22.5 per cent of household waste is actually recycled; and 54 per cent say that they make a conscious effort to take fewer flights, while in fact the number of airline passengers in 2005 was 48 million higher than in 2000.

it is not necessarily a question of hypocrisy, or of evasion, or deception either. Divergence may occur because we simply do not see or realise the consequence of a choice or a particular approach to solving a problem. There are many other reasons for disparities. We may not wish to give offence by a statement that could be seen as controversial or politically incorrect; we also may wish to keep our own views on our most important values and principles to ourselves; we may also tend to look for things we want to see and to ignore what we do not want to see.

Rousseau's suggestion was that in such situations democratic governments should impose their majorities in order to assert the assumed values of society and to rely on what people say their stated values are. This decision rule has already been criticised for its crudity. In the world of informed citizens a more subtle interchange seems to be involved where governments need to give greater weight to what people choose for themselves and what they actually do. It means giving much more weight to what economists refer to as 'revealed preferences' rather than stated preferences. Thus the disparities mentioned above between individual valuations of the use of the car and the stated values of society to restrain car use and between the declared values of people in favour of renewable energy and their actual behaviour in opposing wind farms can be seen as reasons for governments to be cautious about what values they apply in the environmental area. The disparities suggest that people may be looking for higher standards of proof about human causation in global warming and a different burden of proof to justify a particular approach such as the construction of nuclear power stations. It is the purpose of the arena function to illuminate this type of interchange about how to weigh and apply values.

A way of encapsulating the type of interchange involved is to look on democratic politics as a mirror. In this metaphor individual valuations are mirrored against the stated values of society and conversely the stated values of society are mirrored against the actual choices made by people in practice. The democratic institutions find their role in illuminating and facilitating the interchange. The advantage of this metaphor is that it sees the role of linking values as a two-way process. Governments need to be respectful of private values before imposing some assumed public value; by the same measure people themselves also need to be better informed of relevant values so that their own decisions are influenced by a wider range of outside values.

The introduction of values in the democratic process cannot therefore be assigned to a constitution, nor left to a simplified decision rule such as what the majority want, nor just reflect what people say they want, nor what politicians simply assume represent the general values of a society. It involves the elected institutions in providing an arena that illuminates and informs a two-way process.

Inquiry

The question remains as to how representative bodies are to provide such an arena and how they can link these interchanges about values with the judgemental processes based on knowledge. Rousseau himself realised that his majority decision rule was a blunt instrument. He tried therefore to resolve the underlying conflicts he perceived arising between individual and collective judgemental processes and between the values we say we espouse and the values we actually embrace in practice by emphasising the importance of education. Rousseau's emphasis on education suggests that we look at the way in which representative institutions perform their task of enlightening public understanding and illuminating public attitudes.

In politics the educative role of democratic institutions was traditionally perceived as falling particularly on the shoulders of representative assemblies. In traditional accounts of representative democracy it was debates in parliament that were held to be particularly useful for informing and educating the electorate on the great issues of the day. However, nowadays parliamentary debates in old-fashioned chambers are stilted, dated and artificial affairs that capture little attention compared with the immediacy and liveliness of information and views picked up from the media or the Internet. The Gothic-revival chambers of Westminster or Budapest and the neo-classical porticos of Paris or Washington DC are portentous but both deadening and distancing. Even in respect of informing electorates where parties stand on particular issues, parliamentary debates are a poor instrument.

In the new separation of powers the key role of representative assemblies is not in mounting old-fashioned debates between old-fashioned parties in old-fashioned chambers. Equally it is not about trying to compete with the world of media celebrities or reality TV or the passing headline or Internet flash. It is about inquiry.

The advantages of inquiry

The key role of the inquiry function is to bring the world of information and expert knowledge together with the world of instinctive opinion, values and principles so that the distinctions can be seen, understood and fed back.[9] Debates perform such functions very poorly. They are

---

[9] This has been referred to as a 'blending' function of legislatures. See Kingdon (1984: 37).

overloaded with value judgements at the expense of those reflecting knowledge; they stand for what politicians want to be identified with rather than for informing the public about the issues and they are fashioned as adversarial contests rather than as explorations that illuminate.

Inquiries provide a much superior format for bringing the world of knowledge together with political judgements because they allow space for views pertinent to both worlds to be expressed and explored. The evidence is not just the facts but also the sentiments and the opinions. Their scope is not just about how unelected bodies are discharging their missions but also about the objectives themselves. In providing a forum for values and objectives to be discussed, they can help illustrate the dissonances between values being introduced and the values actually practised and reflected in society, and the dissonances between individual values and what are assumed to be held as public values.

If these functions are well performed then they are educative as well. They inform the future decisions of citizens as well as the decisions of governments.

Judgemental processes and the new separation of powers

The self-interest of the traditional institutions in the new separation of powers was described earlier in the negative terms of blame avoidance. But their self-interest in the new separation of powers can be viewed in a much more positive light. The separation of functions enables the representative bodies to focus on the judgemental processes of societies that centre on ethical, moral and political values rather than on the task of gathering information and mobilising expert knowledge. They are free to reshape their problem-solving role by focussing on the general framework within which people make their own choices and to reshape as well the way in which they perform the arena function bringing ethical judgements to bear on that framework.

If the benefits of the new separation of powers are accepted, there arises a hugely important question about how the new branch is to be held accountable and from where it derives its legitimacy. Because many of the bodies in the new branch have been separated out from a previous existence within the executive branch of government, there is a temptation to see their legitimacy as deriving from this previous existence and to look to them to remain accountable in some way to the traditional elective branches – governments and their parliaments. This would be a mistake. A different approach to the legitimacy of the new branch is discussed in the next chapter.

8   The legitimacy of the new branch

The new branch of government needs a firm basis on which to rest its legitimacy. Otherwise its role can be constantly challenged. Politicians will be tempted to interfere from the one side, the judiciary from the other. Conversely, it can itself encroach on the legitimate roles of the other branches of government. A means by which the unelected bodies can be held to account also has to be provided. The new institutions can abuse their powers and the trust placed in them. They too can perform badly and require a means through which poor performance can be corrected.

In the classic form of separation of powers each branch of government rested on its own form of legitimacy. By contrast, each of the conventional attempts discussed earlier, that failed to acknowledge the emergence of a new branch, proposed that the new bodies should rely on a legitimacy derived from the other branches. For those who hold that the unelected bodies operate under some kind of democratic overhead, it is the elected bodies that confer legitimacy. For those who see the unelected bodies operating under the authority of a constitution as part of the rule of law, it is the constitution that confers legitimacy. Only in the case of the 'pragmatic' account of unelected bodies is there an attempt to go beyond a derived legitimacy. This account emphasises the acceptability to the public of the practical functions these bodies perform. They possess therefore, in part, their own form of what is known as 'output' legitimacy.[1] However, even in this case, the acceptability of what they do constitutes only one part of a legitimacy derived in further part from both the judiciary and the elected bodies. Moreover, whether the public acceptability of the role they perform is a satisfactory basis on which to rest their own form of legitimacy is highly questionable.

These accounts of where unelected bodies fit within modern democratic frameworks have all been rejected in the earlier discussion in favour of an account that sees them forming a new branch of government in a new

---

[1] Output legitimacy has been referred to as the 'current standard justification' for non-majoritarian institutions. See Thatcher and Stone Sweet (2002: 18–19).

114

separation of powers. If this approach is to be valid it has therefore to offer an account of how the new branch can rest on its own form of legitimacy.

The analogy with the judiciary

Because the new branch of government has been set deliberately apart from the political branch, the clues to the ways in which it can claim to be legitimate can be found by looking at the branch originally set at a distance from democratic politics – the judicial branch. The first clues concern the way in which the judiciary is positioned in relation to public opinion and to the elected branches of government. On the one hand, the judiciary is neither answerable to the public nor controlled by the elected branches. On the other hand, the independence of the judiciary does not mean indifference either to public opinion or to elected bodies. The further clues concern the way in which the judiciary has developed the grounds for its own form of legitimation.

Public acceptance and public answerability

When one looks at the way the judiciary positions itself in relation to the public it is clear that the judicial branch needs a level of public acceptance for what it does. In many ways it was remarkable that the Supreme Court judgement on the Florida recount in 2000 was accepted by public opinion as a whole, even though the United States had been evenly divided in party political terms in the voting booths. Broadly speaking the judiciary does not require public acceptability of individual decisions, but it does require acquiescence to and support for its role in general. This support for its role enables the public to accept even unpopular or politically charged judgements.

The fundamental reason underlying the need for public support for the judiciary's role is that while it can depend, where needed, on the powers of the state for enforcement of its decisions, its standing would be seriously eroded if it had to rely entirely, or even mainly, on the coercive powers of the state. If courts reached that point they would become merely the instruments of government. If the Florida recount judgement had had to be enforced at gunpoint, questions about the legitimacy of President Bush's election and the quality of American democracy would have had a totally different resonance.[2]

---

[2] The exception to the distancing of the judiciary from the opinion of an electorate is seen in the case of state judges in the United States where many states elect judges in the same way as those running for political office. It is not generally regarded as a good practice. It opens

Public support for the role of an independent judiciary is, however, not at all the same as saying that the judiciary should base its legitimacy on being in some way 'answerable' to the public. In the sense that in the final analysis the public can call the shots. At its crudest this would lead to mob justice or verdicts according to public opinion polls. Mob justice is usually not justice at all. The judiciary and legal processes are there in part to prevent it.

The new unelected bodies stand in exactly the same relationship to the public. They too are not indifferent to public attitudes towards them and see the need for public support and understanding. But again there are limits. The world of information and knowledge is not defined by what meets with public approval. It is one thing to accept the sincerity of the views of creationists who take the bible as literal truth in public debate, but it would be disquieting if such views were held or taken into account by an independent agency with scientific responsibilities.

It is the need for some measure of public support that gives a superficial plausibility to the view that the acceptability of the 'output' of the unelected branch provides a form of direct legitimation. But equally it is the fact that their underlying world of information and knowledge relies on different processes for its findings that undermines any attempt to rest the legitimacy of the new bodies on public approval of their 'output'.

In short, both the judiciary and the new branch need to be concerned that the public generally accepts what they do. However, neither the judiciary nor the institutions of the new branch are answerable to the public.

Relations with the traditional branches – deference not control

There is an analogy too between the way the new unelected bodies should be seen in relation to the elected branches of government and the way in which the judiciary is positioned in relation to the elected branches. In the case of the USA, federal judges and justices of the Supreme Court are nominated by the executive (the President) and approved by the Senate. This means that raw politics enters the nomination process. In the case of the US Supreme Court, the recent politics swirls around the approach of nominees to the question of the interpretation of the constitution and whether they are 'strict constructionists' or 'activists'. These labels stand for what are important, but sometimes highly arcane, arguments among legal theorists about, for example, the 'original intent' of the framers of the American constitution. They also stand much more crudely for party

the door to bribery and intimidation and to a widely varying quality of judges. This in turn leads to allegations of 'venue shopping' where the dodgiest lawyers with the dodgiest cases seek out the dodgiest judges.

political affiliations with 'strict constructionists' likely to be seen as belonging to the right of the Republican party and 'activists' to the Democrats.

Despite the fact that raw politics enters into the relationship between the judiciary and the elected branches through the judicial appointments process, the overriding nature of the relationship is characterised by the tradition of 'deference' or 'mutual respect'. What this means is that, however tense the relationship may become between the different branches, for example between a Congress that is controlled by one party and the White House occupied by another, or, for example, between the Supreme Court and the White House over a claim of executive privilege, or between the judiciary and the Executive Branch over the treatment of prisoners taken in the fight against terrorism, each branch shows its respect for the other. This respect is partly for the office but partly for the powers. In other words neither branch wants to go too far in encroaching on the territory of the other. Each branch wants to respect the office and function of the other even if not the persons who occupy the office. The case of Terri Schiavo where Congress passed a resolution signed by the President 'requiring' a federal court to examine whether life support should be reinstated is very much 'the exception which proves the rule'. The practical effect, however, was to leave the procedures and authority of the court system intact while subjecting Congress to charges of playing politics with human life.

The lesson for the new breed of unelected body is the need to distinguish between 'deference' or mutual respect and 'control'. Despite the politics of the appointment process and the aberration of the Schiavo case, the US Supreme Court cannot be regarded as 'controlled' by either of the other branches. But each branch respects and takes care to defer to the powers of the other. Similarly, with the new breed of institution; it is a mistake to look for them to be 'controlled' by either assemblies or governments, but it is to the advantage of each branch to practise a mutual respect towards the other.

If it is a mistake to look for the elective branches of democracies to 'control' the new branch then the question again is how the powers of the new branch are to be justified as legitimate. Once again the analogy with the judicial branch is helpful.

Legitimating an independent judiciary – the development of own standards

Four different theoretical approaches to the legitimacy of the judicial branch can be distinguished. Although they apply to the law as a whole, in practical terms questions about the legitimacy of the law tend to arise especially in cases involving judicial review of the acts of the other branches – the legislature and the executive.

The first of these approaches is to argue that the judiciary is legitimised by a constitution. This approach is associated in Europe with the theories of Hans Kelsen and his search for the 'basic norm' as a means to ground the rule of law without inviting further question. Kelsen's approach, however, is circular and his quest fails. According to Kelsen, the basic norm is to be found in the constitution and this simply transforms the question about the basic norm back into the question of what legitimises the constitution. There are good constitutions and there are bad – those that would be seen to have democratic legitimacy and those that would not. One can sympathise with Kelsen's overall philosophical quest to analyse the logic of legal systems and to distinguish between what is normative and what is not. Unfortunately, this quest led him to view law as a coercive order distinct from morality in terms perilously close to viewing law simply as an instrument of government.[3]

Principles and legitimation

The second approach to the legitimation of the law is to demand that the judiciary observes certain fundamental moral and political principles in its interpretation and application of the law.[4] These are the principles to be found, for example, in declarations of fundamental rights or under-lying them.[5] A judicial branch that based its approach to the law on these principles would be held to be legitimate and, conversely, one that flouted basic principles would be held to have lost its legitimacy.

The difficulties with this approach revolve around the nature of the guiding principles. One source of difficulty is that even the most basic rights can lead to enormous variations in interpretation – the more general the right the more various the interpretations. A second source of difficulty is that rights or basic principles clash. It is most rare for a situation to involve only one applicable right or principle. When more than one is involved the door is open again for many and various weightings

---

[3] According to Kelsen the validity of a constitution derives from the first constitution and 'one presupposes, as jurist, that one ought to conduct oneself as the historically first constitution prescribes'. See Kelsen (1986: 114).

[4] 'I call a "principle" a standard that is to be observed, not because it will advance or secure an economic, political, or social situation deemed desirable, but because it is a require-ment of justice or fairness or some other dimension of morality.' Dworkin (1977: 22).

[5] See also Dworkin (1996).

of the two or more together. This difficulty has been aggravated in recent decades by the explosion in the variety of claims that are said to involve rights. A third source of difficulty, as mentioned earlier, is that the language of rights is increasingly used to argue about the allocation of resources in society – for example over who should have access to a university place or to a job. This leads the judiciary in the direction of distributive justice. This leads to a fourth source of difficulty – the question of whether the relevant principles and rights for grounding the legitimacy of the law should be limited to those of procedural justice or substantive justice or some combination.

What this means is that the desire to rest the legitimacy of the law on generally accepted principles or rights and to hold it accountable to their observance lands the judicial branch not on safe and uncontroversial ground but, instead, in the middle of hotly disputed territory about substantive values. Moreover, the more that courts move into the territory of interpreting the substantive values of society, the more they are likely to encroach on the territory of legislatures and the political process. This in turn points in the direction of a different approach to legitimating the law where the emphasis is on the procedural standards observed by the law.

Procedural legitimation

Over decades the law has developed procedures fitted to the purposes of the law itself. Anglo-Saxon law has famously developed case law as a method of discovery of legal principles while, where law is based on the Napoleonic code, standards of purposive interpretation have been developed as a means to explore the application of principle to particular circumstances.

The aim of these procedures at a theoretical level is to achieve a law that is known to all, equally applicable to all and offering equal protection to all. At a less abstract level the law tries to develop standards of evidence suited to determining whether or not someone was guilty of the act for which they were charged; standards for apportioning blameworthiness (depending, for example, on whether or not there were attenuating circumstances or a diminished level of responsibility) and standards for levying a penalty proportionate to the offence committed and the degree of blameworthiness.

In the view of some, it is the development of these and other standards of procedure on which the legitimacy and accountability of the law resides. Law that is always obscure, or not equally applicable, or a judiciary that consistently allowed unsafe evidence or made no effort to apportion blame or to deliver remedies proportionate to an offence would eventually find itself discredited.

Principles and procedures

A final approach to the legitimation of the law is to try to bring the principles-based approach together with a procedural legitimation. For example, it has been suggested in the case of the United States, in the context of judicial review, that the key principle in the constitution is the democratic principle – revolutionary in its time. The particular suggestion is that in deciding constitutional cases the Supreme Court can look to what would be 'representation reinforcing'.[6] This suggestion aims to avoid landing the Supreme Court with the task of determining the substantive values to be achieved by the political process but aims to go beyond strict legal proceduralism by identifying the overarching political principle in the constitution through which substantive values can be realised. Another approach that also aims to combine both procedural and substantive components is that of judicial 'minimalism'. Under this approach the procedural component is to try to leave fundamental issues undecided; at the same time the law looks for substantive guidance in adjudication from the core values contained in the constitution (such as religious freedom).[7]

Whether these or other approaches that look beyond strictly procedural standards succeed or not is a matter of continuing debate. What results from this analogy with the way in which the law is legitimised and held accountable is not the resolution of disputes that have raged (politely) in legal circles for hundreds of years. Instead it identifies what is not generally disputed. First, the standards of the law and the ways in which it seeks legitimation have been developed by the judicial branch itself. Secondly, any references to outside norms and principles do not rely for their validation on the legislative or executive branches.[8] In cases where possibly relevant outside norms involve political principles (such as the representation principle), they underpin and validate the political branches too. Thirdly, despite common ground, the procedural standards of the law are not synonymous with the standards that apply to the political branches of government. For example, party politics in a democracy

---

[6] Ely (1980).   [7] For this approach see Sunstein (1999).
[8] There is a long-standing debate about the nature of legal discourse between those who argue that legal principles can be deduced from the language of law itself and those who argue in favour of its roots in outside normative principles. For one view of this debate see Coleman (2001).

involves claim and counter-claim but the claims do not have to pass the kinds of testing and cross-examination familiar to the law. Moreover, the law has developed these standards partly to ward against the dangers flowing from the fact that government is the source of much law and often an interested party in its adjudication. To apply standards that would imply subservience to the political branches would bring the law into disrepute and a judiciary that applied such standards would quickly find itself in trouble. Conversely, political branches that followed standards of the law would also find themselves in difficulty. There are indeed political institutions that have their origin as courts of law – the British House of Commons most notably. In addition, until recently the highest court in the UK was part of the Second Chamber. But these are anachronisms or examples of historical interest only.

The analogy with the law should not be overdrawn. There are a number of ways in which the principles and procedures described below that help legitimate the new breed of unelected body differ from those that apply to the law. However, the fundamental lesson is valid. In a manner analogous to the law, the new branch of government can seek to achieve legitimacy through the development of its own standards appropriate to its own particular role. It too may need to draw on outside principles and procedures but political standards would bring it into disrepute.

The principles and procedures of the new branch

The new branch of government is dealing with the world of scientific and social information and the mobilisation of policy-relevant empirical knowledge drawn from the natural and social sciences. The right place to look for standards that could legitimate its activities is therefore in this world. In order to explore the character of these standards it seems appropriate, as in the case of the law, to distinguish between relevant principles, relevant procedures and approaches that combine both principles and procedures.

Principles and legitimation

There are three basic principles that apply to the world of the natural and social sciences that apply also, with some modification, to the world of the new breed of unelected body:

The first principle is their need to be aware of distinctions between normative analysis and positive analysis (between what should be and what is). Historically, the distinction resonates in the physical and biological sciences where, for so long, observations were clouded or disputed by religious views of what the world and the human species should look like rather than what they did look like. Nowadays, the difficulties in the way of making a clear distinction between normative observations and factual are often emphasised. The social context of research, the impossibility of the unbiased observer, the barriers and value-laden nature of the language in which we conceptualise and communicate are all well-known obstacles. Despite these difficulties, the philosophical distinction that ethical judgements are different from other sorts of judgement remains important.[9] Also, despite the difficulties, our knowledge of the world is not immune to empirical check. Moreover, the effectiveness of knowledge is not mere accident.[10] Both scientific and social reasoning can be said to be constrained by facts.[11] In addition, being aware of making value judgements and trying to make them explicit and transparent remains crucial to the integrity of the methods both of the natural and of the social sciences.[12]

Being 'constrained by facts' and attempting to be transparent about value judgements applies equally well to the world of the unelected bodies. For example, the central banker analysing the behaviour of monetary aggregates or the economic regulator trying to quantify the costs of a proposed regulation are constrained by facts. At the same time, they also have to be clear that they are making normative assumptions about the social virtues of low inflation in the case of the central banker and the social value of competitive markets in the case of the economic regulator. In some cases, as already discussed, the normative may be much more pronounced. A boundary watcher looking at an area such as privacy, for example, is dealing with normative statutory responsibilities in deciding what should be permitted or not. But the constraints and the normative distinctions are still important.

The distinction between the normative and the empirical does not imply that scientists lack humanity or that the officials in unelected bodies are bloodless bureaucrats. Scientists can be impassioned and highly motivated by ethical concerns and so too can the unelected. The passion and the commitment should not, however, interfere with the method of inquiry.

The second principle concerns respect for the evidence. The empirical tradition of the physical and social sciences that, despite recent challenges,

---

[9] See Putnam (2002).   [10] For a discussion of the realist view see Sayer (1984).
[11] For example, Blaug (1980: 510) argues that although economics lacks universal laws of the sort claimed by science nevertheless economic theories still rise or fall depending on how well they link to observable facts or predict relationships not borne out by evidence. For a more assertive attack on epistemological 'relativism' see Riker (1990).
[12] See Hesse (1978: 1–16).

remains the main tradition places enormous importance on data, on the quality of observations and the structuring of experiments so that observations can be measured and tested. Data, the use of data, reporting on the source of data and how it was created are all fundamental aspects of scientific methods.[13] 'Reproducibility' – the possibility for the same conclusions to be reached by a different researcher armed with the same data and assumptions – is a fundamental test of the robustness over time of method, observations and inferences.

Similarly, the unelected bodies have to show a similar respect for evidence. As described earlier, much of their time is spent on data gathering and data analysis and testing the completeness or reliability of data provided by the private sector. 'Reproducibility' is also a test of the robustness of the models they employ. The transparency of critical assumptions is therefore equally important.

The third principle is respect for the uncertainties and what is not known.[14] When asked about their particular field, physical and social scientists will try to give an authoritative judgement based on the current state of knowledge and in the light of the best available evidence. At the same time, they are fully aware that the knowledge is rarely if ever certain, and it is the uncertainties and degrees of confidence that also have to be pointed out in their judgements.[15]

Similarly, the institutions in the new branch have to respect the uncertainties in the world they deal with. There are gaps in data, inadequacies in trying to model the world they deal with and the application of their knowledge often has uncertain effects. Dealing with, allowing for and looking out for 'unintended consequences' is a constant in the life of any body performing regulatory functions. The standard to which unelected bodies operate is not certainty but 'best practice'.

Procedures and legitimation

In addition to the principles described above, there are two key procedures drawn from the world of scientific and social investigation that apply, with some modification, also to bodies in the new branch.

A first procedural standard analagous to those in academic life concerns the importance of an experimental approach. In the world of the

---

[13] See King, Keohane and Verba (1994).
[14] 'No scientific hypothesis is ever proved completely and definitively.' Hempel (1965: 84).
[15] 'Without a reasonable estimate of uncertainty, a description of the real world or an inference about a causal effect in the real world is uninterpretable.' King, Keohane and Verba (1994: 9).

physical sciences this is associated with the laboratory and in the world of the social sciences with developing highly abstract models of individual or group behaviour. Even those who might dispute whether the scientific approach can ever get to the 'truth' nevertheless accept the importance of a methodological approach.[16]

For unelected bodies the difficulty lies in respecting the experimental method at the same time as they are dealing with the real world and when their actions have real-world consequences. While risk aversiveness is a negative characteristic in social science, risk aversiveness may be a very desirable component of a regulator's approach to the real world. For example, as already mentioned, economic regulators do not want to be constantly changing the regulatory framework because stability helps businesses make their decisions. Similarly, independent central banks do not like to surprise financial markets. An important part of the 'professionalism' of regulators is about reducing regulatory uncertainties. At the same time, experimental techniques or techniques that try to reduce the risk of getting it wrong are crucial. For example, independent central banks may change a policy orientation in a series of small steps rather than take a risk of making a large mistake. Similarly, if boundary watchers wish to make a large change in the rules they may wish to pave the way gradually.

The main experimental technique for many of the unelected bodies is to use the techniques of Impact Assessment. Impact Assessments are a tool derived from investment appraisal techniques for exploring alternative approaches to a particular real-world problem and bringing evidence together in a coherent framework.[17] The experimental approach can be supplemented by pilot schemes or test runs before proposals are hardened into regulations or legislation.

The models used in Impact Assessments are highly simplified and imperfect in many ways. The justification for their use, analogous to the claims of applied science, lies in some measure of empirical success, such as their use in harnessing observations or in contributing to practical problem-solving.[18]

A second procedural standard, again drawn from academic precedents, is the importance of exposing data, method of analysis, and inferences drawn from the data and analysis to public inspection. In the natural and social sciences this means being willing to expose methods to peer review.

[16] See Introduction to Gadamer (1994).
[17] For a brief review of these techniques and their role in 'regulating the regulator', see Froud and Boden (1998).
[18] For a typology of empirical success see Solomon (2001: 15–31).

Less rigorous consultation mechanisms have long been used in government in part as a defence against getting it wrong and consultation remains a crucial device for the unelected bodies. But peer review involves a higher standard. It involves review by those professionally qualified to judge proposals and the analysis underpinning draft proposals and not review by those who simply have a view on the subject or are affected by a potential measure. Moreover, those carrying out the peer review are intended to be independent of those whose work is under scrutiny. In the case of the law, standards have developed as to who has 'standing' in a case. Peer review is a different technique for establishing the standing of those able to judge the quality of evidence and techniques of analysis.

Peer review has its critics because, despite its widespread use in the academic world, its own effectiveness and reliability as a technique for determining quality has not been subject to much systematic testing itself. Nevertheless, independent review of the work of the unelected bodies potentially provides an important defence against several different kinds of bias that may afflict them.

First, there is a need for a defence against any professional bias in the agency concerned – for example in the techniques of analysis employed, in the selection of data or in the interpretation of evidence. Sometimes an internal house style, culture, or way of thinking evolves that needs an outside check. Secondly, there is a need for a defence against biases that arise from institutional incentives. Institutions have their own interests at stake and this may colour or distort their better judgements. Confirmation bias, where a regulator or other institution looks for evidence, consciously or unconsciously, that confirms their presuppositions or preferred conclusions is a serious problem. Thirdly, there is a need for a defence against the kind of distortions that can arise from 'game playing' or role playing between an institution and its clients. 'Gaming' arises because the interests affected by an institution may anticipate its actions and adopt positions or present evidence in the light of those anticipations. Similarly, the institution will anticipate a reaction from the interests it reaches and that too may colour its behaviour. Game playing needs to be recognised and this is something that an independent observer may recognise more readily than someone involved in the game itself. There are analogous behaviour and analogous situations in academic life – for example in the application for research grants – that independent peer review is intended to address.

In addition, peer review can provide a defence against formalism or proceduralism. Institutions will feel that they have to do more than simply go through the motions if the substance of their proposals, their actions and their behaviour is going to be submitted to external independent review.

There are difficulties in organising peer review. One difficulty is in finding reviewers who are truly independent and who do not introduce their own biases. This is a problem too in academic life where those working in the same field may recognise the origin of an article or research proposal or research findings that they are meant to evaluate from an independent perspective, or may have their own preconceived orientation towards the field of inquiry. Both may intrude on the evaluation.

Combining procedures and principles

In the case of the law, attempts to combine procedures and principles involve an attempt to reconcile principles of substantive justice, setting out the end results of what the law is to achieve, with procedural norms that set out the way in which the law is to be conducted without specifying any ends. The effort involves proposing a norm of behaviour or interpretation that is both procedural and substantive. In the case of the new unelected institutions, the analogous approach involves recourse to such concepts as 'the public interest' or the 'general economic interest'. These standards are intended to suggest that there is an objective and substantive 'public or general interest' that can be identified in any situation, while the procedures of the unelected bodies should be geared to establishing that general interest. Whether there is in practice a general interest that can be distinguished from many particular interests is a matter of dispute.

The distinctiveness of the new branch's own standards

Rigour

The principles and procedures integral to the workings of the unelected bodies described above set the new branch at a considerable distance from the workings of the traditional elected branches. It is a distance characterised above all by the more rigorous and methodical approach to facts, sources, analysis and uncertainties adopted by the new branch compared with politics. The core features that the new branch shares with the world of scientific and social knowledge – the importance of data quality, of explicit references connecting data to theory and of public testability of any emerging propositions – all distance it from politics by trying to seek and account for facts and evidence more systematically and according to more rigorous principles and procedures. This more rigorous approach to the world of information and knowledge not only sets the new bodies at a distance from the elected bodies but also underpins their own claim for an independent status in a system of government. If the bodies in the new branch were consistently trying to break away from being 'constrained by the facts', disregarded the procedures needed to gather reliable evidence, or introduced their own unacknowledged value judgements into their operations, they would quickly find themselves discredited and their authority undermined.

A disputed standard?

One important possible objection to looking at the world of scientific principles and procedures for the standards that legitimate the new branch of government is that there is today no single account of the principles of scientific investigation that commands general assent. The days when scientific knowledge was viewed as a process where unbiased observers accumulated objective facts about the external world until better explanations or better theories emerged are long gone.[19] Other long-standing controversies within the world of social and scientific investigation also seem to be invoked. For example, bracketing the social sciences together with the natural sciences appears to be taking sides in a long running dispute about how far they both use the same methods and justification for their claims and whether the behaviour of human beings can be explained in similar ways to natural behaviour.[20] The approach appears also to take sides in debates about differences between the standards relevant to pure research and applied research.[21]

None of these reservations is compelling. The question of what legitimates the law also takes place against the background of contested claims about the logic of the law and the nature of legal reasoning. It should not be a surprise if a discussion of the legitimation of the new branch also takes place against the background of contested claims about the logic of scientific and social reasoning. No side needs to be taken on any of the disputes; contestation should be accepted and even welcomed as part of a competition between ideas.[22] For the new branch the claim about the relationship to the methods of the natural and social sciences is about relevance – what types of principles, procedures and combinations are relevant to it. It does not require that these principles and procedures should not be debated or debatable. It certainly does not involve one

---

[19] The key text is Kuhn (1962).
[20] For a discussion see Ryan (1970) and for a brief overview, Ryan (1973: 1–14).
[21] For one account of the differences between pure scientific research and applied research see Argyris, Putnam and McClain Smith (1985).
[22] For a defence of the scientific value of advocacy see Green and Shapiro (1994: 188).

having to take sides on fundamental philosophical disputes about the empirical tradition and its shortcomings.

Validation

The standards relevant to the unelected institutions are not the same as standards that apply to the elected branches, nor do they depend for their relevance on validation by democratically elected bodies. Principles may sometimes overlap. For example, it is important to embody a discovery process in democratic structures as well as in science. But at bottom the methods of science are simply different from those of politics and come from different roots.

The standards most relevant to their world are there to be further developed by the unelected institutions themselves and this development equally does not depend on validation by other branches. In the same way that the law has developed its own standards so too can the new branch develop its. As in the case of the different approaches to the legitimation of the law, there will also be continuing dispute and debate about which particular principles and procedures, or which combination of principle and procedure, are most relevant to the new branch. Nevertheless, unelected bodies that tried to ignore the principles and procedures set out above would find their credibility and authority in tatters. It is by following them that they have their own source of legitimacy.

Outside the context of national systems of democratic government the same need arises for people being able to distinguish between bodies charged with the mobilisation of evidence and knowledge and for the supply of information untainted by politics, and those bodies that make political judgements on that knowledge. But how to organise that distinction so that unelected bodies operating in the supra-national arena can also achieve legitimacy raises different questions. The next two chapters therefore broaden the discussion in order to look at how the arrival of this new branch of government plays out in trans-national contexts – within the European Union and in international regimes more generally. Both the European Union and international regimes lag in their recognition of the significance of the new separation of powers. As a result, their legitimacy is greatly weakened.

9 The new separation of powers and the European Union

The European Union is a paradoxical organisation. Its most important contribution to the post-war world and to the world following the collapse of communism has been the part it has played in anchoring newly democratised countries in Europe to a democratic way of life. Yet at the very same time its own internal organisation lacks a base of democratic principle. The explanation behind this paradox is historical. A desire to make a decisive break from their recent undemocratic past and to seek legitimacy from democratic neighbours propels newly democratised countries to become members in a political union alongside the other democracies. At the same time the historical roots of the European Union itself are anchored in a technocratic vision and not a democratic one.

Notwithstanding multiple treaty revisions and a first attempt to consolidate them in the form of a 'Treaty Establishing a Constitution', the European Union still stands, not for the latest principles of democratic government, but for confusion among different principles of democratic organisation. It has established neither the traditional form of parliamentary democracy practised in the member states, nor the old democratic separation of powers between executive, legislature and judiciary. Nor has it established the new separation of powers.[1]

At the centre of this unhappy story about unprincipled structures lies an unelected body – the Commission. The position it has occupied from the origins of the European Union has resulted in a unique form of power sharing at the highest institutional levels. Beneath the surface, elements of the new separation of powers struggle to emerge.

This chapter looks at the historical dynamic behind power sharing in the EU and at the way in which the EU has taken the first steps to

---

[1] Majone (2005) warns against making an unwarranted assumption that because its members are democracies the EU necessarily has to be democratically organised itself. However, since EU institutions have decision-making powers that can bind its members, it is a reasonable starting point as a normative proposition that its organisation should be consistent with democratic principles.

acknowledge the new separation of powers. It examines to what extent the blending of the new separation of powers together with the old form of power sharing leads to a viable approach to democratic organisation.

The path to power sharing

The explanation of why the European Union has ended up with institutional arrangements at variance with any principles of democratic organisation comes in two parts. The first part focusses on why the original framework was created in the particular form it took. It revolves around the need for what is known as 'credible commitment'. The second part is about what is known as 'path dependency'.[2] What this refers to is that considerable costs were incurred in setting up the EU and for new members to join it and there have been equally large costs to consider in making any new arrangements. As a result it has seemed less costly for the members to try to work around established institutional interests. It is this that has produced the kind of power sharing that can be seen today and remains undisturbed in the proposed Treaty Establishing a Constitution.

Credible commitment

The historical problem confronting the founders of the European Union was that in the post-war world the individual nation-states in Europe seemed to have inherent limitations as problem-solving units. In particular, unilateral actions by individual nation-states seemed to invite a return to the self-destructive national rivalries of the pre-war years. The key task therefore was to replace the cycle of destructive behaviour by a binding commitment to co-operative behaviour.

The idea of credible commitment arises at the intersection of principle–agent theory with game theory. It addresses two aspects of the underlying institutional logic of the EU. First, it refers to the strategies a principal can use to bind an agent to behave in the way the principal intends. In the context of the EU, the principals are the member states and the behaviour they were concerned about was their own. Secondly, it describes a setting where players involved in strategic interactions need reassurance about the resolve of the other player to continue to act in a manner consistent with their original commitment in situations of future uncertainty. From this perspective, the members of the EU each looked for reassurance that other members would continue to act in a manner consistent with their

---

[2] For path dependency see North (1990).

original commitments even if the future were to throw up unexpected surprises and developments.[3] Thus the beginning of the story is about how the members of the EU made institutional arrangements that would make their own commitments seem both credible to other members and lasting.

Two instruments were chosen in order to achieve this breakthrough. The first was the use of treaties as the way to nail down the commitment of participants to co-operation; the second was the creation of a unique body, the Commission, as a way to change the source of political initiative within the EU. Instead of governments pursuing their own national self-interest, they committed themselves to entrust the general European interest to an independent unelected body.

Treaties as commitments

There were two tactical reasons why the founding documents of what is now called the European Union took the form of treaties. The first was that the ultimate political objectives behind the formation of the then European Coal and Steel Community and the Common Market were to be approached indirectly. The idea of an overt political union of states was judged to be premature – premature both for political elites and for public opinion. Instead, the procedure envisaged was to establish a dynamic where one goal would link forward to another more distant goal. It was envisaged that starting from limited economic goals, more expansive goals would emerge and eventually lead to political union. The second tactical reason was that treaties were the normal form of international arrangements between states. Founding the club on the basis of a treaty preserved the view that the states were ultimately in charge, even in cases where they were agreeing to pool their powers and forgoing the possibility of acting unilaterally.

The more important strategic reason for the treaty format was, however, to obtain 'credible commitment'. Each potential member was choosing to pool or delegate powers but needed a mechanism to convince others that they would not backtrack from their commitments if, for example, the party of government changed.[4] Thus, any state seeking to become a member had to enter into a long and formal negotiation. In becoming a member it also had to change some of its own internal policies and commit to change others in future. It also had to make a very visible

---

[3] For the underlying assumptions about the rationality of the actors see Morrow (1994: 7–8). See also the discussion on 'commitment' in Skyrmes (1996: 2–44).
[4] See Majone (2001).

and public commitment to the terms of the treaty, as well as what it had agreed to change internally, according to its own constitutional require- ments. This process resulted in the kind of commitment any new member state would subsequently find very difficult to ignore or to walk away from, even if its domestic politics changed quite radically.[5]

In addition, member states were also acutely aware of the problem that there was, and that there remains to this day, a lack of complete trust between the states in Europe. As a result they took other steps to make their commitment to co-operative behaviour be seen as credible. They established the Court of Justice as an independent body for adjudicating disputes. Much more dramatically, they created a new style of indepen- dent, unelected body – the Commission.

The Commission

The Commission was and remains a unique body. It was not elected and was set deliberately apart from the democratic politics of the member states. The individual commissioners in the College of Commissioners were to be appointed by member states, yet were to be independent and not to take instructions from the governments that appointed them.

This body was deliberately given a mix of powers. In general the mix of powers can be seen as expressing a 'fiduciary relationship' between the principals (the member states) and the agent (the Commission) because they involve above all a duty to act.[6] The key to its power as a political body was the exclusive right to initiate – in other words the right to set, or at least exert a major influence over, the policy and legislative agenda. Furthermore, it was to have a judicial role – the task of ensuring that the terms of the treaty were observed, to investigate non-compliance and to bring infringement proceedings against member states that did not observe the treaty. Its executive powers were more circumscribed. Member states were responsible for implementing what was agreed. But the Commission could regulate directly in some areas and shared a general responsibility for ensuring that member states were implementing in practice what they had agreed to do.

To this day it retains this combination of legislative, executive and judicial functions. To this day it also remains an appointed body rather

---

[5] For a more general treatment of the role of 'credible commitment' in the institutional design of the EU see Pollack (2003: 29–33).

[6] The classic description of a fiduciary relationship lists four key attributes: affirmative duties to disclose; open-ended duties to act; tightly limited bounds in respect of positional advantages and a moral rhetoric. See Clark (1985).

than an elected one. The member states appoint its head, as well as the members of the College of Commissioners, subject to approval by the European Parliament of the choice of the head of the Commission and its composition as a whole.

This arrangement of treaty-based commitments by member states together with a powerful unelected body combining political, executive and judicial functions continues to shape the political landscape of the EU. The original treaty has undergone many revisions, but even the current proposal to turn the treaties into a form of constitution leaves these arrangements substantially intact.

Legacy costs

On the whole, this approach has been a success measured against what the founders set out to achieve. Even the indirect approach to political union has worked until recently. Above all, the commitment of member states to the terms of the treaties has also been credible. Two member states have practised 'empty chair' policies at different times and the Commission continues to take infringement actions against member states when they do not, in its view, observe the terms of the treaties. Nevertheless, at the end of the day, the EU continues to grow in membership, the number of policy objectives pursued collectively also expands, and no major state has yet left the European Union.

At the same time there have been costs to these arrangements – costs that have become more apparent the more time that elapses. To some extent these were foreseen. The decision to approach political union indirectly, as the culmination of a process of economic integration, meant that serious thought about the principles of democratic organisation was deliberately postponed for the future. Moreover, the founders of the treaty were not primarily worried about such democratic concerns as the possibility that the central institutions would abuse their powers. On the contrary, the danger to European construction was seen to be over-mighty member states rather than over-mighty European institutions. What perhaps the founders did not envisage was that the procedures and institutions they had established, in their turn, set up institutional interests that subsequently could not easily be shifted. A form of path dependency was created that continues to frame the way the European Union is evolving.

Path dependency can be defined as a situation where institutional vested interests shape the response to external forces of change in ways that profoundly hamper the ability of a society to adapt. In the case of the EU there have been three key components making change difficult. The first was the size of the set-up costs – those involved in establishing the EU and the costs incurred in adapting for membership. The second has been the ideology surrounding the institutions. Criticism is often denounced as 'anti-European'. The third has been the costs of getting change. Getting everyone to agree on the same change is difficult; getting agreement on flexible arrangements has proved equally difficult.[7]

The particular form that path dependency has taken in the EU has involved a dynamic favouring power sharing. What has happened to the subsequent organisation of powers within what is now the European Union is a process where the powers of the other institutions have been shaped around those of the Commission. Rather than confront the range of its powers directly, the challenge to its role has been indirect. Thus the Commission's right to set the agenda for the EU has been challenged by the creation of the European Council, comprising the heads of government or of state, that has asserted its own right to set the overall political priorities for the EU. In addition, the Council of Ministers from individual member states does much of the work of negotiating laws and regulations and is therefore intimately involved with the Commission in preparing legislation. Equally important, a directly elected Parliament has replaced the original indirectly elected parliamentary body. Its essential role is to revise and amend law-making proposals coming from the Commission and Council and it too tries to assert an agenda-setting role, in part through its power to approve the Commission as a whole or to dismiss it.

The relationship that has been set in train between the institutions is competitive but, above all, collusive. The Parliament competes with the Council to control the Commission but it also sees the Commission as an ally against the Council. The Commission sees the Council as a threat to its agenda-setting role but it also needs the support of the Council in order to make its own voice count. It aims to preserve its role not only by the constant search for allies in the Council but also by finding a pivotal role between the Council and Parliament. Ostensibly above the political fray stands the European Court of Justice asserting the traditional prerogatives of a constitutional court to interpret the treaties and to review the legality of acts of the EU institutions including those of the Commission. But it too has a subtly political role – discreetly watching the temper of the member states as to where the boundaries of union law can be pushed out and with its own self-interest in extending the EU's sphere of competence against competing jurisdictions – the jurisdictions of the member states

---

[7] These key conditions for path dependency are described in North (1990: 95).

themselves. In this vital respect the interests of the Court and of the Commission are aligned.[8]

The end result of this historical legacy of a body, central to the union, but without democratic roots and combining all the traditional functions of the different branches of government, overlaid by a mix of rival claimants to parts of its core functions, is one of inter-institutional bargaining rather than institutional separation. The 'Inter-Institutional Agreement' – an agreement between Council, Commission and Parliament – has become an established formula. Not for nothing have the institutions of the European Union come to be seen in the popular press and in the popular mind as 'Brussels' – in other words, indistinguishable.

What these arrangements mean is that the European Union has never addressed fundamental principles of democratic organisation. The powers of the Commission not only contravened any democratic organisation based on the separation of powers, but they also stood in the way of alternative organising principles for democracy.

The shift towards the new separation of powers

At the same time as the institutions of the European Union have been sharing power between themselves in successive revisions to the treaties, the EU has not been immune to the new developments in the organisation of government happening elsewhere. In order to distinguish these developments from the higher-level jostling for power, they have been introduced under the label of 'governance'. Their adoption has started to lead the EU towards the new separation of powers.

Agencies

The first development consistent with the new separation of powers has taken place through the expansion of the number of independent unelected bodies, mainly but not exclusively, in the form of agencies (see table 6).[9] First and foremost among these bodies is the European Central Bank established by the Maastricht Treaty in emulation of the success of Germany's independent central bank. In total, there are now over thirty independent agencies and other bodies covering fields as diverse as the registration of medicines, food safety and the monitoring

---

[8] 'The European Court of Justice ... acts in concert with other institutions to influence policy outcomes.' Conant (2002: 214).
[9] Bodies governed by European public law, distinct from Council, Parliament and Commission and with their own legal personality.

Table 6: *Independent public bodies in the EU*

Service providers
Agency for Management of Operational Cooperation at External Borders (FRONTEX)
European Agency for Reconstruction (EAR)
European Central Bank (ECB)
European Centre for the Development of Vocational Training (CEDEFOP)
European Foundation for the Improvement of Living and Working Conditions
  (Eurofound)
European Investment Bank (EIB)
European Police Office (EUROPOL)
European Research Council (ERC)
European Union: Institute for Security Studies (EUISS)
European Union Satellite Centre (EUSC)
European Union's Judicial Cooperation Unit (Eurojust)
The Office of Harmonization for the Internal Market (OHIM)

Risk assessors
Community Plant Variety Office (CPVO)
European Aviation Safety Agency (EASA)
European Centre for Disease Prevention and Control (ECDC)
European Chemicals Agency (ECHA)
European Food Safety Authority (EFSA)
European Maritime Safety Agency (EMSA)
European Medicines Evaluation Agency (EMEA)
European Monitoring Centre for Drugs and Drug Addiction (EMCDDA)
European Railway Agency
The European Agency for Safety and Health at Work (EU-OSHA)
The European Environment Agency (EEA)

Boundary watchers
European Fundamental Rights Agency (EFRA)
European Monitoring Centre on Racism and Xenophobia (EUMC)
European Network Information Security Agency (ENISA)

Inquisitors and inspectors
European Court of Auditors

Umpires and whistle-blowers
Court of First Instance
European Data Protection Supervisor (EDPS)
European Ombudsman
Fisheries Control Agency (CFCA)

---

of racial discrimination, including those in the process of being created. For the purposes of this discussion the Court of Auditors is also included among them. As a result there are now agencies and other bodies in all the fields originally identified in the survey mapping the world of unelected bodies. Important omissions from the list are in the field of competition and economic regulation where tasks given to sector regulators or to specialised competition bodies in member states are internalised within the Commission.

The terms of reference of the new agencies have been circumscribed much more rigorously than in the case of independent agencies within the member states. Care has been taken to ensure that they deal mainly with the information base for public policy and not policy itself.[10] This is because neither the Commission nor the Council of Ministers have wished to see their own role in making judgements on policy eroded. The terms of reference of the new bodies stress this non-policy role.

Networking

The second development consistent with the new separation of powers has been the increasing use of networks bringing together national unelected bodies, notably regulatory and competition bodies. The creation of such networks has been partly associated with the establishment of EU agencies that have been required to operate in close association with their national counterparts. But they have also sprung up in the absence of such agencies.

One reason for this development has been to try to offset some of the disadvantages associated with the lengthy and problematic legislative procedures followed by the EU.[11] The second reason for this development has been simply that the information necessary for the EU to carry out its functions does not exist within the Commission or within the machinery of the Council – neither within the Council Secretariat nor within the Permanent Representatives. Information has been deficient in at least two important respects – lack of knowledge about the particular conditions in salient parts of the member states and lack more generally of market knowledge. Networks bring together decentralised sources of information and greater market knowledge. A third reason is that networks can easily cross lines of competence (who is responsible for what) between the EU and the member states and thus reduce friction about the responsibilities of the EU compared with the member states.

The networks now in place include most sectors of economic regulation. They cover financial services, including securities markets, banking and insurance, telecommunications and energy. In addition, cross-sectoral networks have emerged covering topics such as regulatory techniques, competition policy and superior court systems.

---

[10] Majone (1997) notes that they have been 'denied powers that regulatory bodies normally possess'.
[11] For this line of reasoning see Dehousse (1997).

Evidence-based procedures

The third development consistent with the new separation of powers has been the adoption of evidence-based procedures in preparing legislation. Notably there has been an Inter-Institutional Agreement on the introduction and application of Regulatory Impact Analysis to try to ensure that legislation and regulation is based on the best knowledge available about the probable results. This would, in other circumstances, constitute an important step towards distinguishing the information and empirical knowledge relevant to a particular measure from political judgements based on that evidence. In the context of the EU, its effect is somewhat vitiated by the fact that the Commission that is responsible for carrying out impact assessments also wants to make sure that they do not damage or limit its political right of initiative.[12]

The end result of grafting elements of the new separation of powers on to a superstructure where powers are shared is a very uneasy mixture. The independent agencies tend to be out of sight and out of mind. In addition, the networks are accused of usurping legislative functions or of deliberately blurring who is responsible for what. The Commission's impact assessments include political soundings and are more than usually vulnerable to charges that they rationalise what the Commission would like to bring forward as a political objective anyway.

It has become commonplace to justify the overall architecture of the EU as '*sui generis*' – a Latin tag that aims to deflect further thought. The EU has also been called 'a large-scale institutional experiment'.[13] The key question is whether the combination of the new separation of powers and the kind of historic power sharing practised in the EU is internally consistent and compatible with any principles of democratic organisation.

Combining different principles of democratic organisation

In a situation such as in the United States, where the founding democratic principles were based on a separation of powers, the emergence of a new branch for mobilising information and evidence and applying knowledge-

---

[12] The Commission's latest Impact Assessment (IA) Guidelines state, 'The College of Commissioners will take the IA findings into consideration in its deliberations. The IA will not, however, dictate the contents of its final decision. The adoption of a policy proposal is a political decision that belongs solely to the College, not to officials or technical experts.' Source: Impact Assessment Guidelines (SEC (2005) 791), dated 15 June 2005.
[13] Olsen (2001).

based judgements, untainted by the passions of elective politics, simply represents an extension of the old founding principles. Each of the original branches, including the judicial, legislative and particularly the executive branch, cede some of their traditional territory to the new branch, but, as discussed earlier, it is in their own self-interest to do so. The development of the new separation of powers is compatible with the old and, after each branch has adapted to the arrival of the new, may even add to the original system of checks and balances.

European states have followed a different organising principle for their democracies, built around a parliamentary system of government rather than a separation of powers. Although there are differences between different countries, the essential feature of a parliamentary democracy is that electors vote for a party, or parties, to form a government and the composition of a parliament reflects this choice. The result is a fusion of powers between governments and parliaments. In extreme cases, where a government has a large majority of party supporters in parliament, the parliament becomes a 'rubber stamp' and the government what has been called (with exaggeration) 'an elected dictatorship'.

In the case of parliamentary democracies of the kind seen in European countries, it is the government and the executive branch, more than parliaments, that cede territory to the new unelected bodies. Functions that were formerly internalised within the central machinery of government are disestablished and put on a new foundation. However, this development does not in itself disturb the essential electoral connection between government and parliament giving rise to the fusion of their powers. It places both at a distance from the new branch but leaves their own electoral interrelationship intact. Thus, in both the model of democratic organisation based on a parliamentary system of government, as well as the model based on a separation of powers, the emergence of a new branch of government is compatible with the existing organising principles.

The situation in the European Union raises quite different questions. Not only has there never been a traditional separation of powers, but the nature of power sharing between the institutions is also quite different from the fusion of powers in the member states.

The nature of power sharing in the EU

Three factors maintain the original dynamic towards power sharing in the European Union between the main institutions:

The first is institutional weakness. For example, as mentioned above, the Council and Commission jostle over which body is setting the agenda for the policy priorities of the EU and driving it forward. From a theoretical perspective the tussle can be presented as an unresolved issue about which body forms the government of Europe. But from a practical perspective the power sharing between the two bodies is about weakness. The Commission's strength lies in its claim to be able to get things done. It is the Commission's ability to use its right of initiative to forge compromises in the Council, to set objectives and deadlines, and its ability to trigger legal sanctions against treaty infringements that it claims drive the EU. Its weakness is a lack of a democratic base. The Council has a democratic base, but it is a weak body for arriving at collective decisions and weak in the practical follow through to resounding political declarations. Neither body will yield to the other on their strengths; the Council will not concede on democratic legitimacy nor the Commission on effectiveness. But both bodies see a need for the other and a need to work together as a means to compensate for their own areas of weakness.

The Parliament's propensity for power sharing is also an admission of weakness. Its strength lies in the fact that it is the only directly elected body among the EU institutions. However, it has two major weaknesses. Its membership (currently 732 members) is unwieldy and professionally ill equipped to deal with the highly technical issues that it can amend or block. It also has only a weak claim to be representative of any public opinion. There are many reasons for this but chief among them is the fact that politics in Europe remains national politics and even trans-European issues are refracted through national lenses. The first weakness leads the Parliament to look to the Commission for a coherent lead and for technical support. The second weakness leads it to look to deal-making with the Council that can claim to be more representative of public opinion in member states.

The second driving force behind power sharing stems from the nature of what the EU does. Most of what the EU does is about rule-making and regulation in a broad sense. This covers not only the regulatory framework for the internal market area, but also the negotiation of external trade rules and market access as well as safeguarding the monetary rules for the Euro zone. This focus is highly technical. In the original conception the EU was not to get involved in the detail but to focus on framework laws that member states themselves would implement in detail. In practice the framework approach has not worked because member states have wanted detail important to their own situation to be included in any framework. The latest constitutional treaty tries to rationalise the modes of law-making but does not address this basic propensity in favour of rule-making in detail.

The result of the focus on regulation and rule-making again pushes each of the institutions towards the others. Neither the Parliament nor the Commission can ignore the regulatory traditions and experience in the member states reflected in the Council. At the same time the Council lacks trust and confidence in either the Commission or Parliament to get rule-making right on their own. The result is that each delves deeply into the core competences of the others.

The third driving force behind power sharing is about complexity. It is inevitable in a union of twenty-seven states, with additional members yet to come, that broadbrush rule-making will not fit the particular circumstances of each member state or the salient groups within those member states impacted by the proposed rule or regulation. Moreover this problem is compounded by the fact that much of the necessary information in the EU involves not only decentralised sources of knowledge but also information available only in the private sector. The Commission has a comparative advantage in forming an overview of conditions across the EU but it is the member states in the Council that have the knowledge of particular circumstances in their state. None of the institutions can claim much in the way of private sector expertise. These defects also lead in the direction of pooling their resources.

In an ideal world, institutional roles suited to the particular functions of the European Union and with a bedrock of democratic principle should have been worked out long ago. But, as discussed earlier, the historical legacy and the vested interests it created have worked against such a review. Even the Convention that prepared the latest constitutional treaty was sadly defective in representing the existing institutional interests rather than those capable of discussing alternative organising principles. The new separation of powers is potentially compatible with the classic separation of powers. It is also potentially compatible with the fusion of governmental and parliamentary powers seen in the individual member states. However, what the particular form of power sharing practised within the European Union brings is, not only a gross violation of the classic separation of powers, but also incompatibility with the new separation of powers.

The incompatibility

The basic distinction reflected in the new separation of powers, distinguishing between the processes of making knowledge-based judgements and the processes of applying political judgements to that knowledge, cannot be observed with the kind of power sharing arrangements practised in the European Union for two main reasons.

The first incompatibility is in respect of the evidence and knowledge-gathering process itself. That process is compromised from the start. In areas where both the Council and the Commission are in competition, such as in the agenda-setting role, there is a tendency to want to set the agenda in advance of having the evidence. This distorts the evidence-gathering process because, as mentioned above, it means that tools such as impact assessment are seen to represent not impartial assessments of impact but more sophisticated rationalisations of what the institutions want to do anyway. With respect to the Commission's right of initiative, it is not possible to tell whether its proposals for measures to be taken by the EU represent a professional opinion based on evidence of need, or a political judgement reflecting political objectives. Moreover, there will be a suspicion that in searching for relevant evidence, the Commission will be looking for supporting evidence rather than contradictory evidence. Equally, there will be suspicions about the evidence mobilised through the Council, whether it accurately reflects the impact of a measure or has been gathered to support the political judgement of the particular member state. In short, information and knowledge from either Council or Commission will always run the risk of being seen as tainted and viewed with suspicion.

The second incompatibility is that judgemental processes are also undermined. This applies to each of the institutions. For example, the Commission's role in applying competition law or the law against state aids that distort competition should be based strictly on the evidence and professional judgements on that evidence. Its political role introduces the possibility that other factors enter into the judgement. For example, it will find itself accused of not wishing to offend a powerful member state in arriving at a verdict on a state-aid case. Or, if the Commission finds against an American company for anti-competitive behaviour, there will also be the suspicion that what could have swayed the opinion was not questions of market behaviour but questions of EU and US political relationships.

There is damage too to the judgemental role of the Council and Parliament. Under the new separation of powers, their key problem-solving role is to focus on the 'macro' framework and their key role in providing a democratic arena is to reach beyond evidence and expert judgement to outside values in order to arrive at a political judgement of the evidence. Instead of the institutions with an electoral base illuminating judgemental processes in European political life in this way, what they actually get submerged in within the EU is technocratic detail. As a result the institutions with an electoral base provide neither an effective framework for problem-solving nor a framework for a democratic arena.

It has become conventional to blame the shortcomings of Europe's elected institutions on the absence of a Europe-wide public opinion. As mentioned earlier, it indeed remains the case that most of European political life is channelled through national perspectives.[14] The arrangements have also been termed an 'accountability' failure.[15] The reality is a much more fundamental failure of democratic principle stemming from a failure to address the questions for democratic organisation raised by unelected bodies.

The costs of incompatibility

The costs of trying to combine the elements of the new separation of powers with a power sharing arrangement between the key institutions are both economic and political. They are economic because regulating the market framework is a core activity of the European Union and essential to the economic success of the union as a marketplace. The confusion of evidence gathering with political judgement is unlikely to produce either an efficient or competitive marketplace. The costs are also political because electorates are distanced by the monolithic appearance of power sharing and likely to react negatively to Brussels as a source of spin and proselytising.

Trying to disentangle existing power sharing arrangements, to clarify core responsibilities and to combine the new separation of powers either with the old separation of powers or, alternatively, with the principles of parliamentary democracy, will involve huge transitional costs. It is fear of these costs that has led successive revisions of the existing treaty base, including the recently proposed constitutional treaty, in the direction of trying to avoid undue disturbance to existing institutional interests. But the result is the long-term cost of path dependency – the cost of arrangements that do not provide a framework either for the unelected bodies to do best what they are best suited to do or for the elected bodies to do best what they are most suited to do. The costs will be high. The European Union will continue to accrete power but at the same time will be weak in problem-solving and weak also in mirroring the values of its citizens.

---

[14] 'When one compares the abstention figures at European and national elections, one cannot avoid the prima-facie conclusion that the legitimacy of the Union is rather low, and, in particular, that it is appreciably lower than that enjoyed by the member states.' Blondel, Sinnott and Svensson (1998: 55).
[15] Harlow (2002).

10   International institutions: blurring
the boundaries

The world of international institutions seems remote for many people. They grab the headlines when there is a political or humanitarian crisis in the Middle East, Asia or Sub-Saharan Africa but otherwise fade out of sight. Yet it is a misleading impression because it obscures their increasingly important more mundane activities. If a law firm or real estate agent wants a copy of an individual's recent utility bill or passport it could be because the Financial Action Task Force associated with the OECD is promoting a 'know your client' policy across the world,[1] or if the clothes one sees in the shops increasingly carry a 'made in People's Republic of China' label it could be because of action to phase out textile quotas agreed in the World Trade Organization, or if the benefits in a company pension scheme are suddenly reduced it could be because an international accounting organisation has changed the rules of how pension liabilities are to be counted. Away from the spotlight of headline events, international organisations have an increasing influence on the fabric of everyday life. Even when international decision-making becomes highly visible and may have public backing, for example when elected leaders come together as the G8 to agree on debt cancellation for the poorest countries, most people will be stumped to define what the G8 is, how it relates to international organisations such as the United Nations or World Bank or how indeed its declarations feed back into national democratic channels.[2]

---

[1] Since it was established in 1989 the FATF has put in place forty recommendations against money laundering (as well as nine Special Recommendations on terrorist financing). Recommendation 5 requires Customer Due Diligence including identifying and verifying the identity of customers.
[2] The G8 first met in 1975 (as G6) and now comprises heads of government or of state, supported by their foreign ministers, of Canada, France, Germany, Italy, Japan, Russia, the United Kingdom and the United States as well as the President of the European Commission and President of the European Council.

Currently, there are about seventy international organisations in existence.[3] Many people would be hard pressed to define exactly what they do. They belong to the world of unelected bodies by virtue of the fact that they inhabit a world beyond the direct reach of democratic practice. In most cases their members and/or shareholders are governments and this provides them, at best, with an indirect link to democratic practices. Even this link is diluted because about 50 of the 191 governments that are members of the United Nations are not democratic.[4] In addition, a number of international bodies have overlapping or interlocking relationships with unelected bodies in the same field in member states. These relationships are not always very transparent and they encourage a style of rule-making that is also not very transparent. Moreover, the techniques through which governments and international organisations make international rules have themselves been changing. The change has led away from the formality of trying to set out rules through international treaty agreements towards less formal styles of rule-making involving 'soft' understandings or recommendations that nevertheless have 'hard' effects when transposed into national law. Such 'soft' techniques of rule-making also pose a challenge to traditional democratic means of control.[5]

Because of the remoteness of international organisations from popular democratic control, there have been calls in recent years for a clearer form of accountability to be established, including some kind of direct democratic accountability.[6] In addition, non-governmental organisations have pressed their claims for a voice in their policy-making on the basis that they represent the otherwise unheard voice of 'civil society'.

This chapter glances briefly at this world to see whether the kinds of distinctions that have been established in the discussion so far are helpful for defining the place of the international institutions and in assessing the different claims about how to place them within a democratic framework.

Mobilising empirical knowledge

In theory, international organisations exercise powers and responsibilities delegated to them by their members – in most cases governments. They

---

[3] Defined as universal or intercontinental organisations. The number rises to about 250 if regional organisations are included and to over 5,000 on the broadest count. Source: *Yearbook of International Organizations* (2004/5: 33–4).
[4] Countries rated as 'not free' in 2005 by Freedom House.
[5] For a general discussion of the growth of soft law see Shelton (2000). For a discussion in the financial services area see Zaring (2005).
[6] For one view of the democratic 'deficit' that places international organisations in elitist theories of political organisation see Keohane (2002).

offer to their members four main kinds of advantage. First, they make it more difficult for states to renege on global rules they have chosen to put in place – the role discussed earlier of helping to make commitments 'credible'. Secondly, they can help enforce rule-based behaviour by linking issues together – for example, in the world of international finance in the context of debt negotiations, there is an established link between IMF relationships and multilateral debt actions by the Paris Club of creditor nations on bilateral official debt and private creditor actions on debt owed to the private sector. Thirdly, they can increase the amount of information and knowledge available to inform the behaviour of nations – for example, about whether to take action against a possible international pandemic or what constitutes best practice in measures to prevent money laundering.[7] Fourthly, they can reduce some of the costs associated with agreements on international rules – for example by providing a forum for the settlement of disputes arising over their interpretation.[8]

Each of these functions echoes those of independent agencies in national contexts. In addition, in performing these functions, with the great exception of the United Nations, which has an unambiguously political role and a political mandate to help preserve world peace through international co-operation and collective security in the General Assembly and Security Council, most of the international institutions share the characteristics common to unelected bodies within nation-states. That is to say they inhabit a technical world where specialised knowledge is required and they have an important role as information gatherers, in promoting lesson-learning and knowledge transfer. A recent president of the World Bank referred to it as 'a knowledge bank',[9] UNEP refers to its role as facilitating the transfer of knowledge for sustainable development and UNCTAD describes itself as an authoritative knowledge-based institution. In addition, they belong to and help promote epistemic communities – for example the World Trade Organization (WTO) deals mainly with trade specialists, the World Bank with development aid specialists and the World Health Organization with public health specialists.[10] The terrain they cover

---

[7] Ernst Haas (1989: 74) makes a distinction between the two: 'The term knowledge is more appropriate than information because it implies the structuring of information . . . with some theoretical principle.'

[8] For these distinctions see Meersheimer (1994/5). A similar list of functions is provided in Keohane (2002a) and in Held and McGrew (2002).

[9] James D. Wolfensohn. Press Briefing 14 April 2005.

[10] One branch of international relations theory sees such epistemic communities as a key to understanding international relations. See Haas (2004).

Table 7: *A guide to selected international organisations**

Service providers
International Civil Aviation Organization (ICAO)
International Maritime Organisation (IMO)
International Organization for Standardization (ISO)
International Telecommunication Union (ITU)
Interpol
Organisation for Economic Co-operation and Development (OECD)
Universal Postal Union (UPU)
World Meteorological Organization (WMO)

Risk assessors
Financial Stability Forum (FSF)
Food and Agriculture Organization of the United Nations (FAO)
United Nations Environment Programme (UNEP)

Boundary watchers
Bank for International Settlements (BIS)
International Association of Insurance Supervisors (IAIS)
International Bank for Reconstruction and Development (IBRD)
International Labour Organization (ILO)
International Monetary Fund (IMF)
International Organization of Securities Commissions (IOSCO)
United Nations Conference on Trade and Development (UNCTAD)

Inquisitors and inspectors
Financial Action Task Force (FATF)
International Atomic Energy Agency (IAEA)
United Nations Educational, Scientific and Cultural Organization (UNESCO)

Umpires and whistle-blowers
International Centre for Settlement of Investment Disputes (ICSID)
International Court of Justice (ICJ)
International Criminal Court (ICC)
International Tribunal for the Law of the Sea (ITLOS) (Hamburg, Germany)
International Whaling Commission (IWC)
United Nations Children's Fund (UNICEF)
United Nations High Commissioner for Refugees (UNHCR)
World Trade Organization (WTO)

* For details see Appendix.

also parallels the range of activities of the unelected bodies in nation-states.

Table 7 divides a selection of international bodies into the general categories identified earlier. As before there are some organisations that fit more than one category.

Expertise and the incentives to blur

Table 7 suggests that most international organisations, other than the United Nations itself, can be categorised as belonging to a world with a pattern of activities analogous to those handled by unelected bodies within states. Nevertheless there are two important differences. First, their connection with the private sector is very much reduced – most of their contact with the outside world is mediated through governments. Secondly, the distinction between judgements that are based on evidence and empirical knowledge and judgements that are political is one that is typically blurred. The first of these differences is discussed at a later point in this chapter. The second is discussed now.

International institutions and political 'interference'

Allegations that international organisations play a political role are often based on the simple perception that they stand in opposition to what are labelled 'independent' nation-states. For example, when the IMF attaches policy conditions to a balance of payments loan to a developing country, opponents will immediately cry 'political interference'. The outward appearance is of an institution playing a political role that goes far beyond the advisory, regulatory and executive roles of unelected bodies within states.

This appearance is misleading because it misconstrues the relationship between international organisations and the so-called 'independent' nation-state. The two phenomena are linked – but not in opposition to each other as is frequently claimed – but in symbiosis. The growth of international rule-making makes it possible for even very small states to survive and flourish without fear of discrimination by larger or hostile neighbours. Thus, the growth of international organisations and international rule-making is closely linked with an increase in the number of so-called 'independent' nation-states.[11] States may find it useful to complain to domestic audiences about 'interference' from international organisations but it is the states themselves that have created this world and it is this world that provides the environment where they can thrive. Moreover, the rules are those to which the countries themselves subscribe as members of the organisation.

Charges that international organisations inhabit a political world because they 'interfere' with domestic politics therefore should not be

---

[11] The original membership of the United Nations in 1945 totalled only 51 countries compared with the 192 today in 2007.

taken at face value. Nevertheless, the institutions themselves do blur the boundaries between knowledge-based judgements and value-laden activities. This is for three different reasons. The first is that many international organisations adopt a self-imposed role as advocacy bodies – trying as hard as possible to argue for a cause. The second is the desire of international organisations to shape policy of member governments. The third is that the framework of rules that they are called on to enforce, or to operate within, is still contested, at least by some. Each is discussed below.

Advocacy

One reason why international institutions blur boundaries is that many see themselves as advocates of a cause. For example, the World Bank sees itself as an advocate for developing countries, UNICEF for children and UNEP for a greener and safer global environment. The cause itself may well be 'good'. But the problem with such advocacy is that it brings value judgements into play of the type that cross over into the world of politics. Advocacy also tends to override the kinds of statements that can be made on the basis of knowledge and evidence alone and damages the professional reputation of the organisation itself. For example, the World Bank was at one time a strong advocate of so-called integrated rural development projects that aimed to bring large numbers of the rural poor into the cash economy – it was an advocacy that outran the evidence and later investigations showed that few of the claims made on the behalf of such projects were justified.[12] One reason why the World Bank pushed such claims on the behalf of rural development projects was the simple desire to highlight the moral imperative of reaching the poorest part of the population in the poorest countries. The moral imperative is clear enough but it confused the professional question of what type of assistance could be effective.[13]

Advocacy of scientific or sociological propositions can, as mentioned earlier, play a useful role in encouraging competition between ideas or in changing policy priorities. However, this does not mean that unelected bodies should themselves be advocates of a contested view. Unelected bodies within nation-states play a key role in navigating between

---

[12] The World Bank's 1992 Portfolio Management Task Force (known as the Wapenhans report) found that over one-third of projects completed in 1991 were failures, up from 15 per cent in 1981.

[13] Haas suggests that international organisations can attain success when they are supported by stable coalitions of like-minded states and where there is sufficient consensual knowledge to provide a moral context for solutions. See Haas (1989: 164).

competing ideas and disputes within the scientific community and this largely precludes an advocacy role. The same applies to international organisations.

Shaping policy

The second factor that has led international organisations to go beyond an evidence-gathering and expert role into judgements that essentially belong in the realm of politics is their desire to shape the international policy of governments. Governments are their members, shareholders and clients and a key target of their activities. If governments pay no attention to what they do or say then the existence of an international organisation is called into question. On the other hand the desire to influence governments can lead organisations into making judgements that are political rather than evidence-based – based on a desire to please or not to offend rather than a desire to tell the truth.[14] For example, there is a contested relationship about whether tax competition between high-tax jurisdictions and low-tax jurisdictions is conducive to economic growth and development. The division of expert opinion among economists has not stopped the OECD from appearing to be trying to mobilise international tax policy against tax competition on the grounds of an association between low-tax jurisdictions and tax evasion and money laundering. The reason for the OECD's apparent bias in the dispute is that it listens to representatives of the tax-collecting authorities rather than to independent economists. It regards the tax collectors as the constituency it wishes to be in good standing with.

These incentives to blur boundaries, because of a desire to act as advocate or to have policy influence, are not easily held in check. The terms of reference of international bodies tend to be drawn in rather broad terms, partly for reasons of compromise between different member interests, and thus the founding articles often do not themselves set limits or clearly defined objectives. Moreover, terms of reference are difficult to revise because international agreements and treaties require unanimity or high majorities to amend. In addition, there are well-known propositions from public choice theory which argue that institutions will try to set their own agenda in order to maximise their internal objectives for bureaucratic growth.

---

[14] Recently the Governor of the Bank of England in discussing the need to reform the IMF called upon it to engage in 'ruthless truth telling'. The implication is that currently it does not.

In theory the governments that are the members of the organisations and provide their executive boards should be able to exert control over such tendencies. However, governments may very well have mixed motives – including a desire to suppress unflattering international comparisons or embarrassing information. They may thus use their influence to dilute the information and knowledge role of the institution. International organisations thus inhabit an uncomfortable half-way house – too far removed from the democratic institutions of member states to claim a democratic basis for their activities but too close to governments to be able to make independent and unfettered empirical judgements.

Moreover, when institutions pursue roles that extend beyond their information and knowledge transfer role the difficulties already discussed for principals to control agents become relevant once again. International organisations illustrate in the clearest way possible the difficulties of control when there are multiple principals with different and conflicting objectives. In order to be able to pursue agendas that reach beyond an information and knowledge transfer role the institutions have the maximum possibility to play one group against another. For example, World Bank management can play members that borrow resources against members that provide resources, or the IAEA can play off non-nuclear powers against nuclear powers. The difficulties in trying to exercise control in such situations lead to crude and potentially damaging practices. Members try to exercise 'control' by withholding budget monies or capital subscriptions or by trying to place their nationals in key management positions. Once again international institutions find themselves in the highly unsatisfactory situation where they hesitate or find it impolitic to 'tell it as it is' but at the same time have sufficient 'wriggle room' to pursue their own agendas.

Another important symptom of dissatisfaction with struggles to set clear boundaries for international organisations is a turn by governments to utilise international networks of national regulators as well as national courts for international rule-making purposes. Indeed it has been suggested that in seeing states acting at this 'disaggregated' level we are seeing a new form of global governance emerge, pioneered, it is claimed, by the European Union.[15] It may well be the case that networks of national regulators and national courts are providing a more effective and reliable way for states to go about international rule-making than through their previous dependence on more formal international

---

[15] See Slaughter (2004).

organisations. But this 'solution' to the problem of global governance turns the argument back to the way in which national unelected bodies can themselves be held to be acting legitimately and accountably. Nor, as discussed in the previous chapter, does the EU in its current state supply a model of how to provide a democratic framework for unelected bodies and networks.

The framework

A final reason why international institutions are seen to be 'political' rather than basing their activities on evidence, expertise and the latest knowledge available is that the rules they administer, or police, or operate within are more contentious in a global setting than in a national context. For example, national economic regulators in Europe and the United States operate within a context where, broadly speaking, the benefits of a market economy are accepted. The areas of controversy, in Europe at least, concern just how far open and competitive markets will also produce social benefits and to what extent certain kinds of social goals justify exclusions from competition policy. These are important differences, but in the case of the international setting the rules are even less accepted. Even public opinion in a market economy such as the United States has difficulty in accepting the advantages of rules that safeguard free trade when it is associated with the outsourcing of jobs or the shrinking of the textile and steel and other industries. In addition, there is a vocal minority in most countries in the world that does not accept the rules at all.

Part of the questioning of the rules stems from the fact that international acceptance of the market economy as the least bad way to organise economic activity is relatively recent. Thus the perception of international organisations as 'political' bodies may diminish in time. A different part of the response is for international organisations to improve the transparency of what they do. Unelected bodies within nation-states take care to achieve public understanding of their role and approach to it. This is not just or even mainly a question of public relations. It is much more a question of following procedures that allow for evidence to be gathered, reviewed and rebutted. International organisations have extensive and expensive public relations departments, but they have far to go in developing transparent evidence-based procedures.

If it is accepted that many international organisations should see themselves as 'knowledge' institutions in the way that the World Bank and others proclaim their knowledge roles, then the earlier discussion of what legitimises the activities of unelected bodies within states becomes relevant to international bodies too. In other words it would be a mistake to try to base the legitimacy of their activities on democratic political processes, either direct or indirect. Instead the legitimacy of their activities would flow from how well they observe the principles and procedures that tie them to the world of the natural and social sciences.

If international institutions were to seek legitimacy in this way, then the temptation to blur boundaries between the evidence-based and the political might diminish. In such circumstances, the diversity of shareholder and member views in international organisations would no longer be a negative factor impeding 'control' but become, instead, a positive feature precisely because political control would be difficult. Moreover, a diversity of views should be helpful in the discovery process. Equally they would find it easier to establish a principled relationship with NGOs and organisations claiming to represent civil society. Against the standards applicable to knowledge-based institutions, the claims of NGOs to provide a form of democratic input would be misconceived. NGOs would have a role only in so far as they could mobilise evidence that would otherwise be excluded from the knowledge base or by promoting transparency in international organisations. There are some NGOs that may very well be in such a position to bring evidence to the table, but it is a different kind of role and justification for their contribution.

Procedures

There seems little doubt that international organisations could adopt, in cases where they have not already adopted them, the kind of procedures that unelected bodies need to follow in order to legitimate their activities. They can make their information gathering a more open process, extend their consultation procedures to allow for input from more sources with relevant evidence, expose their preliminary findings to systematic independent peer review and allow for rebuttal and counter-evidence. Many have already gone some way down this route. For example, IMF and World Bank reports are placed in the public domain after completion and can be independently scrutinised and criticised. However, for many there is much further to go.

In looking at the obstacles that international organisations face in developing their procedures in this direction, there is one contrast with the practices and procedures of unelected bodies within nation-states that stands out – that is their comparative lack of openness to the private sector. One reason for this is that they deal with governments, many of which claim a privileged status for, and confidentiality in respect of, the information they provide. Thus, for example, a draft report is typically discussed with the government concerned but not typically subject to independent review by outside experts. The other reason is less obvious and more difficult to address and concerns their lack of market knowledge and lack of openness to market signals about their operations.

Openness

A lack of market knowledge in international organisations stems in part from staffing structures. Unelected bodies within states have taken advantage of their independence from central government to widen their recruiting patterns and to hire from the private sector. By contrast, international organisations remain overwhelmingly staffed by bureaucrats without market experience. A position in an international organisation is often a reward for bureaucratic service within a member state. The lack of market knowledge is compounded by a lack of openness to market signals. This situation is well illustrated by the case of the World Bank.

The World Bank takes no credit risk on the loans it makes out of its borrowings because it seeks, and is provided with, 'preferred creditor status'.[16] This means that it does not normally reschedule its loans and always gets repaid even if its loans have yielded no positive benefits. Market signals about the quality of its lending decisions are therefore suppressed. The World Bank also takes no borrowing risk. The capital of its wealthiest member governments effectively gives it privileged access to capital markets and is available to back its borrowings if all else fails. Signals from capital markets about its performance are therefore also suppressed. It also takes no budgetary risks. It lends at a spread above borrowing costs and can always expand its own budget as long as lending volume is maintained. The kind of signals that a private company would get if its internal cost structure got out of hand, or if its resources were being poorly deployed, are also therefore lacking. The net result of these practices is that the World Bank cuts itself off from all normal sources of market information about what it is doing. Combined with a lack of market expertise among staff, this means it cannot perform as good a job as it might as a 'knowledge' institution.

The World Bank is probably in a unique category, along with other development banks, in closing itself to market signals in this way. But the point is a more general one. Markets are extraordinary sources of

---

[16] The International Development Association credits sourced from the budgetary contributions of members and from repayments of previous credits may be rescheduled. The G8 agreement in 2005 on debt cancellation appears to offer 'compensation' for any financial pain.

information. International organisations are not as open as they need to be to the information that markets provide.[17]

Principles

It was suggested in the case of the unelected bodies in national settings that their legitimacy rested in part on the procedures they followed, and in part on the principles they followed. The principles in this case were also those consistent with the world of the natural and social sciences – a commitment to the integrity of the research process; a respect for evidence and its limitations; a commitment to the experimental approach to knowledge and openness to question, inspection and refutation. All of these apply to those international institutions that belong essentially to the knowledge world and could be followed by them as a means to bolster both the effectiveness of what they do and the legitimacy of their activities.[18] There is, however, a well-established practice and doctrine of international organisations which flies against a fundamental aspect of a principles-based approach. That practice revolves around the doctrine of 'neutrality' towards the regimes they deal with.

Neutrality

The doctrine of neutrality means in practice that any country that is a member of the United Nations may become a member of another international universal organisation and access the benefits of membership. This means that members include those that are autocratic and dictatorial as well as democratic and those that do not pursue the goal of a competitive market economy but practise various forms of state intervention, or what is termed 'crony capitalism', where those with political power manipulate the market in ways to reward themselves or their friends. The membership of such countries has been justified on the grounds that international organisations should be 'neutral' in dealing with non-democratic as compared with democratic regimes and neutral as between market economies and non-market or pseudo-market economies where political elites control the market.

From one perspective the doctrine of neutrality can be seen as a willingness or need to deal with the world as it is rather than as it would be in an

---

[17] The dangers of international organisations becoming insulated and shutting themselves off from effective feedback is discussed with other sources of failure in Barnett and Finnemore (1999).
[18] The need for independent external audit is emphasised in Stiglitz (2003).

ideal state of affairs. There may indeed be a case for this in connection with
bodies with a political role – notably the United Nations. However, it is not
easy to justify in the case of knowledge institutions. In their case the
doctrine of neutrality appears to fit in with the idea of international organisations as apolitical, technocratic bodies – but it is a false fit. It is false
because those governments that deny democratic expression and suppress
market signals are essentially cutting themselves off from information and
discovery. This undercuts the principles that knowledge-based institutions
need to respect. It is also likely to mislead their own operations. Prior to the
collapse of communism both the IMF and the World Bank had offered
what turned out to be grossly inflated estimates of the size and prosperity of
communist economies – no amount of massaging of output figures could
compensate for the absence of a market test.

What this means is that if international institutions are to develop as
other unelected bodies and seek legitimacy as knowledge bodies then they
have to examine quite critically some of the assumptions under which
they have traditionally operated. They will need not only to follow a
clearer set of principles and procedures in their activities but also be
much more open to market sources of information and much more
questioning of members whose posture is hostile to discovery processes.

Legitimising the United Nations

While the majority of international institutions can be seen as belonging
to a family of knowledge-based bodies and potentially legitimated in the
same way by reference to the principles and procedures they follow in
their operations, the situation is quite different in respect of the United
Nations because it is a body that, in the workings of its General Assembly
and Security Council, has an explicit political role. Given this political
role, the question is whether its activities too can be legitimated through
reference to relevant procedures and principles or whether some kind of
overt democratic sanction of its activities is also necessary.

The idea that an unelected body such as the United Nations could have
some kind of direct link to democracy in the way that it is practised within
a single state, for example having members of the General Assembly or
the UN Secretary General elected by global suffrage, seems hugely ideal-
istic and has had few supporters. Opposition remains current.[19] Certainly

---

[19] 'The prospect of world government is as undesirable as it is unrealistic. If the world has
learned one thing from the bloody history of the twentieth century, it is that highly
centralized, top–down systems of governance are economic and political nightmares.'
Florini (2003: 11).

to the great powers, victorious at the end of the Second World War, that established the UN, it was clear that the UN had to be established on the basis of states not peoples. The approach to the legitimation of its role has had to rest therefore on the principles and procedures it represents.

The twin pillars

The two key pillars on which the United Nations has rested since its formation are first on an appeal to values that are claimed to be universal, provided by the United Nations Universal Declaration of Human Rights (adopted in 1948), and secondly on the principle of non-intervention in the internal arrangements within member states contained in the UN Charter itself.[20] Both pillars are now under challenge. As a result the legitimacy of the UN is itself under challenge.

In order to assess how well these twin pillars serve the purpose of legitimising the UN, and in order to understand why they are now being challenged, it is useful to look at their rationale from three different perspectives. One perspective is to see them as a straightforward compromise between realism about the role of states and ethical principles that relate to people rather than to states. A second perspective is to take them in historical context and look at their background in long-standing attempts to find a normative basis for international law at the same time as recognising the need for accommodation between different normative conceptions. A third perspective is to see them as representing the kinds of 'outputs' from the UN that would legitimise its activities through beneficial end results.

Realism about states combined with ethics for peoples

The first way of looking at the two pillars is to see them as an attempt to reconcile 'realism' with ethical principles in the particular circumstances after the end of the Second World War.[21] The principle of non-intervention stood for 'realism' and was a way of recognising the role of states in the UN regardless of the nature of their internal regime. Recognising the role

[20] See in particular Article 2 paragraph 7 of the UN Charter and Article 51.
[21] This reflects the main divide in international relations theory after the Second World War between the realists or neo-realists placing the emphasis on the role of the state and those stressing the interdependence of states, the role of non-state actors, the role of normative principles and more holistic approaches. For an overview of the 'realist' tradition and its variants see Buzan (1993). For different methodological approaches to modelling international relations see Wendt (1999). For a survey of normative approaches see Hoffman (1994: 27–44).

of states provided a justification for the inclusion in the membership of the United Nations of all regimes in control of territory regardless of the political and ethical coloration of the regime. It also justified realism in the formation of the Security Council with its permanent members representing the key powers in the immediate post-war world – again regardless of their political coloration.[22] From a theoretical perspective, 'realism' meant recognising states as the most important actors in world politics and as unitary actors pursuing their own interests in a rational way.[23]

This emphasis on the role of states can be seen in retrospect as far-sighted. The number of states in the world has grown substantially in the post-war world and continues to grow. Despite the emergence of regional groupings such as the European Union, and despite the growth of non-state actors and transnational networks, states remain the main organisational unit in the world. The emphasis on the role of states also has contemporary resonance in the current debate about how to deal with the problems posed by 'failed states'.

At the same time the founders of the United Nations realised that an institution that was based simply on 'realism' would be open to challenge. There needed too to be a normative basis for international behaviour. They solved this dilemma by coupling the emphasis on the role of states in the United Nations with the Universal Declaration of Human Rights. The United Nations would thus stand for the most important values in the world and could be measured against them. Its activities could be sanctioned by an appeal to principles nobody could object to and were supported by everyone.

These twin pillars stood in deliberate contrast to a different way of organising international behaviour – through empire. The old imperial powers, notably the UK and France, had lost both the political will and the capacity to maintain their empires, and in the post-war setting the swing away from empire towards emphasising both the role of independent states and the role of universal principles seemed both realistic and normatively desirable. The contemporary emergence of the United States as the world's only 'superpower' has revived debate about the oscillation between empire and other principles of international organisation in the new clothes of debate about 'unilateralism' versus 'multilateralism'.

---

[22] 'So long as the major states are the major actors, the structure of international politics is defined in terms of them.' Waltz (1979: 94).

[23] For a definition of the core assumptions of the realist tradition see Keohane (1986: 164–5).

Although the twin pillars can be viewed in this way as an attempt in the post-war period to combine 'realism', in the form of recognising the world of states with all their blemishes, with ethical principle, in the form of a commitment to universal values and norms of behaviour, both pillars possess deep historical roots and appeal to a wider set of values. The second way of looking at the pillars is therefore to view them against their more deep-rooted historical background in attempts to establish normative principles for international law while recognising the value of accommodation between opposing viewpoints.

International norms combined with the virtues of accommodation

The historical roots of the Universal Declaration of Human Rights can be traced back to a desire in early medieval times to establish universal ethical principles on a basis other than divine authority or revelation. Eventually this led to the first attempts to provide a theory for an international rule of law based on the principles of natural law and the idea of a normatively ordered universe.[24] The Charter thus stands in a long tradition of attempts to establish the principles and procedures of international law applying equally to all peoples everywhere.[25]

Similarly, the principle of non-intervention also has a long historical background, emerging from a desire to put an end to religious wars in Europe and to limit empire-building rivalries outside Europe. The principle of non-intervention therefore stands for more than window-dressing for 'realism' in the recognition of the role of states. It has a background in tolerance, defined as the need to accept that different cultural and belief systems have to find a way of living together. 'Accommodation' seemed vital in the immediate post-Second World War divide between communism and liberal political and market orders and has continuing relevance for the divides in the contemporary world.

Tolerance defined as 'accommodation' or 'live and let live' may not seem very glorious as a normative principle and this aspect has presented difficulties to defenders of tolerance as a virtue. In the constant everyday tension between principle and accommodation in the workings of the United Nations, it is often principles that seem to be the loser. However, in this respect the workings of the UN are little different from the

---

[24] Developed in the seventeeth century by Grotius and Pufendorf. There are differences in emphasis between theories of natural law and theories of rights.

[25] Richard Tuck (1999: 14) comments, 'It cannot be a coincidence . . . that the modern idea of natural rights arose in the period in which the European nations were engaged in their dramatic competition for the domination of the world.'

workings of democratic states. In the world of democratic politics it is indeed often the case that policies will stray far from what is 'best'. The search is often for the practical solution, or the policy that works, or the median that leaves nobody hugely upset.

Output legitimacy

The third perspective on the twin pillars is to see them in terms of 'output' legitimacy. As earlier noted, what this refers to is the idea that bodies that cannot claim legitimacy by virtue of a democratic input can still claim legitimacy through their output. Under this approach the United Nations could appeal to the outcome of its activities. If its actions bring about peace and dispute resolution in practice between governments, then that in itself provides a form of legitimation.[26] This would also provide the justification of its 'realist' approach to membership. If the inclusion of members of even highly undesirable regimes works in practice to help achieve world peace, then there is a compelling argument for their inclusion. Similarly, in a peaceful world the values reflected in the Universal Declaration of Human Rights would more likely flourish.

In the context of the UN, notions of 'output legitimacy' have to contend with perceptions of 'ineffectiveness'. In the post-war world there have been three long-standing UN 'failures' – over Palestine, the Korean Peninsula and Kashmir – as well as other disasters such as the Rwanda genocide. Ineffectiveness was also a key issue in the run-up to the Iraq war. Notwithstanding such 'failures', the idea that the UN can rest its claim to legitimacy in part on its actual contribution to such goals as world peace is often appealed to.

The weakness of the approach to legitimating UN activities by appealing to its 'output' is that the principles and values represented by the outcomes may be questioned. Even the value of world peace, on the grounds that peace allows all other values to be realised, is a value that itself has to be defended. History unfortunately provides many examples where what is most valued has had to be fought for.

Nevertheless, what this discussion shows is that the twin pillars on which the UN has rested its legitimacy do not just involve a balancing of universal values against 'realism' but can also be seen as balancing concepts of the international rule of law, applicable to all, against concepts of tolerance and accommodation of diversity, and of balancing an

---

[26] The concept of 'output legitmacy' has been developed by Scharpf in the context of the European Union. He views intergovernmental agreement as one of the instruments of output legitimation. See Scharpf (1999: 13–22).

appeal to universal values against an appeal to practical and beneficial end results. Unfortunately, whichever of these perspectives is taken, the twin pillars still have shortcomings as legitimating principles.

The shortcomings

One fundamental weakness centres on the non-observance of, or non-compliance with, the Universal Declaration of Human Rights by many of the UN members. Its principles cannot be regarded as sincerely held when there are members of the organisation that flout them every day and have little or no intention of observing them and for whom there is no penalty in non-observance. The institutionalised hypocrisy was illustrated in 2003 when Libya, a country not hitherto noted for its observance of human rights, was placed in charge of the UN Human Rights Commission.[27]

The second fundamental weakness concerns the question of the mutual consistency of the two principles. The principle of non-intervention tries to ring-fence behaviour that is of concern only to a state itself and behaviour that is of concern to other states. In this sense it is analogous to principles that try to ring-fence individual behaviour from behaviour that is of concern to society at large. In today's world the borders are permeable in both cases. No bright lines can be drawn. Moreover, the principles in the Universal Declaration of Human Rights go in the opposite direction of saying that certain principles of procedural and substantive justice should apply in all cases and situations. Their application does not stop at national boundaries.

Thirdly there is a deliberate disconnect with democracy. The non-intervention principle implies that whether a state is democratic or not is of no concern to its neighbours or to the world at large. This is untenable on two grounds. Empirically, there does seem to be a connection between democracy and peaceful behaviour. This is not because democracies do not go to war.[28] But it has to do with the fact that democratic leaders are constrained in their behaviour by having to explain what they do to their electorate and by the need to achieve electoral support for continuing in office. Their behaviour is thus likely to be

---

[27] A body since replaced by the UN Human Rights Council in an attempt to restore credibility. Countries holding seats on the 47-member Council include Cuba and China.

[28] A view that has been advanced in recent times by John Rawls: 'Constitutional democracies do not go to war with one another ... because they have no cause to go to war with one another.' See Rawls (1999: 8). Among the early theorists, Rousseau argued more perceptively that 'well-governed republics' might go to war with each other because of conflict over different conceptions of justice. See Rousseau (1992 [1775]: 144).

more predictable and more restrained.[29] Democratic powers may also be more inclined to accumulate influence by building winning coalitions rather than pursuing power at the expense of others.[30] Secondly it leads again to an inconsistency between the twin pillars. The procedural principles in the UN Universal Declaration of Human Rights are those observed in democracies and flouted in undemocratic regimes. The principle of non-intervention suggests that their application is a matter of choice rather than a matter of obligation.

In the case of accommodation between conflicting beliefs within democratic states, the virtues of accommodation can be justified by the value of democracy as such – the overriding importance of having procedures that take everybody's views into account. In the case of the United Nations it is also important to take everybody's views into account. However, because the link with democracy is absent, the normative values that are being achieved through accommodation are missing. The policy of accommodation becomes an end in itself – separated both from principle and from democratic practice.

At the end of the day the twin principles on which the United Nations attempts to rest its legitimacy as a political body are simply not compatible with the present membership. One can attempt to justify a universal body on the 'realist' grounds of the need to include every state for practical reasons or for purposes of peaceful 'accommodation', or one can justify it on the grounds of establishing and enforcing universal principles. But in practice the two do not combine. The fatal flaw is the disconnect with democracy. Undemocratic countries undermine the principles contained in the Universal Declaration of Human Rights. At the same time, they undermine the principle of accommodation.

The democratisation of global politics

If the legitimation of the political role of the United Nations cannot rest just on the twin principles of universalism and non-intervention, then the focus turns again to establishing a clearer connection with democracy.

Direct

One approach would be to attempt to democratise the United Nations directly. This would mean, for example, converting the General Assembly into a body that represented peoples rather than states and

---

[29] See the analysis in Reitter and Stam (2002).   [30] See Brawley (1993).

perhaps converting the Security Council into an upper chamber of states with a weighting that favoured the most powerful states.[31] The case for democratisation at the global level rests partly on well-known propositions about the limitations of nation-states as problem-solvers in the face of global issues such as environmental degradation or new forms of pandemics. More fundamentally, it rests on the case that persons should become the focus of international organisation rather than states.[32]

Such an approach still seems very far from reality and democratisation in any direct form is advocated only by a few.[33] In the meantime, the importance of NGOs as a way to reflect 'civil society' is seen as a step on the way and a form of 'associative democracy' at the international level. Even that is hardly convincing. It rests on the tenuous claims of NGOs to be 'representative'.[34]

Indirect

In the absence of direct democratisation of a political organisation such as the UN, the alternative is to look again for an indirect link. This means looking for the member governments of the UN to provide the link with democracy through their own connections with their own electorates. Alternatively, one could just accept that international organisations, including those with a political vocation, will remain not recognisably democratic.[35]

An indirect approach can be criticised on the grounds that democracy inside states still does not lead to democracy at the global level so that international problem-solving would remain without a democratic base.[36] What, however, the indirect approach would achieve is to remove the inconsistency between the twin principles on which the UN tries to base its legitimacy. Member states would no longer be insincere in their commitment to human rights and a generalised policy of non-intervention would more easily be justified.

This suggests a different approach to the legitimation of a world political order. It suggests that it is a mistake to look for a universal

---

[31] See Laslett (2003: 212–24).   [32] For a classic statement see Beitz (1979).
[33] For a restatement of the case for democracy at the global level see Archibugi (2003).
[34] A variant of this position is to stress the importance of relying on increased transparency of international organisations and the role that NGOs can play in promoting transparency. See Florini (2003).
[35] The position adopted by Dahl (1999: 23): 'I suggest that we treat them as bureaucratic bargaining systems.'
[36] The case is set out in Held (2003).

government that rests on the same kind of democratic mechanisms as the government of a state and that instead we should look towards a world order that comprises democratic and market-oriented societies that would enable the UN to rest on a base of shared political principles and procedures. It would be a democratic order in the sense it would be based on the principles and procedures necessary for democracies. Such an indirect approach would still be a major step beyond recognising international organisations simply as bureaucratic conveniences because they would also be seen as organisations conducive to the maintenance of democracies.

It suggests that attempts to democratise international behaviour should focus less on trying to democratise the UN and focus instead on democratising states.

Distinguishing between international bodies

This brief and very incomplete excursion into the world of international organisations from the perspective of the legitimacy of unelected bodies suggests that a major distinction should be made between those international organisations that fall within the knowledge world and those, notably the UN General Assembly and Security Council, that are inherently political. The legitimacy of those that belong to the knowledge world can be rested, in the same way as with unelected bodies within member states, on the principles and procedures that they follow in their activities. It is a mistake to look for a base of popular democratic assent. The UN, however, falls into a quite different category. In the absence of a direct link to democratic assent for its activities, it has tried to rest its legitimacy on principle and procedure in a manner analogous to that of other unelected bodies. This too is a mistake. It does not work because in the absence of a world composed only of democratic states the principles are incompatible.

11 Conclusions: the accountability of the new branch

The new separation of powers in context

Modern democratic practice offers a very confusing kaleidoscope of impressions. A court decides one US presidential election and moral values swing another; an international commission dealing with human rights abuses is presided over by the representative of a country where human rights are barely recognised; heads of agencies resign in response to public criticism even though they are not elected to their positions; a political union is created in Europe to deal with those large issues that flow across national boundaries and ends up intrusively quibbling about technical details and national particularities; central bankers speak and international financial markets sit up and listen, while, when finance ministers speak, markets pay no attention. This book has therefore attempted to sort out these different impressions and try to discern an underlying pattern.

That underlying pattern involves a basic distinction between the ways in which democratic systems of government now try to mobilise information and the latest state of empirical knowledge for public policy-making, untainted by political judgements, and the different ways in which democratic societies draw upon values to pass political judgement on that information and knowledge. It involves an institutional distinction between those bodies, outside elective politics, that have a special role in gathering and analysing information, bringing to bear relevant empirical knowledge, including navigating through contested areas, and those bodies, belonging to elective politics, that bring ethical and political values to bear in the judgemental processes of democratic societies. The same forces that enable an unelected central bank governor to speak with authority, so that markets listen, also devalue the words of an elected finance minister whose words might be regarded as spin and that can be discounted by markets. The same forces that lie behind the rise of unelected bodies and place a court in the role of deciding one US presidential election at the same time place more of an onus on elected institutions to reflect those moral and ethical values that turn out to be decisive in the following election. Much of the confusion in modern democratic practice arises when the institutional distinction is not observed.

The new separation of powers does not hinge on philosophical distinctions between facts and values. It hinges on the fact that in the real world it is possible to distinguish between the evidence and empirical reasoning that go into public policy and the value judgements. Unbundling institutional responsibilities helps to distinguish between and to illuminate the two different components. In this world, unelected bodies are better than the elected alternatives as gatherers of information and mobilisers of empirical knowledge, less likely to conceal or distort information and more likely to be trusted than elected bodies as vehicles for the dissemination of facts and as sources of empirical judgement. The distinction is not rigid. In some cases unelected bodies will be required to make social or ethical judgements. But, even in such cases, they will remain better able to help people distinguish between what is empirical and what are value judgements. The separation is a story that perhaps starts with the BBC charter in 1927 separating broadcasting from government, continues through the ruling of the California Court of Appeal in 1957 in favour of patients being enabled to give their informed consent and continues with the debacle over the treatment of information leading up to the Iraq war.

Framing the debate

Unelected bodies now perform many of the practical day-to-day tasks that enable democracies to function. Their rise poses an enormous challenge both to the theory and to the practice of modern democracy. At a practical level the traditional democratic institutions seem to be relegated to the role of merely symbolic actors. Even worse, parliaments, prime ministers and presidents appear to maintain a smokescreen of democratic organisation while concealing the apparently undemocratic means through which societies actually work.

This book has explored various ways of defining the challenge. Some see the question in terms of an ancient contest between democratic forms of government and elites. According to this view the unelected are the new elites. Their rise brings about a commensurate loss to democracy. This way of looking at the challenge has been rejected. When unelected bodies strip away official secrecy, or provide more trustworthy information or guidance untarnished by spin, democracy is the gainer not the loser. New methods of redress for citizen complaints are also a plus for democracy. The new separation of powers and the growth of unelected bodies mark a potentially important advance for democracies precisely because they are consistent with a better and more reliably informed body of citizens, more questioning of those who possess political power, better equipped to make decisions for themselves and also better equipped with means of redress when things go wrong.

Another way of looking at the challenge presented by the unelected is to see it in terms of the means through which democratic societies harness sources of authority, notably the authority of those who are competent and skilled in difficult fields. This perspective gets us closer to what is going on. But the role of the unelected extends well beyond the exercise of skill and competence, even though they need both. Unelected bodies demarcate the boundaries between state and market and watch over some of the most sensitive boundary issues where empirical appraisal lies side by side with matters of great social or ethical concern. They are much better equipped than elected bodies to provide services, to assess risk and to deal with conflicts of interest in the new forms in which they arise in modern societies. They solve many of the practical problems of relevance to modern electorates. Skill and competence alone are not enough to explain the scope and range of their activities.

The book has examined in much greater detail the framework provided by mainstream accounts of democracy. These attempt to place unelected bodies within traditional accounts of democracy that hinge on the exercise of the vote, or political bargaining, or political persuasion or notions of the rule of law. Yet on examination it is impossible to escape the conclusion that this traditional framework does not marshal what is going on. The rise of the unelected makes democratic participation and deliberation seem much less important to citizens and emphasises the weakest points in accounts of the rule of law. Nor is there any easy way to rescue these mainstream accounts. The idea that the rule of law can be easily extended through the application of new constitutional rules is open to both practical and theoretical objection. The idea that active participation in traditional politics still makes sense because traditional bodies can continue to exercise meaningful control over the new bodies lacks plausibility. The idea that 'pragmatism' is all that societies need to solve their problems ignores the expressive side of social and political debate entirely.

The book has therefore argued that the rise of the unelected should be framed in terms of what it is – a new separation of powers – and that the logic of separation can provide the framework for assessing what the rise of the unelected means for democratic theory and practice.

The implications of the new separation of powers

The advantages of pursuing the analysis of the rise of the unelected through the logic of a new separation of powers are that it focusses attention on the dynamic effects of the new branch on the other traditional branches, the elected bodies and the judiciary; it provides a different way of looking at the legitimacy of the new branch – one that focusses on the roots of its own claim to legitimacy rather than looking to a legitimacy derived from the other branches; and, finally, the subject of this chapter, it provides a more precise approach to questions related to the accountability of the new branch.

The dynamic impact of the unelected on the traditional elected bodies suggested a much more profound and radical effect than appears at first sight. The classic separation of powers was radical because by unbundling the main branches of government it paved the way for democratic government itself. The new separation of powers is radical because by unbundling the different kinds of judgements that go into policy-making it changes the relationship between electorates and their representatives. In turn, the arrival of the informed citizen, coupled with the superior problem-solving capacities of the unelected bodies, brings about an alteration in the role to be played by elected bodies. The elected bodies are propelled to change both the way they discharge their problem-solving role and the way in which they provide an arena for the expression of values in society. Politicians should not sit back and bemoan the lack of trust shown in them by capricious and volatile electorates, nor should they try to recapture ground lost to the rise of unelected bodies. Instead they need to accept a new focus for their activities.

The examination of the legitimacy of the new branch suggested that at the heart of the activities of the new bodies, and what distinguishes them above all from elected bodies, are a more rigorous approach to facts and empirical knowledge, a greater incentive and willingness to disseminate information and a more open acknowledgement of the incompleteness, uncertainties and disputes that accompany facts and empirical knowledge. It is by following the principles and procedures that underpin this greater rigour that the unelected earn their legitimacy. The implications extend beyond the democratic life of nations to include the legitimacy of the regional and international networks and organisations that increasingly affect people's lives.

At the same time there is a final challenge. The challenge concerns the way in which the new separation of powers provides for a system of democratic accountability. It is on accountability therefore that this closing chapter focusses.

Accountability and the new checks and balances

Democratic theory has a long and honourable tradition of distrust of experts and elites. There are also many warnings about thinking that democracy can be based on enlightened reason. Because the new branch is overwhelmingly composed of experts, and its legitimacy depends on the rigour and method with which it mobilises facts and evidence, this same distrust and these same warnings apply to it too. It is owing to these reservations that if the new branch is to be accepted as belonging to democratic systems of government, rather than to elitist systems, it has to find a place within a system of democratic accountability.

The components of accountability

The separation of powers makes an important distinction between what makes a branch legitimate and what makes it accountable. Legitimacy and accountability are closely related concepts but they are not the same. Legitimacy asks how powers are justified. Accountability focusses on how powers are exercised. In democracies, those who hold power must be able both to justify their powers and also to be held to account for the way in which they exercise them. 'Accountability' is a term that is often used very broadly and in the most abstract of ways.[1] It is also sometimes tied to rather general notions of 'responsibility' and powers exercised in the pursuit of a general public interest.[2] There are, however, three distinct and very practical components that are distinguished in the classic American description of the separation of powers.

First, there is accountability in the sense of being 'answerable' for the ways in which powers have been exercised. In general terms this means that elected politicians have to provide reasons to an electorate as to why they should be given or retain office and courts have to offer explanations for their judgements. The classic theory of the separation of powers also defined answerability in a more precise way by relating different forms of answerability to the different ways in which each branch could claim legitimacy. In the case of the American Constitution, as originally conceived, the members of the House of Representatives were answerable directly to the people, senators to the states and the President to a 'compound' mix of both. In the case of the judiciary, the debate revolved around the question as to whether all cases should involve trial by jury. The Founders rejected such a provision because they saw a key component of

---

[1] For a discussion see Schedler (1999).
[2] See Harlow (2002: 6–24), in particular chap. 1 'Thinking about Accountability'.

the rule of law lying in the need for the judiciary to apply general rules supported by specialised reasoning. In other words the judiciary was held answerable to the logic of the law rather than to the vagaries of juries.

Secondly, there is accountability in the sense of powers that are exercised only within defined limits. In a separation of powers this means that courts should not step into politics and elected politicians should not try to tamper with the law. The classic separation between legislature, executive and judiciary held out the prospect that each branch of government would help keep the other in check. The paradox is that the idea of checks and balances significantly modifies any idea that complete separation should exist between the different branches. In the case of the United States separation is in practice far from absolute.[3] For a system of checks and balances to work effectively, the key is not to establish complete separation but, instead, to identify the areas of potential overlap and ensure that they do not compromise the core functions of any of the branches.

Thirdly, there is accountability in the sense of an ability somewhere within the system of government to apply sanctions if powers are misused. This means, not only that electorates should be able to get rid of politicians if they abuse the confidence placed in them, but it also means that an ability to sanction may be needed in respect of the other branches as well. The classical system of checks and balances also provided forms of sanction in the event that powers were misused. The President could be impeached and the courts asserted the right of judicial review over the legislature. Sanction in the case of the judicial branch was limited by America's Founding Fathers to cases of misbehaviour.[4] This reflected the view of the Founding Fathers that as long as it remained independent from the other branches, the judiciary was not a threat to liberty and mainly needed to be defended against attacks from the other branches.[5]

These distinctions remain applicable to the new branch today. Unelected bodies need to give public reasons as a way of answering for their decisions; they too should act within their proper limits and respect the core functions of the other branches and they too should also be capable of being sanctioned.

---

[3] Bruce Ackerman (1984) has argued that in times of major structural change, such as the New Deal, the branches converge in their actions.

[4] 'The tenure by which the judges are to hold their places is, as it unquestionably ought to be, that of good behaviour.' Madison, Federalist Paper no. 39, in Hamilton, Madison and Jay (1987 [1788]: 192).

[5] See Hamilton, Federalist Papers nos. 78 and 81. 'There never can be danger that the judges, by a series of deliberate usurpations on the authority of the legislature, would hazard the united resentment of the body entrusted with it, while this body was possessed of the means of punishing their presumption by degrading them from their stations.' Hamilton, Madison and Jay (1987 [1788]: 414).

The classic separation of powers had one final advantage as a system of accountability. The system of checks and balances was designed to operate in a way that would add to the democratic character of the whole. In one important respect the Founding Fathers of the American system failed in this aim. The separation of powers did not act to preserve the distinctions they made between the powers of the central (federal) government and the powers of the states. The Founding Fathers underestimated the extent to which the different branches of the central government would find it in their joint interests to expand their collective jurisdiction over the states. But the idea that a system of separation of powers could add to the democratic character of the whole remains valid. The key questions, therefore, are whether a system of checks and balances still provides a way of making the new branch accountable in the three classic senses of the term and whether the new branch can also be seen as adding to the democratic character of modern systems of government as a whole.

Making the unelected branch answerable

As mentioned above, the Founding Fathers of American democracy did not regard the judiciary as answerable to the people or even bound throughout to a system of juries. Instead, the judiciary had to provide reasons for its judgements that were explainable in terms of established legal principles and precedents. The same approach applies to the new breed of unelected bodies. As discussed earlier in Chapter 7, they are not answerable to the people but they do have to offer public reasons for their actions. In turn these reasons need to flow from the rigour and application of an empirical methodology that underpins the legitimacy of the new branch.

Holding the unelected branch within the limits of its power

On the whole it seems unlikely that unelected bodies will want to take on core functions belonging to the elected branches or to the judiciary. Unelected bodies are unlikely to be tempted to stray into territory that belongs to a government or legislature because it invites retaliation in ways that would curtail their statutory powers. Similarly, they are unlikely to want to encroach on the judiciary. In some cases the boundary with the traditional judiciary is still unclear. Tasks that in some countries are entrusted to a specialised unelected institution may still, in another country, be entrusted to an ordinary court of law. Nevertheless, as discussed below, the judiciary possesses an important power to sanction unelected bodies and those unelected bodies are unlikely to wish to provoke its use. Instead, where the danger of the misuse of the powers of the unelected lies is in relation to private interests.

The traditional doctrine of checks and balances focussed particularly on the risk of the misuse of power by the elected branches of government. It paid much less attention to the possibility that power could be captured by private interests. Here the Founding Fathers of the American system looked at the power of 'faction' and attempted to address it through the way in which powers were divided between the federal and state levels. In practice, private interests have been much more troublesome for modern systems of government than anticipated by the American Founding Fathers and the new branch of government is vulnerable to misusing its powers in relation to them.

The dangers of the misuse of powers for promoting private interests by the unelected bodies arise on several different fronts. There is the risk that they will be captured by the interests they are dealing with, or will develop client and complicit relationships rather than arm's-length relationships with important constituencies. They are also susceptible to manipulation by NGOs and so-called 'civil society organisations' that have a strong interest or advocacy position in the same field of activity.

There is no doubt that such dangers exist. This is in part because the procedures and principles under which the new institutions operate are themselves still evolving. The defence against such dangers stems, in part, from the development of procedural safeguards such as peer review. But there is also a defence provided by the other branches. 'Capture' by a particular interest is likely to lead either to challenge in the courts, or to a challenge by the elected branches as other interests protest their exclusion. Checks and balances still operate even against powerful private interests.

Sanctioning the unelected branch

The new branch can be sanctioned both by the judiciary and by the elected branches. The law can sanction the new branch through judicial review that can overturn the decisions of the unelected bodies. The emphasis is on due process. This involves due process in the gathering of information and evidence, in disseminating information to those with a need to know, in allowing time for comment on draft decisions and rules, and in such matters as the need to allow for a right of appeal against findings. Due process offers a defence against capricious judgements or arbitrary determinations by institutions in the new branch. The new bodies take decisions or arrive at conclusions that can have a major impact on citizens or businesses or on government. It is therefore important that they provide an opportunity for all the evidence to be presented and an opportunity for its rebuttal by those claiming to have counter-evidence. If such standards are not followed, or if the institution is wrong on the facts, then an avenue for challenge is open through judicial review.

Not all activities of unelected bodies lend themselves to judicial review and sanction. For example, the judgemental decisions that independent central banks take to maintain the purchasing power of the currency do not offer opportunities for review by the judiciary. But in cases of serious and persistent poor performance by unelected bodies, sanctions by the elected branch become relevant.

The elected branches can sanction the new branch through their power to redefine the statutory basis of the unelected bodies. As discussed earlier, few have constitutional protection. The elected branch can also sanction through the use of the powers of appointment and dismissal and through budget controls in cases where the unelected bodies are financed by the government budget rather than through other means such as levies and charges.

The theory of the 'democratic overhead' concerns itself as to whether these powers of sanction are sufficient for the elected branches to 'control' the new branch. This is the wrong end of the telescope. The proper question is not whether these possibilities of sanction are sufficient for control, but whether they are excessive in allowing for too much intrusion into the core functions of the new branch. The main risks associated with the new bodies arise not from insufficient powers of the elected branches to apply sanctions but from the possibility of political interference as elected politicians try to reconcile the independence they have granted with the opportunities for continuing control. A similar risk applies in the case of judicial review. Courts may still be tempted to get into the substantive decision-making of the new unelected bodies rather than limiting their review to due process and material omissions.

The Founding Fathers were concerned about whether the judicial branch could resist the encroachments of the other branches. The same perspective is appropriate to the new branch. The chief means that the new bodies possess to resist such encroachment revolves around their superior access to reliable information, specialised knowledge and the rigour with which they deploy the information and knowledge available to them. The more that unelected bodies establish their own authority the riskier it becomes for politicians to try to interfere.[6] The riskier it becomes

---

[6] Rose points out that civil servants are 'trebly handicapped' if they try to interfere in the world of experts. They are handicapped by ignorance, by low status and by the fact that the experts are 'off-line'. The same applies to politicians with an itch to interfere. See Rose (1986: 6).

also for non-specialised courts of the traditional judicial branch to try to interfere with the substance of decisions.

Adding to the sum of the total

The new branch also adds to the sum of the advantages of the other separate branches. Compared with ordinary courts of law and standard judicial processes the new branch offers two advantages. The first is the advantage of specialisation. The new institutions can mobilise the expertise of economists or scientists or other disciplines that may be in short supply within the judiciary. The second is the ability of new institutions to work outside the discipline of case law and precedent. Case law and precedent offer important procedural defences against adventurous judges or wayward juries but they also limit what the law can investigate. The judiciary has to await a case and that case is likely to be highly specific. The new institutions do not have to await a case in order to investigate a situation and they can assess the generality of a situation rather than the specifics of a particular instance. In the language of economists, they economise on transaction costs. More importantly, these two features both help to protect the domain of the new branch and add to what the judicial branch can do on its own.

The new branch adds to the total benefits of a separation of powers in other less tangible ways. It exerts influence on the law in encouraging the law to broaden its own approach to the gathering of evidence. It encourages the law to move away from doctrines of authorising norms in treaties, constitutions and declarations of rights as a sufficient basis for adjudication, to examine in addition the economic and social evidence and reasoning that is involved.

At the same time the potential for the elective branches of government to be halted and held in check by the new branch in a manner that strengthens the democratic character of the whole has already been described. The new branch checks the executive by largely eliminating the claim of governments to have superior knowledge or any claim to know better. It checks the abuse of power by old-style civil service departments because it discourages a culture of secrecy. It checks the legislative branch because it places pressure on legislatures to ensure that legislation and regulation are rooted in evidence.

It seems, therefore, that a system of checks and balances can provide a framework of accountability for the new bodies in all three senses of the term 'accountability' and that, in addition, the new separation of powers also adds potentially to the good functioning of a democratic system as a whole.

Legitimacy and accountability together

The different perspectives on legitimacy and accountability that have now been discussed are summarised in figure 1. The argument of this book has been that unelected bodies have their own claim to legitimacy based on following the principles and procedures appropriate to the world of empirical knowledge. Figure 1 shows that the legitimacy of the new branch is not derived from contracts with the elected political branch, nor are the principles and procedures the same as those that underpin the rule of law. The new branch needs the support and understanding of the public, but it goes too far to say that the legitimacy of the new bodies rests on the acceptability of the outcomes they bring about, or on constitutional consent.

The argument has also been made that the new branch can be held to account through the checks and balances offered by a separation of powers. Figure 1 shows that the new bodies should not be viewed as agents to be controlled either by contractual undertakings with politicians or by subservience to the judiciary. Nor should the new bodies be seen as accountable to the public on a case-by-case basis for particular decisions. A separation of powers provides the other branches with the power of sanction but it is organised around a mutual respect for core functions. Thus, figure 1 shows the new branch viewed on its own terms and not as a

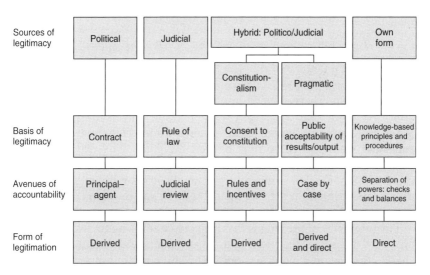

Figure 1: Unelected bodies: alternative democratic frameworks

branch that derives its claims to authority and respect from the other branches.

It is this perspective on the new branch that provides insight into the reforms needed in modern democratic systems of government, both at the national level and in respect of regional and international arrangements.

The reform agenda

Following the analysis above, the reforms needed at the national, regional and international levels need to focus on both the way in which the new branch claims legitimacy and the mechanisms by which it can be held to account in the different meanings of the term.

Reforming national democratic systems

Reforms in national systems of government need to focus on two critical elements in the arrangements for accountability. The first concerns the way in which the core responsibilities are defined so that the unelected bodies have no temptation to stray into areas that belong to politics and elected bodies lose the temptation to interfere with the unelected; the second concerns the need to restrain the sanctioning power of the political branch which, if misused, can convert unelected bodies back into adjuncts of electoral politics.

Defining core functions in the new separation of powers

The terms of reference of the new bodies need to respect the new separation of powers. The most difficult aspect arises in cases where the new institutions are charged with implementing values – for example the utility regulator that is charged with ensuring universal service or the water regulator that has to meet an environmental standard. In these particular examples there may be no ambiguity. The problems arise where an unelected body is given conflicting duties, or has to weigh one value with another, or is given very general social or ethical responsibilities. In such situations they are invited to stray into the arena that belongs to the elected bodies. They should be avoided.

The other side of the coin is that if elected bodies are to discharge their own core 'blending' function, both governments and assemblies have to change the way in which they can best illuminate the value judgements made in democratic societies. Traditionally, among the elected institutions, it was democratically elected assemblies that were looked to in order to express, articulate and debate the moral ethos of society. In modern democracies it is presidents and prime ministers that are involved as much or more than assemblies in setting a tone or reflecting a national mood, but the reform implications are more sweeping for assemblies. Unless elected bodies can provide better forums for the discussion of values and how to weigh different values that may be in conflict, then discussion of much that is important to modern societies is left to the media.

The most important change that representative assemblies can make towards improving the judgemental processes of society is to move away from the sterile exchanges of party political debate in the assemblies as a whole in order to spend much more time and resources on committee-style inquiries. Traditional set-piece debates on the floor of assemblies rehearse what is already known in terms that are already discounted. At the same time as assemblies move in the direction of becoming inquiry chambers rather than debating chambers, they have to greatly increase their own ability to understand the evidence, the information and the knowledge base and the procedures behind them. If they cannot do this, they will be unable either to judge the output of the new branch or to assess opinions of those with competing claims to the right interpretation to place on the evidence. This means either bringing outside expertise into the committee hearings or building their own research capacity or both.[7]

The most difficult lesson for the elected branches is to accept the change in the nature of their core problem-solving role. This involves stepping back from detailed problem-solving of a micro nature to focussing instead on the macro framework. At the micro level, people will be taking more decisions for themselves and in addition much detailed problem-solving in society will be done by the new branch. Governments have to switch away from the micro and from attempting to run services in education, health or welfare that involve micro-management decisions. This means relying still further on independent service providers and regulators as well as accepting market signals, including price signals, and moving away from administrative targets.

Political sanctions and the unelected

The relationship between the new branch and the traditional branches of democratic systems of government has been characterised as one that

---

[7] A report by the Select Committee on the Constitution of the UK's Upper Chamber noted, 'Parliament lacks the mechanism for consistent and coherent scrutiny of regulation.' See House of Lords, Select Committee on the Constitution (2004, Vol. I: 7).

should rest on mutual respect for the core roles of each other, and not one of control. The risk is not a lack of sanctioning power but of excessive political interference.

In general the risk of political interference is not so much from direct intervention by elected bodies in the statutory duties carried out by the unelected as from indirect means of influence, notably from the power to hire and fire the heads of agencies or their boards. The power to hire and fire may be represented as 'democratic control'. In practice it is often something else entirely. All too often it is a pretext for the exercise of patronage by those with political power and it risks politicising those unelected bodies that are intended to be independent in making empirical judgements. The risks are well illustrated by the politicisation of recent appointments to the US Supreme Court and by the unseemly deal-making that surrounded the first appointments to the head of the European Central Bank.

A complete separation of powers is not essential. On the other hand, non-political methods of appointment are a safeguard against indirect means of influence. Similarly, the sanction of dismissal is open to misuse by elected politicians. It seems appropriate that terms for those heading up unelected bodies should be for a fixed duration, with dismissal needing to be grounded on incompetence or misdemeanour – a judicial rather than a political procedure.

There remains a role for political review that does not take the elected branches into the realm that belongs to the unelected. More specifically, elected assemblies can oversee and comment on the activities of the new branch of government that do not fall within the normal purview of courts. For example, assemblies can use their inquiry role to highlight the findings of independent audit, evaluation and review. They can check whether the agencies are taking on board these and other techniques for ensuring the quality of their work. The scope of this political review falls short of sanction.

One development that is an obstacle to this review function is the sheer proliferation of the number of unelected bodies and the complexities introduced by differences in legal form. In countries such as the UK the need to reduce their number is already recognised. A reduction in the number of bodies, however, does not reduce the scope of their role.

Developing the legitimacy of the new branch

The final area where reforms may be needed concerns the development of the principles and procedures that legitimise the new branch. This means giving attention to consultation processes so that a distinction is made between the gathering of evidence and expert knowledge compared with the sounding of those groups that have opinions and views on that knowledge and evidence. It also means more rigorous evidence-gathering techniques through impact assessment, the greater use of methods of testing the applicability of findings, as well as ensuring independent peer review for findings.

These principles and procedures are important in their own right but they serve another purpose in protecting the new separation of powers and the independence of the new branch. A practice of mutual respect for core competences will be strengthened by the development of the principles and procedures of the new branch itself. Differences in methodological rigour are key.

National systems of democratic government that respect the classic form of separation of powers or follow a parliamentary system of fused powers will find the reform implications of the new separation of powers more challenging than they expected when they began the process of separating out the new branch. The reform implications are even more challenging where powers have been deliberately intermingled and where the distinction between knowledge-based processes and the task of making political value judgements on that knowledge has been deliberately blurred. This is the case in the European Union and in international settings.

Reforming the EU

The European Union illustrates what can go wrong when an unelected body (the Commission) is given duties that belong to other branches of government including, notably, the elected branches. The powers of the Commission lie at the heart of the failure of the European Union as a democratic construction. The historical means chosen to accomplish union have set up inter-institutional relationships that now stand as an enormous obstacle to a legitimate and democratically accountable system of government for the EU. The public policies of democratic systems of government need to be able to mobilise the latest empirical knowledge and to mirror the social and ethical judgements of the public on the application of that knowledge. Present arrangements offer Europe the worst of two worlds – over-regulation instead of empirical judgement, bombast and hypocrisy instead of citizen expression.

The new separation of powers provides a model for the Commission and the other institutions that may help reduce the transitional costs of moving to a principled reform of the EU. The new separation of powers delineates two alternative futures for the Commission. Either the

Commission takes on the role of an elected government and becomes a body entrusted with making political judgements and carrying political responsibilities and sheds its other roles, or it continues down the judicial and regulatory path in which case it needs to be freed of its political role. It cannot do both. Moreover, the failure to examine the functions of the Commission constitutes an obstacle to the reform of the other institutions as well. The power sharing that occurs between the institutions in Brussels is not only incompatible with democracy based on a separation of powers, both classical and new, it is also incompatible with models of fused powers drawn from member states.

The costs of this transition to a democratically accountable system of government in the EU will be high. So too, however, are the costs of continued path dependency. The new separation of powers offers the promise that the long-run benefits of breaking out of the original institutional arrangements for the EU will outweigh the transitional costs.

Reforming the international system

Finally the new separation of powers has profound implications for how to make the unelected bodies in the international system more accountable. Two fundamental weaknesses have been identified. One is the difficulty of legitimising a political body, the United Nations, on the basis of principles alone. The second is the tendency of bodies that are essentially about information gathering, lesson learning and knowledge transfer, to overstep the limits of their competence in order to play a political role. This overstepping may be overt or it may be more oblique through their advocacy of values that belong to the political rather than the evidence-gathering process. It damages the role of bodies such as the World Bank or IMF in the knowledge branch of international governance structures.

In the case of knowledge bodies, such as the OECD or the Bretton Woods institutions, the issue is not to encourage their further politicisation by seeking to democratise them in some way. It is also a mistake to attempt to move in this direction by granting special status to NGOs that allegedly 'represent' civil society. The idea that the unelected can confer democratic legitimacy on the unelected is simply misconceived. Independence from politics and pressure groups is a virtue for most international bodies as it is for similar bodies in national politics. Reforms should move them in the other direction – towards greater rigour in what they do.

The essential problem in respect of the UN is that in bringing outside values and principles to bear on international decision-taking, it brings to the table the values of governments. Those governments include the corrupt, the undemocratic and the tyrannical. This places limits on the role the UN can currently play as a legitimising organisation and it means efforts to hold it to account are also frustrated.

In the national context unelected bodies can indeed develop principles and procedures that legitimise their activities. But there are limits to how far this approach can be carried into the world of making value judgements in international politics. As long as there is a significant number of governments that are not democratic, the attempt to set normative standards through the Universal Declaration of Human Rights will be discredited by non-enforcement and there will be respect neither for democratic principles nor for procedures. Undemocratic countries also pose the main threat to the principle of accommodation and tolerance. As a practical matter this means that the task of legitimising international actions will remain resting uneasily between a deeply flawed UN and the actions of clubs of concerned democracies.

In the final analysis a different approach to the international rule of law is needed that places primary emphasis on democratising states. A world of democracies will still be a divided world, because there will remain deep differences between the interpretation of key values and how to apply them in particular circumstances, but it can become a more peaceful and cosmopolitan world.

The least dangerous branch?

This book has looked at the rise of the unelected from the perspective of the emergence of a new branch of government in a revised separation of powers. What at first sight looks like a threat to democracy has turned out to be a benefit. When citizens are more reliably informed, when politicians face a greater challenge when they claim that they know best, and individuals can safely take more decisions for themselves, democracy is strengthened not weakened.

When the Founding Fathers of the American Constitution looked at the separation of powers, Hamilton declared that the judicial branch should be seen as 'the least dangerous' to the democratic aims of the Constitution. It had neither the force of the executive branch nor the law-making powers of the legislative. It relied on the quality of its judgements for its authority. In practice, the authority of the judiciary is more powerful than Hamilton allowed and the judiciary can act as a threat to other and lesser jurisdictions. It can also act in collusion with the other branches.

From one perspective the new branch of government might be viewed as the new claimant for the title of the 'least dangerous' branch. The bodies that belong to it have limited executive powers, they rely for the statutory definition of their roles on the legislative branch, and they lack the long tradition that imparts an embedded authority to the law. The underlying ability of the new bodies to command respect and authority hinges on how well they muster and deploy reliable analysis and information.

In the final analysis, however, the search for the 'least dangerous' branch is a misguided one. Each branch presents its own dangers in its own ways. This is as true for the new branch of government as it is true of the old branches. Although the work of unelected bodies at both the national and international levels is often highly specific and highly technical, at the same time unelected bodies take decisions that have enormous practical influence. This operational function can be abused and can also be performed badly in ways that damage societies.

The rise of the unelected thus presents dangers as well as benefits to a democratic system of government. If the new branch follows the right principles and procedures that legitimate its activities, and if other branches adapt their own functions in the new separation of powers in order to hold it to account, it is the benefits that can prevail.

Appendix: List of unelected bodies referred to in the text

Selected independent bodies in the UK

Adult Learning Inspectorate (ALI)
Adventure Activity Licensing Authority (AALA)
Arts Council
Audit Commission
Bank of England
British Broadcasting Corporation (BBC)
British Council
Care Standards Tribunal (CST)
Charity Commission
Child Support Agency
Civil Aviation Authority (CAA)
Commission for Racial Equality (CRE)
Commission for Social Care Inspection (CSCI)
Competition Appeals Tribunal
Council for Healthcare Regulatory Excellence (CHRE)
Council on Tribunals
Dental Vocational Training Authority (DVTA)
Disability Rights Commission (DRC)
Economic and Social Research Council (ESRC)
Electoral Commission
Employment Appeal Tribunal
English Heritage
English Nature
Environment Agency
Equal Opportunities Commission (EOC)
Family Health Services Appeal Authority (FHSAA)
Financial Reporting Council (FRC)
Financial Services Authority
Food Standards Agency

Football Licensing Authority (FLA)
Gambling Commission
Gangmasters Licensing Authority (GLA)
Health and Safety Commission (HSC)
Health Protection Agency
Human Fertilisation and Embryology Authority (HFEA)
Independent Police Complaints Commission (IPCC)
Information Commissioner
Information Tribunal
Law Commission
Legal Services Complaints Commissioner (OLSCC)
Medical Research Council (MRC)
National Audit Office (NAO)
National Consumer Council (NCC)
National Institute of Health and Clinical Excellence (NICE)
National Lottery Commission (NLC)
National Patient Safety Agency (NPSA)
Occupational Pensions Regulatory Authority (OPRA)
Office for the Commissioner for Public Appointments (OCPA)
Office of Communications (OFCOM)
Office of Fair Trading
Office of Gas and Electricity Markets (OFGEM)
Office of National Statistics (ONS)
Office of Rail Regulation (ORR)
Office of the Telecommunications Adjudicator (OTA)
Office of Water Services (OFWAT)
Pensions Ombudsman
Qualifications and Curriculum Authority (QCA)
Reviewing Committee on the Export of Works of Art (RCEWA)
Standards Board for England
The Health Commission
Training and Development Agency (formerly TTA)

Selected independent bodies in the USA

Centers for Disease Control and Prevention (CDC)
Commodity Futures Trading Commission (CFTC)
Consumer Product Safety Commission
Environmental Protection Agency (EPA)
Equal Employment Opportunity Commission (EEOC)
Federal Communications Commission (FCC)
Federal Election Commission

Federal Reserve System (FRS)
Federal Trade Commission (FTC)
Financial Accounting Standards Board (FASB)
Food and Drug Administration
Government Accountability Office (GAO)
Merit Systems Protection Board (MSPB)
National Aeronautics and Space Administration (NASA)
National Institute of Justice (NIJ)
National Railroad Passenger Corporation (AMTRAK)
National Science Foundation
National Transportation Safety Board
Nuclear Waste Technical Review Board (NWTRB)
Office of Government Ethics (USOGE)
Office of Special Counsel (OSC)
Office of the Comptroller of the Currency (OCC)
Pension Benefit Guaranty Corporation (PBGC)
Securities and Exchange Commission
Small Business Administration
US Commission on Civil Rights
US Postal Service
US Sentencing Commission

Selected independent bodies in Australia

Administrative Appeals Tribunal (AAT)
Administrative Review Council (ARC)
Aged Care Standards and Accreditation Office
Australian Accounting Standards Board (AASB)
Australian Broadcasting Corporation (ABC)
Australian Bureau of Statistics (ABS)
Australian Communications and Media Authority (ACMA)
Australian Competition and Consumer Commission (ACCC)
Australian Competition Tribunal
Australian National Audit Office (ANAO)
Australian Research Council (ARC)
Australian Safety and Co-operation Council (ASCC)
Australian Securities and Investments Commission (ASIC)
Child Support Agency (CSA)
Commonwealth Ombudsman
Curriculum Corporation
Human Rights and Equal Opportunities Commission
National Heritage Trust (NHT)

National Industrial Chemical Notification and Assessment Scheme
(NICNAS)
National Institute of Clinical Studies (NICS)
Office of the Gene Technology Regulator (OGTR)
Office of the Privacy Commissioner
Reserve Bank of Australia
Social Security Appeals Tribunal (SSAT)

Selected independent bodies in member states of the European Union

Alien Appeals Board (Sweden)
Centro de Investigaciones Sociologicas (CIS) (Spain)
Children's Ombudsman (Sweden)
Court of Accounts (France)
Deutsche Bundesbank (Germany)
Equal Opportunities Commission (Sweden)
Federal Agency for Nature Conservation (BfN) (Germany)
Federal Cartel Office (Germany)
Federal Institute for Risk Assessment (BfR) (Germany)
Financial Markets Authority (FMA) (France)
Food Safety Authority of Ireland (FSAI)
French Agency for Food Sanitary Safety (AFSSA)
French Office for the Protection of Refugees and Stateless
German Financial Supervisory Authority (BaFiN)
High Authority against Discrimination and for Equality
(HALDE) (France)
Instituto Nacional de Investigacion y Tecnologia Agraria
(INIA) (Spain)
Irish Human Rights Commission (IHRC)
Irish Social Services Inspectorate (ISSI.IE)
Irish Water Safety
Medical Products Agency (Sweden) (MPA)
National Board of Health and Welfare (Sweden)
National Council for Curriculum and Assessment (NCCA) (Ireland)
National Institute for Consumer Protection (France)
National Institute for Public Health and the Environment (RIVM)
(Netherlands)
National Research and Safety Institution for the Prevention of
Occupational Accidents and Diseases (INRS) (France)
Office of the Data Protection Ombudsman (Finland)
Office of the Pensions Ombudsman (Belgium)

Ombudsman for Children (OCO) (Ireland)
Royal Meteorological Office (Netherlands)
Swedish Forest Agency (SFA)
The Federal Court of Auditors (Germany)
The Swedish Environmental Protection Agency (EPA)
The Swedish National Post and Telecom Agency (PTS)

Selected independent bodies of the European Union

Agency for Management of Operational Co-operation at External
   Borders (FRONTEX)
Community Plant Variety Office (CPVO)
Court of First Instance
European Agency for Reconstruction (EAR)
European Aviation Safety Agency (EASA)
European Central Bank (ECB)
European Centre for Disease Prevention and Control (ECDC)
European Centre for the Development of Vocational Training
   (CEDEFOP)
European Chemicals Agency (ECHA)
European Court of Auditors
European Food Safety Authority (EFSA)
European Foundation for the Improvement of Living and Working
   Conditions (Eurofound)
European Fundamental Rights Agency (EFRA)
European Investment Bank (EIB)
European Maritime Safety Agency (EMSA)
European Medicines Evaluation Agency (EMEA)
European Monitoring Centre for Drugs and Drug Addiction
   (EMCDDA)
European Monitoring Centre on Racism and Xenophobia (EUMC)
European Network Information Security Agency (ENISA)
European Police Office (EUROPOL)
European Railway Agency
European Research Council (ERC)
European Union: Institute for Security Studies (EUISS)
European Union Satellite Centre (EUSC)
European Union's Judicial Cooperation Unit (Eurojust)
The European Agency for Safety and Health at Work
   (EU-OSHA)
The European Environment Agency (EEA)
The Office of Harmonization for the Internal Market (OHIM)

Selected independent international organisations

Bank for International Settlements (BIS)
Basel Committee on Banking Supervision (BCBS)
Financial Action Task Force (FATF)
Financial Stability Forum (FSF)
Food and Agriculture Organization of the United Nations (FAO)
International Accounting Standards Board (IASB)
International Association of Insurance Supervisors (IAIS)
International Atomic Energy Agency (IAEA)
International Bank for Reconstruction and Development (IBRD)
International Centre for Settlement of Investment Disputes (ICSID)
International Civil Aviation Organization (ICAO)
International Court of Justice (ICJ)
International Criminal Court (ICC)
International Labour Organization (ILO)
International Maritime Organization (IMO)
International Monetary Fund (IMF)
International Organization for Standardization (ISO)
International Organization of Securities Commissions (IOSCO)
International Telecommunication Union (ITU)
International Tribunal for the Law of the Sea (ITLOS)
International Whaling Commission (IWC)
Interpol
Organisation for Economic Co-operation and Development (OECD)
United Nations Children's Fund (UNICEF)
United Nations Conference on Trade and Development (UNCTAD)
United Nations Educational, Scientific and Cultural Organization
    (UNESCO)
United Nations Environment Programme (UNEP)
United Nations High Commissioner for Refugees (UNHCR)
Universal Postal Union (UPU)
World Meteorological Organisation (WMO)
World Trade Organisation (WTO)

Bibliography

Ackerman, B. 1984. 'The Storrs Lectures: Discovering the Constitution', *Yale Law Journal*, 93 (6): 1013–72.

Archibugi, Daniele (ed.) 2003. *Debating Cosmopolitics*. London: Verso.

Argyris, Chris, Putnam, Robert and McClain Smith, Diana (eds.) 1985. *Action Science*. San Francisco: Jossey Bass.

Arkes, Hal R. and Hammond, Kenneth R. (eds.) 1986. *Judgement and Decision Making: An Interdisciplinary Reader*. Cambridge: Cambridge University Press.

Arrow, Kenneth J. 1985. 'The Economics of Agency', in Pratt, John W. and Zeckhauser, Richard J., *Principals and Agents: The Structure of Business*. Boston, MA: Harvard Business School Press, 37–51.

Barber, Benjamin R. 1984. *Strong Democracy: Participatory Politics for a New Age*. Berkeley, CA: University of California Press.

Barberis, P. 1998. 'The New Public Management and a New Accountability', *Public Administration*, 76 (3): 451–70.

Barnett, Michael N. and Finnemore, Martha 1999. 'The Politics, Power and Pathologies of International Organizations', *International Organization*, 53: 699–732.

Bawm, Kathleen 1995. 'Political Control versus Expertise: Congressional Choice about Administrative Procedures', *American Political Science Review*, 89 (1): 62–73.

Beitz, Charles R. 1979. *Political Theory and International Relations*. Princeton, NJ: Princeton University Press.

Bekke, Hans A. G. M., Perry, James L. and Toonen, Theo A. J. (eds.) 1996. *Civil Service Systems in Comparative Perspective*. Bloomington, IN: Indiana University Press.

Bergman, Torbjörn, Müller, Wolfgang C. and Strøm, Kaare 2000. 'Parliamentary Democracy and the Chain of Delegation', *European Journal of Political Research*, 37 (3): 255–60.

Blaug, M. 1980. *The Methodology of Economics*. Cambridge: Cambridge University Press.

Blondel Jean, Sinnott, Richard and Svensson, Palle 1998. *People and Parliament in the European Union: Participation, Democracy and Legitimacy*. Oxford: Clarendon Press.

Bodin, Jean 1955 [1576]. *Six Books of the Commonwealth* (trans. M. J. Tooley). Oxford: Blackwell.

Bohman, James 1996. *Public Deliberation: Pluralism, Complexity and Democracy.* Cambridge, MA: MIT Press.

Bohman, James and Rehg, William (eds.) 1997. *Deliberative Democracy: Essays on Reason and Politics.* Cambridge, MA: MIT Press.

Boulding, Kenneth E. 1956. *The Image: Knowledge in Life and Society.* Ann Arbor: University of Michigan Press.

Braithwaite, John 1999. 'Accountability and Governance under the New Regulatory State', *Australian Journal of Public Administration,* 58 (1): 90–3.

Brawley, Mark R. 1993. *Liberal Leadership: Great Powers and their Challengers in Peace and War.* Ithaca, NY: Cornell University Press.

Brennan, Geoffrey and Hamlin, Alan 2000. *Democratic Devices and Desires.* Cambridge: Cambridge University Press.

2002. 'Expressive Constitutionalism', *Constitutional Political Economy,* 13 (4): 300–11.

Breyer, Stephen G., Stewart, Richard B., Sunstein, Cass R. and Spitzer, Matthew L. 1998. *Administrative Law and Regulatory Policy.* New York: Aspen Law and Business.

Brione, Paul 2005. 'Politicians' Itch to Interfere', *Central Banking,* 15 (3): 27–32.

Buchanan, James M. 1990. 'The Domain of Constitutional Economics', *Constitutional Political Economy,* 1 (1): 1–18.

Buzan, Barry, Jones, Charles and Little, Richard 1993. *The Logic of Anarchy.* New York: Columbia University Press.

Calvert, Randall, McCubbins, Mathew D. and Weingast, Barry R. 1989. 'A Theory of Political Control and Agency Discretion', *American Journal of Political Science,* 33 (3): 588–66.

Clark, Robert C. 1985. 'Agency Costs versus Fiduciary Duties', in Pratt, John W. and Zeckhauser, Richard J., *Principals and Agents: The Structure of Business.* Boston, MA: Harvard Business School Press, 55–79.

Coen, David and Thatcher, Mark 2005. 'The New Governance of Markets and Non-Majoritarian Regulators', *Governance: An International Journal of Policy, Administration and Institutions,* 18 (3): 329–46.

Coleman, Jules L. 2001. *The Practice of Principle: In Defence of a Pragmatist Approach to Legal Theory.* Oxford: Oxford University Press.

Conant, Lisa 2002. *Justice Contained: Law and Politics in the European Union.* Ithaca, NY: Cornell University Press.

Crouch, Colin 2004. *Coping with Post Democracy.* London: Polity Press.

Dahl, Robert A. 1970. *After the Revolution? Authority in a Good Society.* New Haven, CT: Yale University Press.

1989. *Democracy and its Critics.* New Haven, CT: Yale University Press.

1998. *On Democracy.* New Haven, CT: Yale University Press.

1999. 'Can International Organizations be Democratic? A Skeptic's View', in Shapiro, Ian and Hacker-Cordon, C. (eds.), *Democracy's Edges.* Cambridge: Cambridge University Press, 19–40.

Dalton, Russell 2004. *Democratic Challenges, Democratic Choices: The Erosion of Political Support in Advanced Industrial Democracies.* Oxford: Oxford University Press.

2006 *Citizen Politics: Public Opinion and Political Parties in Advanced Industrial Democracies*. Washington, DC: CQ Press.

Dehousse, Renaud 1997. 'Regulation by Networks in the European Community: The Role of European Agencies', *Journal of European Public Policy*, 4 (2): 246–61.

Denzou, Arthur T. and North, Douglass C. 2000. 'Shared Mental Models: Ideologies and Institutions', in Lupia, Arthur, McCubbins, Mathew D. and Popkin, Samuel L. (eds.), *Elements of Reason: Cognition, Choice and the Bounds of Rationality*. Cambridge: Cambridge University Press, 23–46.

Diggins, John Patrick 1994. *The Promise of Pragmatism: Modernism and the Crisis of Knowledge and Authority*. Chicago: University of Chicago Press.

Douglas, Mary 2002. *Risk and Blame: Essays in Cultural Theory*. London: Routledge.

Dworkin, Ronald 1977. *Taking Rights Seriously*. Cambridge, MA: Harvard University Press (9th impression 1990).

1996. *Freedom's Law*. Oxford: Oxford University Press.

Electoral Commission and Hansard Society 2006. *An Audit of Political Engagement 3*. Electoral Commission. London.

Elster, Jon 1992. *Local Justice*. Cambridge: Cambridge University Press.

(ed.) 1998. *Deliberative Democracy*. Cambridge: Cambridge University Press.

1999. *Alchemies of the Mind: Rationality and the Emotions*. Cambridge: Cambridge University Press.

Ely, John Hart 1980. *Democracy and Distrust*. Cambridge, MA: Harvard University Press.

Epstein, David 1999. *Delegating Powers: A Transactions Cost Politics Approach to Policy Making under Separate Powers*. Cambridge: Cambridge University Press.

Epstein, David and O'Halloran, Sharyn 1994. 'Administrative Procedures, Information and Agency Discretion', *American Journal of Political Science*, 38 (3): 697–722.

1999. 'Asymmetric Information, Delegation and the Structure of Policy Making', *Journal of Theoretical Politics*, 11 (1): 37–56.

Florini, Ann 2003. *The Coming Democracy: New Rules for Running a New World*. Washington, DC: Island Press.

Froud, Julie and Boden, Rebecca 1998. *Controlling the Regulators*. Basingstoke: Macmillan.

Fukuyama, Francis 1995. *Trust: The Social Values and the Creation of Prosperity*. Harmondsworth: Penguin.

Gadamer, Hans Georg 1989. 1994 (2nd edn). *Truth and Method*. New York: Continuum Books.

Gigerenzer, Gerd 2002. *Reckoning with Risk*. Harmondsworth: Penguin.

Gillroy, John Martin and Wade, Maurice (eds.) 1992. *The Moral Dimension of Public Policy Choice*. Pittsburgh, PA: University of Pittsburgh Press.

Goddard, Eileen 2005. *Public Confidence in Official Statistics*. ONS Omnibus Survey, Office for National Statistics, London.

Goldman, Alvin I. 1986. *Epistemology and Cognition*. Cambridge, MA: Harvard University Press.

192   Bibliography

Green, Donald P. and Shapiro, Ian 1994. *Pathologies of Rational Choice Theory.* New Haven, CT: Yale University Press.

Greenawalt, Kent 2002. 'Constitutional and Statutory Interpretation', in Coleman, Jules and Shapiro, Scott (eds.), *The Oxford Handbook of Jurisprudence and Philosophy of Law.* Oxford: Oxford University Press, 268–310.

Haas, Ernst B. 1989. *When Knowledge is Power: Three Models of Change in International Organizations.* Berkeley, CA: University of California Press.

Haas, Peter M. 1989. 'Do Regimes Matter?' *International Organization,* 43 (3): 377–403.

2004. 'When Does Power Listen to Truth?' *Journal of European Public Policy,* 2 (4): 569–92.

Hamilton, Alexander, Madison, James and Jay, John 1787/8. 1987 (2nd edn ed. Beloff). *The Federalist.* Oxford: Basil Blackwell.

Hammond, Kenneth R. and Adelman, Leonard 1986. 'Science, Values and Human Judgement', in Arkes, Hal R. and Hammond, Kenneth R. (eds.), *Judgement and Decision Making: An Interdisciplinary Reader.* Cambridge: Cambridge University Press, 127–43.

Harlow, Carol 2002. *Accountability in the European Union.* Oxford: Oxford University Press.

Held, David 2003. 'Cosmopolitanism: Ideas, Realities and Deficits', in Held, David and McGrew, Anthony (eds.), *Governing Globalization: Power, Authority and Global Governance.* Cambridge: Polity Press, 305–24.

Hempel, C. G. 1965. *Aspects of Scientific Explanation.* New York: Free Press.

Hesse, Mary 1978. 'Theory and Values in the Social Sciences', in Hookway, Christopher and Pettit, Philip (eds.), *Action and Interpretation: Studies in the Philosophy of the Social Sciences.* Cambridge: Cambridge University Press, 1–16.

Hoffman, Mark 1994. 'Normative International Theory: Approaches and Issues', in Groom A. J. R. and Light, Margot (eds.), *Contemporary International Relations: A Guide to Theory.* London: Pinter, 27–44.

Hollis, Martin 1994. *The Philosophy of Social Science: An Introduction.* Cambridge: Cambridge University Press.

Hood, Christopher 1998. *The Art of the State.* Oxford: Clarendon Press.

2002. 'The Risk Game and the Blame Game', *Government and Opposition,* 37 (1): 15–37.

Hood, Christopher, Rothstein, Henry and Baldwin, Robert 2001. *The Government of Risk.* Oxford: Oxford University Press.

Hood, Christopher and Schuppert, Gunnar Folke (eds.) 1988. *Delivering Services in Western Europe.* London: Sage Publications.

Horn, Murray J. 1995. *The Political Economy of Public Administration.* Cambridge: Cambridge University Press.

House of Lords. Select Committee on the Constitution (2004). *The Regulatory State: Ensuring its Accountability.* London: The Stationery Office.

Huber, John D. and Pfahler, Madelaine 2001. 'Legislatures and Statutory Control of Bureaucracy', *American Journal of Political Science,* 45 (2): 330–45.

Huber, John D. and Shipan, Charles R. 2000. 'The Costs of Control: Legislators, Agencies and Transactions Costs', *Legislative Studies Quarterly,* 25 (1): 25–52.

2002. *Deliberate Discretion: The Institutional Foundations of Bureaucratic Autonomy*. Cambridge: Cambridge University Press.

Hughes, Owen 1998. *Public Management and Administration*. Basingstoke: Palgrave Macmillan.

Kaplan, Mark 2002. 'Decision Theory and Epistemology', in Moser, Paul K. (ed.), *The Oxford Handbook of Epistemology*. Oxford: Oxford University Press, 434–62.

Kelsen, Hans 1986 [1964]. 'The Function of a Constitution' (trans. Stewart), in Tur, R. and Twining, W. (eds.), *Essays on Kelsen*. Oxford: Oxford University Press, 109–19.

Keohane, Robert O. (ed.) 1986. *Neorealism and its Critics*. Princeton, NJ: Princeton University Press.

2002a. 'Governance in a Partially Globalized World', in Held, David and McGrew, Anthony (eds.), *Governing Globalization: Power, Authority and Global Governance*. Cambridge: Polity Press, 325–47.

2002b. *Power and Governance in a Partially Globalized World*. London: Routledge.

Key, V. O. 1948. *Politics, Parties and Pressure Groups* (2nd edn). New York: Thomas Y. Crowell Co.

King, Gary, Keohane, Robert and Verba, Sidney 1994. *Designing Social Inquiry: Scientific Inference in Qualitative Research*. Princeton, NJ: Princeton University Press.

Kingdon, J. W. 1984. 1995 (2nd edn). *Agendas, Alternatives and Public Policies*. New York: Longman.

Kolm, Serge-Christophe 1996. *Modern Theories of Justice*. Cambridge, MA: MIT Press.

Krehbiel, Keith 1998. *Pivotal Politics*. Chicago: University of Chicago Press.

Krishna, A. 2002. 'Enhancing Political Participation in Democracies: What is the Role of Social Capital?' *Comparative Political Studies*, 35 (4): 437–60.

Kuhn, Thomas 1962. *The Structure of Scientific Revolution*. Chicago: University of Chicago Press.

Kydland, Finn and Prescott, E. 1977. 'Rules Rather than Discretion: The Inconsistency of Optimal Plans', *Journal of Political Economy*, 85 (3): 473–90.

Lane, Jan Erik 2005. *Public Administration and Public Management: The Principal–Agent Perspective*. London: Routledge.

Laslett, Peter 2003. 'Environmental Ethics and the Obsolescence of Existing Political Institutions', in Fishkin, James S. and Laslett, Peter (eds.), *Debating Deliberative Democracy*. Oxford: Blackwell, 212–24.

Lindblom, C. E. 1959. 'The Science of Muddling Through', *Public Administration Review*, 19: 79–88.

Lupia, Arthur and McCubbins, Mathew D. 1998. *Democratic Dilemma: Can Citizens Learn What they Need to Know*. Cambridge: Cambridge University Press.

Lupia, Arthur, McCubbins, Mathew D. and Popkin, Samuel L. (eds.) 2000. *Elements of Reason: Cognition, Choice and the Bounds of Rationality*. Cambridge: Cambridge University Press.

Lynn, Laurence E. 1987. *Managing Public Policy*. Boston: Little Brown.

Lynn, Laurence E., Heinrich, Carolyn J. and Hill, Carolyn J. 2001. *Improving Governance: A New Logic for Empirical Research.* Washington, DC: Georgetown University Press.

Mair, P. and von Biezen, I. 2001. 'Party Membership in Twenty European Democracies 1980–2000', *Party Politics,* 7 (1): 5–21.

Majone, Giandomenico 1997. 'The New European Agencies: Regulation by Information', *Journal of European Public Policy,* 4 (2): 262–75.

2001. 'Two Logics of Delegation: Agency and Fiduciary Relations in EU Governance', *European Union Politics,* 2: 103–21.

2005. *Dilemmas of Integration.* Oxford: Oxford University Press.

Marin, Bernd and Mayntz, Renate (eds.) 1991. *Policy Networks.* Boulder, CO: Westview Press.

Matheson, Alex and Kwon Hae-Sang 2003. 'Public Sector Modernisation: A New Agenda', *OECD Journal on Budgeting,* 3 (1): 7–23.

Meersheimer, John 1994/5. 'The False Promise of International Institutions', *International Security,* 19 (3): 5–49.

Mele, Alfred R. 2004. 'Motivated Irrationality', in Mele, Alfred R. and Rawling, Piers (eds.), *The Oxford Handbook of Rationality.* Oxford: Oxford University Press, 240–56.

Misztal, Barbara A. 1996. *Trust in Modern Societies.* Cambridge: Polity Press.

Morgan, Bronwen 2003. 'The Economization of Politics: Meta-Regulation as a Form of Nonjudicial Legality', *Social and Legal Studies,* 12 (4): 489–523.

Morrow, James D. 1994. *Games Theory for Political Scientists.* Princeton, NJ: Princeton University Press.

Norris, Pippa 2002. *Democratic Phoenix: Reinventing Political Activism.* Cambridge: Cambridge University Press.

North, Douglas C. 1990. *Institutions, Institutional Change and Economic Reform.* Cambridge: Cambridge University Press.

OECD 2002. 'Public Sector Modernisation: A New Agenda'. GOV/PUMA 2002, version 2 (Oct. 2002).

Office of Management and Budget 2004. 'Progress in Regulatory Reform: 2004 Report to Congress on the Costs and Benefits of Federal Regulations and Unfunded Mandates on State, Local and Tribal Entities'. Washington, DC.

Olsen, J. P. 2001. 'Garbage Cans, New Institutionalism and the Study of Politics', *American Political Science Review,* 95 (1): 191–7.

Osborne, David and Gaebler, Ted 1992. *Reinventing Government.* New York: Addison-Wesley.

Owens, Susan, Raynor, Tim and Bina, Olivia (2004). 'New Agendas for Appraisal: Reflections on Theory, Practice and Research', *Environment and Planning,* 36: 1943–59.

Pateman, Carole 1970. *Participation and Democratic Theory.* Cambridge: Cambridge University Press.

Pattie, Charles, Seyd, Patrick and Whiteley, Paul 2004. *Citizenship in Britain. Values, Participation and Democracy.* Cambridge: Cambridge University Press.

Peters, B. Guy 1996. *The Future of Governing: Four Emerging Models.* Lawrence: University Press of Kansas.

Pettit, Philip 2001. *A Theory of Freedom: From the Psychology to the Politics of Agency*. Cambridge: Polity Press.

Pettit, Philip and Smith, Michael 2004. 'The Truth in Deontology', in Jay, Wallace R., Pettit, Philip, Scheffler, Samuel and Smith, Michael (eds.), *Reason and Value*. Oxford: Clarendon Press, 153–75.

Pollack, Mark A. 2003. *The Engines of European Integration*. Oxford: Oxford University Press.

Pollitt, Christopher and Bouckaert, Geert 2000. *Public Management Reform: A Comparative Analysis*. Oxford: Oxford University Press.

Pollitt, Christopher and Talbot, Colin (eds.) 2004. *Unbundled Government: A Critical Analysis of the Global Trend to Agencies, Quangos and Contractualisation*. London: Routledge.

Pollitt, Christopher, Talbot, Colin, Caulfield, Janice and Smullen, Amanda. 2004. *Agencies*. Basingstoke: Palgrave Macmillan.

Posner, Richard A. 2003. *Law, Pragmatism and Democracy*. Cambridge, MA: Harvard University Press.

Power, Michael 1997. *The Audit Society: Rituals of Verification*. Oxford: Oxford University Press.

Power Inquiry. 2006. *The Report of Power: An Independent Inquiry into Britain's Democracy*. York: York Publishing Distribution.

Pratt, John W. and Zeckhauser, Richard J. 1985a. 'Principals and Agents: An Overview', in Pratt, John W. and Zeckhauser, Richard J. (eds.), *Principals and Agents: The Structure of Business*. Boston, MA: Harvard Business School Press, 1–36.

1985b. *Principals and Agents: The Structure of Business*. Boston, MA: Harvard Business School Press.

Putnam, Hilary 2002. *Collapse of the Fact/Value Dichotomy and Other Essays*. Cambridge, MA: Harvard University Press.

Putnam, Robert D. 2002. *Bowling Alone: The Collapse and Revival of American Community*. New York: Simon and Schuster.

Putnam, Robert D., Leonardi, Robert and Nanetti, Rafaella 1993. *Making Democracy Work: Civic Traditions in Modern Italy*. Princeton, NJ: Princeton University Press.

Rawls, John 1999. *The Law of the Peoples*. Cambridge, MA: Harvard University Press.

Reitter, Dan and Stam, Allan C. 2002. *Democracies at War*. Princeton, NJ: Princeton University Press.

Riker, William H. 1990. 'Political Science and Rational Choice', in Alt, James E. and Shepsle, Kenneth A. (eds.), *Perspectives on Positive Political Economy*. Cambridge: Cambridge University Press, 163–81.

Rose, Richard 1986. *Giving Direction to Civil Servants: Signals from the Law, Expertise, the Market and the Electorate*. Glasgow: Centre for the Study of Public Policy, University of Strathclyde.

2005. *Learning from Comparative Public Policy*. London: Routledge.

Rousseau, J. J. 1755, 1992. 'Discourse on Political Economy', in Masters, Roger D. and Kelly, Christopher (eds.), *The Collected Writings of Rousseau*, Vol. III. Hanover, NH: University Press of New England.

Ryan, Alan 1970. *The Philosophy of the Social Sciences*. London: Macmillan.
  (ed.) 1973. *The Philosophy of Social Explanation*. Oxford: Oxford University
  Press.
Sabatier, Paul A. (ed.) 1999. *Theories of the Policy Process*. Boulder, CO: Westview
  Press.
Sayer, Andrew 1984. *Method in Social Science: A Realist Approach*. London:
  Routledge.
Scharpf, Fritz 1999. *Governing in Europe: Effective and Democratic?* Oxford:
  Oxford University Press.
Schedler, Andreas 1999. 'Conceptualizing Accountability', in Schedler, Andreas,
  Diamond, Larry and Plattner, Marc F. (eds.), *The Self-Restraining State*.
  Boulder: Lynn Riesner, 13–28.
Schedler, Andreas, Diamond, Larry and Plattner Marc F. (eds.) 1999. *The Self-
  Restraining State. Power and Accountability in New Democracies*. Boulder: Lynn
  Rienner.
Scheufele, D. and Shah, D. 2000. 'Personality Strength and Social Capital: The
  Role of Dispositional and Informational Variables in the Production of Civic
  Participation', *Communication Research*, 27: 107–31.
Shapiro, Ian and Hacker-Cordon, C. (eds.) 1999a. *Democracy's Value*. Cambridge:
  Cambridge University Press.
  (eds.) 1999b. *Democracy's Edges*. Cambridge: Cambridge University Press.
Shelton, Dinah (ed.) 2000. *Commitment and Compliance: The Role of Non-Binding
  Norms in the International Legal System*. Oxford: Oxford University Press.
Simon, Herbert A. 1986. 'Alternative Visions of Rationality', in Arkes, Hal R.
  and Hammond, Kenneth R. (eds.), *Judgement and Decision Making: An
  Interdisciplinary Reader*. Cambridge: Cambridge University Press, 97–113.
Skyrmes, Brian 1996. *Evolution of the Social Contract*. Cambridge: Cambridge
  University Press.
Slaughter, Anne-Marie 2004. *A New World Order*. Princeton, NJ: Princeton
  University Press.
Slote, Michael 1989. *Beyond Optimizing: A Study in Rational Choice*. Cambridge,
  MA: Harvard University Press.
Solomon, Miriam 2001. *Social Empiricism*. Cambridge, MA: MIT Press.
Statistics Commission. 2005. Report No. 24. 'Official Statistics: Perceptions and
  Trust'. London.
Steunenberg, Bernard 1996. 'Agency Discretion, Regulatory Policy Making and
  Differential Institutional Arrangements', *Public Choice*, 86: 309–39.
Stiglitz, Joseph E. 2003. 'Democratizing the International Monetary Fund and
  the World Bank: Governance and Accountability', *Governance*, 16 (1):
  111–39.
Strøm, Kaare, Müller, Wolfgang C. and Bergman, Torbjörn (eds.) 2005.
  Delegation and Accountability in Parliamentary Democracies. Oxford: Oxford
  University Press.
Sunstein, Cass R. 1996. *Legal Reasoning and Political Conflict*. Oxford: Oxford
  University Press.
  1999. *One Case at a Time: Judicial Minimalism on the Supreme Court*. Cambridge,
  MA: Harvard University Press.

Thatcher, Mark 1998. 'The Development of Policy Network Analysis', *Journal of Theoretical Politics*, 10 (4): 389–416.

2005. 'The Third Force? Independent Regulatory Agencies and Elected Politicians in Europe', *Governance: An International Journal of Policy, Administration, and Institutions*, 18 (3): 347–73.

Thatcher, Mark and Stone Sweet, Alec 2002. 'Theory and Practice of Non-Majoritarian Institutions', *West European Politics*, 25 (1): 1–22.

True, James L., Jones, Bryan D. and Baumgartner, Fred R. 1999. 'Punctuated Equilibrium Theory', in Sabatier, Paul A. (ed.), *Theories of the Policy Process*. Boulder, CO: Westview Press, 97–115.

Tsebelis, George 2002. *Veto Players: How Political Institutions Work*. New York: Russell Sage Foundation.

Tuck, Richard 1999. *The Rights of War and Peace*. Oxford: Oxford University Press.

Union of International Associations (ed.) 2004/5. Edition 41. *Yearbook of International Organisations*, Vol. V. Munich: K. G. Saur.

Vibert, Frank 2001. *Europe Simple, Europe Strong*. Cambridge: Polity Press.

Waltz, Kenneth 1979. *Theory of International Politics*. Reading, MA: Addison Wesley.

Weaver, R. Kent 1986. 'The Politics of Blame Avoidance', *Journal of Public Policy*, 6 (4): 371–98.

Wendt, Alexander 1999. *Social Theory of International Politics*. Cambridge: Cambridge University Press.

West, William 1995. *Controlling the Bureaucracy: Institutional Constraints in Theory and Practice*. Armonk, NY: M. E. Sharpe.

Zakaria, Fareed 2003. *The Future of Freedom: Illiberal Democracy at Home and Abroad*. New York: W.W. Norton and Co.

Zaring, David 2005. 'Informal Procedure, Hard and Soft, in International Administration', *Chicago Journal of International Law*, 5 (2): 547–603.

Index